The Essential Guide to HTML5

Using Games to Learn HTML5 and JavaScript

Jeanine Meyer

an *Apress* company

Games to Learn HTML5 and JavaScript

Copyright © 2010 by Jeanine Meyer

ISBN-13 (pbk): 978-1-4302-3383-1

ISBN-13 (electronic): 978-1-4302-3384-8

Distributed to the book trade worldwide by Springer Science+Business Media LLC., 233 Spring Street, 6th Floor, New York, NY 10013. Phone 1-800-SPRINGER, fax (201) 348-4505, e-mail orders-ny@springer-sbm.com, or visit www.springeronline.com.

For information on translations, please e-mail rights@apress.com or visit www.apress.com.

Apress and friends of ED books may be purchased in bulk for academic, corporate, or promotional use. eBook versions and licenses are also available for most titles. For more information, reference our Special Bulk Sales–eBook Licensing web page at www.apress.com/info/bulksales.

The source code for this book is freely available to readers at www.friendsofed.com in the Downloads section.

Credits

To Daniel, Aviva, Anne, Esther, and Joseph, who is still in our lives, and for the newest members of the family: Allison, Liam, and Grant.

Contents at a Glance

Contents

About the Author

 **Jeanine Meyer** is a Full Professor at Purchase College/State University of New York. She teaches courses for mathematics/computer science and new media majors, as well as a mathematics class for humanities students. The web site for her academic activities is `http://faculty.purchase.edu/jeanine.meyer`. Before coming to academia, she was a Research Staff Member and Manager at IBM Research, working on robotics and manufacturing research and later as a consultant for IBM's educational grant programs.

For Jeanine, programming is both a hobby and a vocation. Every day she plays computer puzzles online (set game, kakuru, hashi, hitori and—often, still—tetris), and she does the crossword puzzle and ken ken in the newspaper (by hand and in ink—it's easier that way). She enjoys cooking, baking, eating, gardening, travel, and a moderate amount of walking. She greatly enjoys listening to her mother play piano and occasionally plays the flute. She is an active volunteer for progressive causes and candidates.

About the Technical Reviewer

Cheridan Kerr has been involved in Web Development and Design since 1997 when she began working in a research team for the Y2K Millennium Bug. It was here she learned about the Internet and promptly fell in love with the medium. In her career she has been responsible for web sites in the early 00s such as Weight Watchers Australia and **Quicken.com.au**, and she worked as Creative Services Manager of Yahoo!7 in Australia on clients such as Toyota, 20th Century Fox, and Ford. Currently she is working as Head of Digital for an Australian advertising agency.

Acknowledgments

Much appreciation to my students and colleagues at Purchase College/State University of New York for their inspiration, stimulation, and support.

Thanks to the crew at friends of ED: Ben Renow-Clarke, who encouraged me even before I quite grasped the idea of writing this book; Debra Kelly, who is an excellent project manager—which I needed; Cheridan Kerr, the technical reviewer, who provided important suggestions; and the art manager and many others I don't know by name.

And lastly, thanks to you, the reader. I am confident you can build on these ideas to make wonderful web sites.

Introduction

There's been considerable enthusiasm about the new capabilities of HTML5, and even suggestions that no other technologies or products are necessary to produce dynamic, engrossing, interactive web sites. That may be overstating things, but it is true the new features are exciting. It now is possible, using just HTML5, Cascading Style Sheets, and JavaScript, to draw lines, arcs, circles and ovals on the screen and specify events and event handling to produce animation and respond to user actions. You can include video and audio on your web site with standard controls, or place the video or audio in your application exactly when needed. You can create forms that validate the input and provide immediate feedback to users. You can use a facility similar to cookies to store information on the client computer. And you can use new elements, such as header and footer, to help structure your documents.

This book is based on my teaching practices and past writings. Delving into the features of a technology or general programming concepts is best done when there is a need. Games, especially familiar and simple ones, supply the need and thus the motivation and much of the explanation. When learning a new programming language, my first step is to program the game of craps. If I can build a ballistics simulation with animation, such as the slingshot game, and make a video or audio clip play when a specific condition occurs, I am happy. If I can construct my own maze of walls, draw a stick figure for hangman, and store information on the player's computer, I am ecstatic. And that's what we do in this book. As you see how to build these simple games, you'll build your expertise as well.

This goal of this book, developed with considerable help from the friends of ED staff and the technical reviewer, is to prepare you to produce your own web sites, including games and other dynamic applications, with a gentle introduction to the essentials of HTML5 and programming.

At the time of writing this book, not all browsers support all the HTML5 features. The applications have been tested using Chrome, FireFox, and Safari.

Who is this book for?

This book is for people who want to learn how HTML 5 can help build dynamic, exciting web sites. It's for you if you know something about programming and want to see what HTML 5 brings to the table. And it's also for you if you have no programming experience whatsoever. Perhaps you're a web designer or web site owner and you want to know how to make things happen behind the scenes. With this book, we want to showcase the new features of HTML5 and demystify the art of programming. Programming is an art, and creating appealing games and other applications requires real talent. However, if you can put together words to form sentences and sentences to form paragraphs, and you have some sense of logic, you can program.

How is this book structured?

The book consists of 10 chapters, each organized around a familiar game or similar application. There is considerable redundancy among the chapters so you can skip around if you like, though the games do get more complex. Each chapter starts by listing the technical features that will be covered and describing the application. We look first at the critical requirements in a general sense: what do we need to implement the application, independent of any specific technology. We then focus on the features of HTML5, CSS,

JavaScript, or general programming methodology that satisfy the requirements. Finally, we examine the implementation of the application in detail. I break out the code line by line in a table, with comments next to each line. In the cases where multiple versions of a game are described, only the new lines of code are annotated. This isn't to deprive you of information, but encourage you to see what is similar, what is different, and how you can build applications in stages. Each chapter includes suggestions on how to make the application your own, and how to test and upload the application to a web site. The summary at the end of each chapter highlights what you've learned and what you'll find ahead.

Conventions used in this book

The applications in this book each are HTML documents. The JavaScript is in a script element in the head element and the CSS is in the style element in the head element. The body element contains the static html, including any canvas elements. Several examples depend on external image files and one example requires external video files and another external audio files.

Layout conventions

To keep this book as clear and easy to follow as possible, the following text conventions are used throughout:

- Important words or concepts are normally highlighted on the first appearance in *italic type*.
- Code is presented in `fixed-width font`.
- The complete code for each application is presented in table with the left hand column holding each statement and the right hand column holding an explanatory comment.
- Pseudo-code is written in *`italic fixed-width font`*.
- Sometimes code won't fit on a single line in a book. Where this happens, I use an arrow like this: ➡.

So, with the formalities out of the way, let's get started.

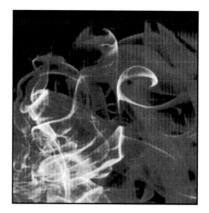

Chapter 1

The Basics

In this chapter, we will cover

- the basic structure of an HTML document
- the html, head, title, script, style, body, img, and a elements
- a Cascading Style Sheet (CSS) example
- a JavaScript code example, using Date and document.write

Introduction

Hypertext Markup Language (HTML) is the language for delivering content on the Web. HTML is not owned by anyone, but is the result of people working in many countries and many organizations to define the features of the language. An HTML document is a text document which you can produce using any text editor. HTML documents contain elements surrounded by tags—text that starts with a < symbol and ends with a > symbol. An example of a tag is `<img src="home.gif"/>`. This particular tag will display the image held in the file home.gif. These tags are the *markup*. It is through the use of tags that hyperlinks, images, and other media are included in web pages.

Basic HTML can include directives for formatting in a language called Cascading Style Sheets (CSS) and programs for interaction in a language called JavaScript. Browsers, such as Firefox and Chrome, interpret the HTML along with any CSS and JavaScript to produce what we experience when we visit a web site. HTML holds the content of the web site, with tags providing information on the nature and structure of the content as well as references to images and other media. CSS specifies the formatting. The same content can be formatted in different ways. JavaScript is a programming language that's used to make the web site dynamic and interactive. In all but the smallest working groups, different people may be responsible for the HTML, CSS, and JavaScript, but it's always a good idea to have a basic understanding of how these different tools work together. If you are already familiar with the basics of HTML and how CSS and JavaScript can be added together, you may want to skip ahead to the next chapter. Still, it may be worth casting your eye over the content in this chapter, to make sure you are up to speed on everything before we start on the first core examples.

The latest version of HTML (and its associated CSS and JavaScript) is HTML5. It is generating considerable excitement because of features such as the canvas for displaying pictures and animation; support for video and audio; and new tags for defining common document elements such as header, section, and footer. You can create a sophisticated, highly interactive web site with the new HTML5. As of this writing, not all browsers accept all the features, but you can get started learning HTML5, CSS, and JavaScript now. Learning JavaScript will introduce you to general programming concepts that will be beneficial if you try to learn any other programming language or if you work with programmers as part of a team.

The approach I'll use in this book is to explain HTML5, CSS, and JavaScript concepts in the context of specific examples, most of which will be familiar games. Along the way, I'll use small examples to demonstrate specific features. Hopefully, this will help you both understand what you want to do and appreciate how to do it. You will know where we are headed as I explain the concepts and details.

The task for this chapter is to build a web page of links to other web sites. In this way, you'll get a basic understanding of the structure of an HTML document, with a small amount of CSS code and JavaScript code. For this and other examples, please think of how to make the project meaningful to you. The page could be a list of your own projects, favorite sites, or sites on a particular topic. For each site, you'll see text and a hyperlink. The second example includes some extra formatting in the form of boxes around the text, pictures, and the day's date and time. Figure 1-1 and Figure 1-2 show the different examples I've created.

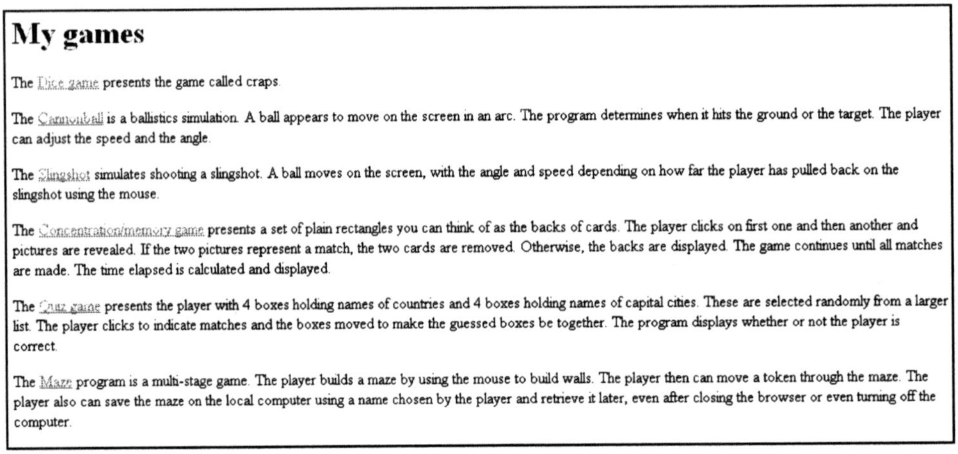

Figure 1-1. An annotated list of games

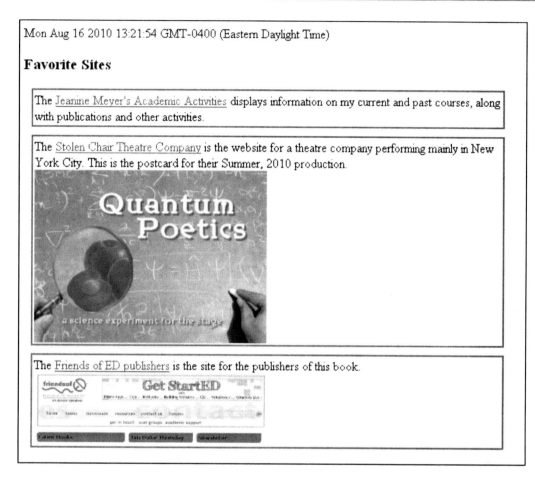

Figure 1-2. Favorite sites, with extra formatting

When you reload the Favorite Sites page, the date and time will change to the current date and time according to your computer.

Critical requirements

The requirements for the list of links application are the very fundamental requirements for building a web page containing text, links, and images. For the example shown in Figure 1-1, each entry appears as a paragraph. In the example shown in Figure 1-2, in contrast, each entry has a box around it. The second example also includes images and a way to obtain the current day, date, and time. Later applications will require more discussion, but for this one we'll go straight to how to implement it using HTML, CSS, and JavaScript.

HTML5, CSS, and JavaScript features

As I noted, HTML documents are text, so how do we specify links, pictures, formatting, and coding? The answer is in the markup, that is, the tags. Along with the HTML that defines the content, you'll typically find CSS styles, which can be specified either inside the HTML document or in an external document. You might also include JavaScript for interactivity, again specified in the HTML document or in an external document. We'll start with a look at how you can build simple HTML tags, and how you can add inline CSS and JavaScript all within the same document.

Basic HTML structure and tags

An HTML element begins with a starting tag, which is followed by the element content and an ending tag. The ending tag includes a / symbol followed by the element type, for example /head. Elements can be nested within elements. A standard HTML document looks like this:

```
<html>
    <head>
        <title>Very simple example
        </title>
    </head>
    <body>
        This will appear as is.
    </body>
</html>
```

Note that I've indented the nested tags here to make them more obvious, but HTML itself ignores this indentation (or whitespace, as it's known), and you don't need to add it to your own files. In fact, for most of the examples throughout this book I won't be indenting my code.

This document consists of the html element, indicated by the starting tag <html> and ending with the closing tag: </html>.

HTML documents typically have a head and a body element, as this one has. This head element contains one element, title. The HTML title shows up different places in different browsers. Figure 1-3 shows the title, "Very Simple Example" at the top-left portion of the screen and also on a tab in Firefox.

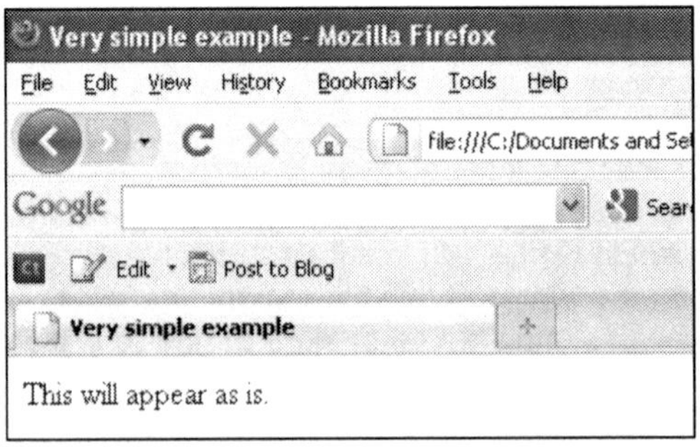

Figure 1-3. The HTML title in two places in Firefox

In most cases, you will create something within the body of the web page that you'll think of as a title, but it won't be the HTML title! Figure 1-3 also shows the body of the web page: the short piece of text. Notice that the words html, head, title and body do not appear. The tags "told" the browser how to display the HTML document.

We can do much more with text, but let's go on to see how to get images to appear. This requires an img element. Unlike html, head, and body elements that use starting and ending tags, the img element just uses one tag. It is called a singleton tag. Its element type is img (not image) and you put all the information with the tag itself using what are termed attributes. What information? The most important item is the name of the file that holds the image. The tag

```
<img src="frog.jpg"/>
```

tells the browser to look for a file with the name frog and the file type jpg. In this case, the browser looks in the same directory or folder as the HTML file. You can also refer to image files in other places and I'll show this later. The src stands for source. It is termed an attribute of the element. The slash before the > indicates that this is a singleton tag. There are common attributes for different element types, but most element types have additional attributes. Another attribute for img elements is the width attribute.

```
<img src="frog.jpg" width="200"/>
```

This specifies that the image should be displayed with a width of 200 pixels. The height will be whatever is necessary to keep the image at its original aspect ratio. If you want specific widths and heights, even if that may distort the image, specify both width and height attributes.

> Tip: You'll see examples (maybe even some of mine) in which the slash is omitted and which work just fine, but it is considered good practice to include it. Similarly, you'll see examples in which there are no quotation marks around the name of the file. HTML is more forgiving in terms of syntax (punctuation) than most other programming systems. Finally, you'll see HTML documents that start with a very fancy tag of type !DOCTYPE and have the HTML tag include other information. At this point, we don't need this so I will keep things as simple as I can (but no simpler, to quote Einstein).

Producing hyperlinks is similar to producing images. The type of element for a hyperlink is a and the important attribute is href.

```
<a href="http://faculty.purchase.edu/jeanine.meyer">Jeanine Meyer's Academic
Activities </a>
```

As you can see, this element has a starting and ending tag. The content of the element, whatever is between the two tags—in this case, Jeanine Meyer's Academic Activities—is what shows up in blue and underlined. The starting tag begins with a. One way to remember this is to think of it as the most important element in HTML, so it uses the first letter of the alphabet. You can also think of an anchor, which is what the a actually stands for, but that isn't as meaningful for me. The href attribute (think hypertext reference) specifies the web site where the browser goes when the hyperlink is clicked. Notice that this is a full Web address (called a Universal Resource Locator, or URL, for short).

We can combine a hyperlink element with an img element to produce a picture on the screen that a user can click on. Remember that elements can be nested within other elements. Instead of putting text after the starting <a> tag, put an <img> tag:

```
<a href="http://faculty.purchase.edu/jeanine">
<img src="jhome.gif" width="100" />
</a>
```

Let's put these examples together now:

```
<html>
<head>
<title>Second example </title>
</head>
<body>
This will appear as is.
<img src="frog.jpg"/>
<img src="frog.jpg" width="200"/>
<a href=http://faculty.purchase.edu/jeanine.meyer>Jeanine Meyer's Academic↪
 Activities </a>
<a href=http://faculty.purchase.edu/jeanine.meyer><img src="jhome.gif"/></a>
</body>
</html>
```

I created the HTML file, saved it as second.html, and then opened it up in the Chrome browser. Figure 1-4 shows what is displayed.

Figure 1-4. Example with images and hyperlinks

This produces the text; the image in its original width and height; the image with the width fixed at 200 pixels and height proportional; a hyperlink that will take you to my web page (I promise); and another link that uses an image that will also take you to my web page. However, this isn't quite what I had in mind. I wanted these elements spaced down the page.

This demonstrates something you need to remember: HTML ignores line breaks and other white space. If you want a line break, you have to specify it. One way is to use the br singleton tag. I'll show other ways later. Take a look at the following modified code. Notice that the <br/> tags don't need to be on a line by themselves.

```
<head>
<title>Second example </title>
<body>
This will appear as is. <br/>
<img src="frog.jpg"/>
<br/>
<img src="frog.jpg" width="200"/>
<br/>
<a href=http://faculty.purchase.edu/jeanine.meyer>Jeanine Meyer's Academic↪
 Activities </a>
<br/>
<a href=http://faculty.purchase.edu/jeanine.meyer><img src="jhome.gif"/></a>
</body>
</html>
```

Figure 1-5 shows what this code produces.

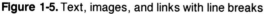

Figure 1-5. Text, images, and links with line breaks

There are many HTML element types: the h1 through h6 heading elements produce text of different sizes; there are various elements for lists and tables, and others for forms. CSS, as we'll see in a moment, is also used for formatting. You can select different fonts, background colors, and colors for the text, and control the layout of the document. It's considered good practice to put formatting in CSS, interactivity in JavaScript, and keep the HTML for the content. HTML5 provides new structural elements, such as article, section, footer, and header, and this makes it even easier to put the formatting in CSS. Doing this lets you easily change the formatting and the interactions. Formatting, including document layout, is a large topic. In this book, I stick to the basics.

Using cascading style sheets

CSS is a special language just for formatting. A style is essentially a rule that specifies how a particular element will be formatted. This means you can put style information in a variety of places: a separate file, a style element located in the head element, or a style within the HTML document, perhaps within the one element you want to format in a particular way. The styling information cascades, trickles down, unless a different style is specified. To put it another way, the style closest to the element is the one that's used. For example, you might use your official company fonts as given in the style section in the head element to flow through most of the text, but include specification within the local element to style one particular piece of text. Because that style is closest to the element, it is the one that is used.

The basic format includes an indicator of what is to be formatted followed by one or more directives. In the application for this chapter (available at www.friendsofed.com/downloads.html), I'll specify the formatting for elements of type section, namely a border or box around each item, margins, padding, and alignment, and a background of white. The complete HTML document in Listing 1-1 is a mixture (some would say a mess!) of features. The elements body and p (paragraph) are part of the original version of HTML. The section element is one of the new element types added in HTML5. The section element does need formatting, unlike body and p, which have default formatting that the body and each p element will start on a new line. CSS can modify the formatting of old and new element types. Notice that the background color for the text in the section is different from the background color for the text outside the section.

In the code in Listing 1-1, I specify styles for the body element (there is just one) and the section element If I had more than one section element, the styling would apply to each of them. The style for the body specifies a background color and a color for the text. CSS accepts a set of 16 colors by name, including black, white, red, blue, green, cyan, and pink. You can also specify color using RGB (red green blue) hexadecimal codes, but you'll need to use a graphics program, such as Adobe Photoshop, Corel Paint Shop Pro, or Adobe Flash Professional to figure out the RGB values, or you can experiment. I used Paint Shop Pro to determine the RGB values for the green in the frog head picture and used that for the border as well.

The text-align directives are just what they sound like: they indicate whether to center the material or align it to the left. The font-size sets the size of text in pixels. Borders are tricky and don't appear to be consistent across browsers. Here I've specified a solid green border of 4 pixels. The width specification for section indicates that the browser should use 85 percent of the window, whatever that is. The specification for p sets the width of the paragraph at 250 pixels. Padding refers to the spacing between the text and the borders of the section. The margin is the spacing between the section and its surroundings.

Listing 1-1. A Complete HTML Document with Styles

```
<html>
<head>
<title>CSS example </title>
<style>
body {
        background-color:tan;
```

```
        color: #EE015;
        text-align:center;
        font-size:22px;
}
section {
        width:85%;
        border:4px #00FF63 solid;
        text-align:left;
        padding:5px;
        margin:10px;
        background-color: white;
}

p {
        width: 250px;
}
</style>
</head>
<body>
The background here is tan and the text is the totally arbitrary RED GREEN BLUE↪
 value #EE015. <br/>
<section>Within the section, the background color is white. There is text with↪
 additional HTML markup, followed by a paragraph with text. Then, outside the↪
 section there will be text, followed by an image, more text and then a↪
 hyperlink. <p>The border color of the section matches the color of the↪
 frog image. </p></section>
<br/>
As you may have noticed, I like origami. The next image represents a frog head.<br/>
<img src="frogface.gif"/> <br/>If you want to learn how to fold it, go to

<a href=http://faculty.purchase.edu/jeanine.meyer/origami>the Meyer Family↪
 Origami Page <img src="crane.png" width="100"/></a>

</body>
</html>
```

This produces the screen shown in Figure 1-6.

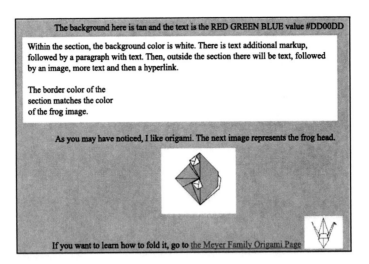

The background here is tan and the text is the RED GREEN BLUE value #DD00DD

Within the section, the background color is white. There is text additional markup, followed by a paragraph with text. Then, outside the section there will be text, followed by an image, more text and then a hyperlink.

The border color of the section matches the color of the frog image.

As you may have noticed, I like origami. The next image represents the frog head.

If you want to learn how to fold it, go to the Meyer Family Origami Page

Figure 1-6. Sample CSS styles

Tip: Don't be concerned if you don't understand everything immediately—you'll find lots of help on the Web. In particular, see the official source for HTML 5 at http://dev.w3.org/html5/spec/Overview.html.

There are many things you can do with CSS. You can use it to specify formatting for types of elements, as shown above; you can specify that elements are part of a class; and you can identify individual elements using the id attribute. In Chapter 6 where we create a quiz, I use CSS to position specific elements in the window and then JavaScript to move them around.

JavaScript programming

JavaScript is a programming language with built-in features for accessing parts of an HTML document, including styles in the CSS element. It is termed a scripting language to distinguish it from compiled languages, such as C++. Compiled languages are translated all at once, prior to use, while scripting languages are interpreted line by line by browsers. This text assumes no prior programming experience or knowledge of JavaScript, but it may help to consult other books, such as *Getting Started with JavaScript*, by Terry McNavage (friends of ED, 2010), or online sources such as http://en.wikipedia.org/wiki/JavaScript. Each browser owns its version of JavaScript.

An HTML document holds JavaScript in a script element, located in the head element. To display the time and date information as shown in Figure 1-2, I put the following within the head element of the HTML document:

```
<script>
document.write(Date());
</script>
```

JavaScript, like other programming languages, is made up of statements of various types. In later chapters, I'll show you assignment statements, compound statements such as if and switch and for statements, and statements that create what are called programmer-defined functions. A function is one or more statements that work together in a block and can be called anytime you need that functionality. Functions save writing out the same code over and over. JavaScript supplies many built-in functions. Certain functions are associated with objects (more on this later) and are called methods. The code

```
document.write("hello");
```

is a JavaScript statement that invokes the write method of the document object with the argument "hello". An argument is additional information passed to a function or method. Statements are terminated by semicolons. This piece of code will write out the literal string of characters h, e, l, l, o as part of the HTML document.

The document.write method writes out anything within the parentheses. Since I wanted the information written out to change as the date and time change, I needed a way to access the current date and time, so I used the built-in JavaScript Date function. This function produces an object with the date and time. Later, you'll see how to use Date objects to compute how long it takes for a player to complete a game. For now, all I want to do is display the current date and time information, and that's just what the code

```
document.write(Date());
```

does. To use the formal language of programming: this code calls (invokes) the write method of the document object, a built-in piece of code. The period (.) indicates that the write to be invoked is a method associated with the document produced by the HTML file. So, something is written out as part of the HTML document. What is written out? Whatever is between the opening parenthesis and the closing parenthesis. And what is that? It is the result of the call to the built-in function Date. The Date function gets information maintained by the local computer and hands it off to the write method. Date also requires the use of parentheses, which is why you see so many. The write method displays the date and time information as part of the HTML document, as shown in Figure 1-2. The way these constructs are combined is typical of programming languages. The statement ends with a semi-colon. Why not a period? A period has other uses in JavaScript, such as indicating methods and also for decimal points for numbers.

Natural languages, such as English, and programming languages have much in common: different types of statements; punctuation using certain symbols; and a grammar for the correct positioning of elements. In programming, we use the term notation instead of punctuation, and syntax instead of grammar. Both programming languages and natural languages also let you build up quite complex statements out of separate parts. However, there is a fundamental difference: As I tell my students, chances are good that much of what I say in class is not grammatically correct, but they'll still understand me. But when you're "talking" to a computer via a programming language, your code must be perfect in terms of the grammatical rules of the language to get what you want. The good news is that unlike a human audience, computers do not exhibit impatience or any other human emotion so you can take the time you need to get things right. There's also some bad news that may take you a while to appreciate: If you make a mistake in grammar— termed a syntactic error—in HTML, CSS, or JavaScript, the browser still tries to display something. It's up to you figure out what and where the problem is when you don't get the results you wanted in your work.

Building the application and making it your own

You build an HTML document using a text editor and you view/test/play the document using a browser. Though you can use any text editor program to write the HTML, I suggest TextPad for PCs and TextWrangler for Macs. These are shareware, which makes them relatively inexpensive. Don't use a word processing program, which may insert non-text characters. Notepad also works, though TextPad has benefits such as color-coding that I'll demonstrate. To use the editor, you open it up and type in the code. Figure 1-7 shows what the TextPad screen looks like.

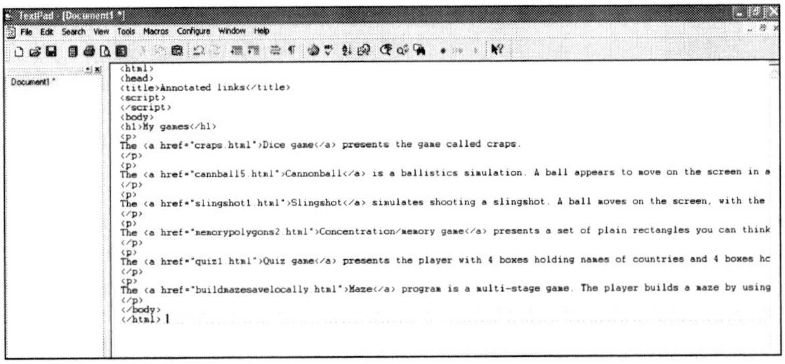

Figure 1-7. Starting off in TextPad

You will want to save your work frequently and, most important, save it as the file type .html. In TextPad, click on **File ➤ Save As** and then change the **Save as type** to HTML, as shown in Figure 1-8.

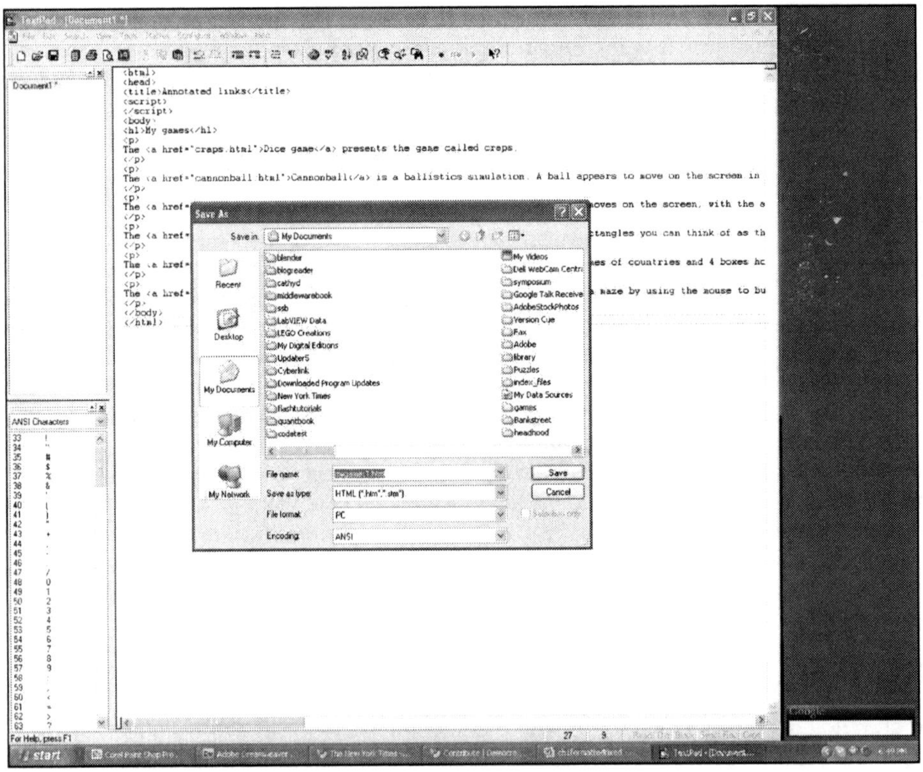

Figure 1-8. Saving a file as type HTML

Notice that I gave the file a name and that I can also change the folder from My Documents to something else if I want. After saving the file, and clicking on Configure ➤ Word Wrap (to make the long lines visible on the screen), the window appears as shown in Figure 1-9.

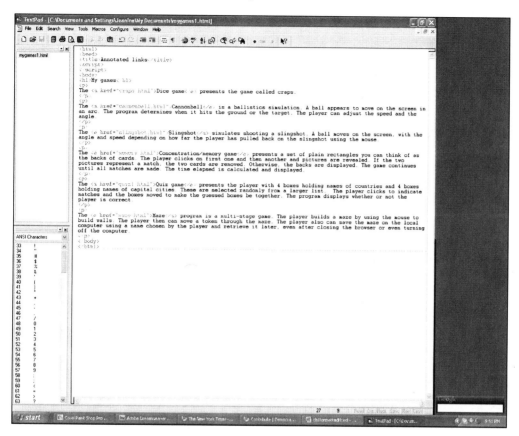

Figure 1-9. After saving the file as HTML and invoking word wrap

The color coding, which you'll see only after the file is saved as HTML, indicates tags and quoted strings. This can be valuable for catching many errors.

Now let's delve into the HTML coding, first for the list of annotated links and then for the favorite sites. The code uses the features described in the previous section. Table 1-1 shows the complete code for this application: paragraphs of text with links to different files, all located in the same folder.

Table 1-1. The "My games" Annotated Links Code

Code	Explanation
`<html>`	Opening `html` tag
`<head>`	Opening `head` tag
`<title>Annotated links</title>`	Opening `title` tag, the title text and closing `title` tag
`<body>`	Opening `body` tag
`<h1>My games</h1>`	Opening `h1` tag, text and then closing `h1` tag. This will make "My games" appear in a big font. The actual font will be the default.
`<p>`	Opening `p` for paragraph tag
The `<a href="craps.html">Dice game</a>` presents the game called craps.	Text with an `a` element. The opening `a` tag has the attribute `href` set to the value craps.html. Presumably this is a file in the same folder as this HTML file. The contents of the `a` element—whatever is between the `<a>` and the `</a>`—will be displayed, first in blue and then in mauve once clicked, and underlined.
`</p>`	Closing `p` tag
`<p>`	Opening `p` tag
The `<a href="cannonball.html">Cannonball</a>` is a ballistics simulation. A ball appears to move on the screen in an arc. The program determines when the ball hits the ground or the target. The player can adjust the speed and the angle.	See the previous case. The `a` element here refers to the cannonball.html file and the displayed text is Cannonball.
`</p>`	Closing `p` tag
`<p>`	Opening `p` tag

Code	Explanation
The `<a href="slingshot.html">Slingshot</a>` simulates shooting a slingshot. A ball moves on the screen, with the angle and speed depending on how far the player has pulled back on the slingshot using the mouse.	See previous. This paragraph contains the hyperlink to slingshot.html.
`</p>`	Closing p tag
`<p>`	Opening p tag
The `<a href="memory.html">Concentration/memory game</a>` presents a set of plain rectangles you can think of as the backs of cards. The player clicks on first one and then another and pictures are revealed. If the two pictures represent a match, the two cards are removed. Otherwise, the backs are displayed. The game continues until all matches are made. The time elapsed is calculated and displayed.	See previous. This paragraph contains the hyperlink to memory.html.
`</p>`	Closing p tag
`<p>`	Opening p tag
The `<a href="quiz1.html">Quiz game</a>` presents the player with 4 boxes holding names of countries and 4 boxes holding names of capital cities. These are selected randomly from a larger list. The player clicks to indicate matches and the boxes are moved to put the guessed boxes together. The program displays whether or not the player is correct.	See previous. This paragraph contains the hyperlink to quiz1.html
`</p>`	Closing p tag
`<p>`	Opening p tag

Code	Explanation
The `<a href="maze.html">Maze</a>` program is a multi-stage game. The player builds a maze by using the mouse to build walls. The player then can move a token through the maze. The player can also save the maze on the local computer using a name chosen by the player and retrieve it later, even after closing the browser or turning off the computer.	See previous. This paragraph contains the hyperlink to maze.html.
`</p>`	Closing `p` tag
`</body>`	Closing `body` tag
`</html>`	Closing `html` tag

The Favorite Site code has the features of the annotated list with the addition of formatting: a green box around each item and a picture in each item. See Table 1-2.

Table 1-2. The Favorites Sites Code

Code	Explanation
`<html>`	Opening `html` tag
`<head>`	Opening `head` tag
`<title>Annotated links</title>`	Complete `title` element: opening and closing tag and Annotated links in between
`<style>`	Opening `style` tag. This means we're now going to use CSS.
`Article {`	Start of a style. The reference to what is being styled is all `section` elements. The style then has a brace - {. The opening and closing braces surround the style rule we're creating, much like opening and closing tags in HTML.
`width:60%;`	The `width` is set to 60% of the containing element. Note that each directive ends with a ; .
`text-align:left;`	Text is aligned to the left
`margin:10px;`	The margin is 10 pixels

Code	Explanation
`border:2px green double;`	The border is a 2-pIxel green double line
`padding:2px;`	The space between the text and the border is 2 pixels
`display:block;`	The article is a block, meaning there are line breaks before and after
`}`	Closes the style for `article`
`</style>`	Closing `style` tag
`<script>`	Opening `script` tag. We are now writing JavaScript code
`document.write(Date());`	One statement of code: write out what is produced by the `Date()` call
`</script>`	Closing `script` tag
`<body>`	Opening `body` tag
`<h3>Favorite Sites</h3>`	Text surrounded by h3 and /h3 tags. This make the text appear somewhat larger than the norm.
`<article>`	Opening `article` tag
`The <a href="../index.html">Jeanine Meyer's Academic Activities</a> displays information on my current and past courses, along with publications and other activities.`	This text will be subject to the style specified. It includes an a element. Notice that the value for the `href` attribute is a relative reference: it says: go to the parent folder of the current folder and then to the index.html file. Two periods (..) is computer-speak for "go back a folder level", so if we were in the tree/fruit/apple folder, then ../index.html would take us back to the fruit folder to find the index file, and ../../index.html would take us back to the tree folder.
`</article>`	Closing `article` tag
`<article>`	Opening `article` tag

Code	Explanation
The `<a href="http://stolenchair.⤶ org">Stolen Chair Theatre Company</a>` is the web site of a theatre company performing mainly in New York City. This is the postcard for their Summer, 2010 production.` `	See previous. Notice that the value for the `href` attribute here is a full Web address, and that the HTML includes a ` ` tag. This will force a line break.
`<img src="postcard.jpg" width="300"/>`	An `img` tag. The source of the image is the file postcard.jpg. The width is set at 300 pixels.
`</article>`	Closing `article` tag
`<article>`	Opening `article` tag
The `<a href="http://friendsofed⤶ .com/">friends of ED publishers</a>` is the site for the publishers of this book. ` `	See previous. This also refers to a Web address. A ` ` tag will force a line break before the image.
`<img src="friendsofed.gif" width="300"/>`	An `img` element. The source is friendsofed.gif. The width is set at 300 pixels.
`</article>`	Closing `article` tag
`</body>`	Closing `body` tag
`</html>`	Closing `html` tag

It is pretty straightforward how to make this application your own: use your own favorite sites. In most browsers, you can download and save image files if you want to use a site logo for the hyperlink, or you can include other pictures. It is my understanding that making a list of sites with comments and including images such as logos is within the practice called "fair use," but I am not a lawyer. For the most part, people like links to their sites. It doesn't affect the legal question, but you can also choose to set the `src` in the `img` tag to the Web address of the site where the image lives if you'd rather not download a particular image file to your computer and then upload it to your web site.

Web addresses can be absolute or relative. An absolute address starts with http://. A relative address is relative to the location of the HTML file. In my example, the postcard.jpg and the friendsofed.gif are both located in the same folder as my HTML file. They are there because I put them there! For large projects, many people put all the images in a subfolder called images and write addresses as "images/postcard.gif".

You also can make this application your own by changing the formatting. Styles can be used to specify fonts, including specific font, font family, and size. This lets you pick a favorite font, and also specify what font to use if the preferred font is not available on the user's computer. You can specify the margin and padding or vary independently the margin-top, margin-left, padding-top, and so forth.

Testing and uploading the application

You need to have all the files, in this case the single HTML file plus all image files, in the same folder unless you are using full Web addresses. For the links to work, you need to have the correct addresses for all href attributes. My examples show how to do this for HTML files in the same folder or for HTML files somewhere else on the Web.

You can start testing your work even if it is not completely done. For example, you can put in a single img element or a single a element. Open up a browser, such as Firefox, Chrome, or Safari (I didn't mention Internet Explorer because it does not yet support some of the HTML5 features I'll be using in other tutorials, though support is coming in IE9). In Firefox, click on File and then Open file and browse to your HTML file. In Chrome, press Ctrl on the PC (CMD on the MAC) and o and then browse to the file and click OK to open it. You should see something like my examples. Click on the hyperlinks to get to the other sites. Reload the page using the reload icon for the browser and observe the different time. If you don't see what you expect—something like my examples—you need to examine your code. Common mistakes are

- missing or mismatched opening and closing tags.
- wrong name for image files or HTML files, or wrong file extension for the image files. You can use image files of type JPG, GIF, or PNG but the file extension named in the tag must match the actual file type of the image.
- missing quotation marks. The color coding, as available in TextPad and some other editors, can help you identify this.

Summary

In this chapter, you learned how to compose HTML documents with text, images, and hyperlinks. This included

- the basic tags, including html, head, title, style, script, body.
- the img element for displaying images.
- the a element for hyperlinks.
- simple formatting using a style element written following Cascading Style Sheet (CSS) rules.
- a single line of JavaScript code to provide date and time information.

This chapter was just the beginning, though it's possible to produce beautiful and informative web pages using basic HTML, with or without Cascading Style Sheets. In the next chapter, you will learn how to include randomness and interactivity in an application, and how to use the canvas element, the critical feature of HTML5.

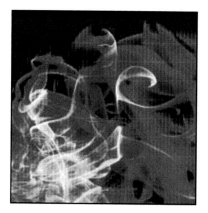

Chapter 2

Dice Game

In this chapter, we will cover

- drawing on canvas
- random processing
- game logic
- form output

Introduction

Among the most important new features in HTML5 is the `canvas`. This element provides a way for developers to make line drawings, include images, and position text in a totally free-form fashion, a significant improvement over the older HTML. Although you could do some fancy formatting in the earlier versions, layouts tended to be boxy and pages less dynamic. How do you draw on the canvas? You use a scripting language, usually JavaScript. I will show you how to draw on canvas and I'll explain the important features of JavaScript that we'll need to build an implementation of the dice game called craps: how to define a function, how to invoke what is termed *pseudo-random behavior*, how to implement the logic of this particular game, and how to display information to a player. Before we go any further, though, you need to understand the basics of the game.

The game of craps has the following rules:

The player throws a pair of dice. The sum of the two top faces is what matters so a 1 and a 3 is the same as 2 and 2. The sum of two 6-sided dice can be any number from 2 to 12. If the player throws a 7 or 11 on the first throw, the player wins. If the player throws a 2, 3, or 12, the player loses. For any other result (4, 5, 6, 8, 9, 10), this result is recorded as what is called the player's point and a follow-up throw is required. On follow-up throws, a throw of 7 loses and a throw of the player's point wins. For anything else, the game continues with the follow-up throw rules.

Let's see what our game play might look like. Figure 2-1 shows the result of a throw of two ones at the start of the game.

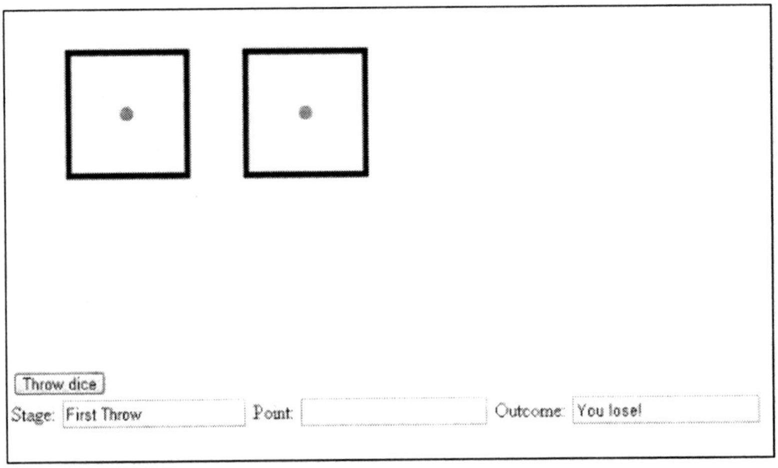

Figure 2-1. First throw, resulting in a loss for the player

It is not apparent here, but our dice game application draws the die faces each time using the `canvas` tag. This means it's not necessary to download images of individual die faces.

A throw of two 1s means a loss for the player since the rules define 2, 3, or 12 on a first throw as a loss. The next example shows a win for the player, a 7 on a first throw, as shown in Figure 2-2.

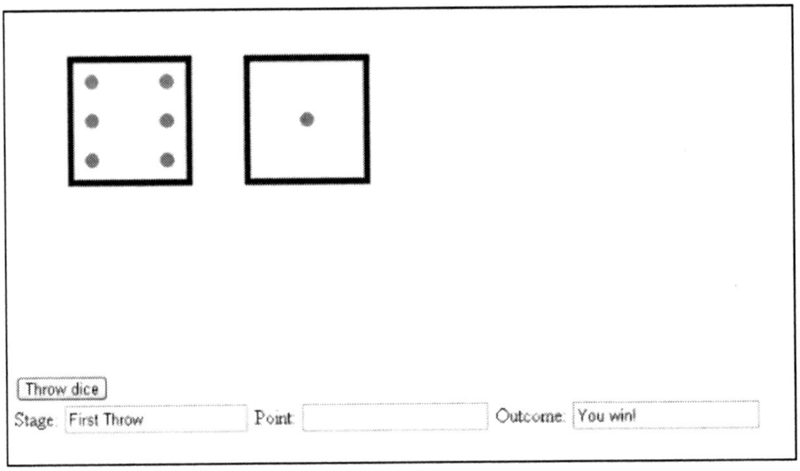

Figure 2-2. A 7 on a first throw means the player wins.

Figure 2-3 shows the next throw—an 8. This is neither a win nor a loss, but means there must be a follow-up throw.

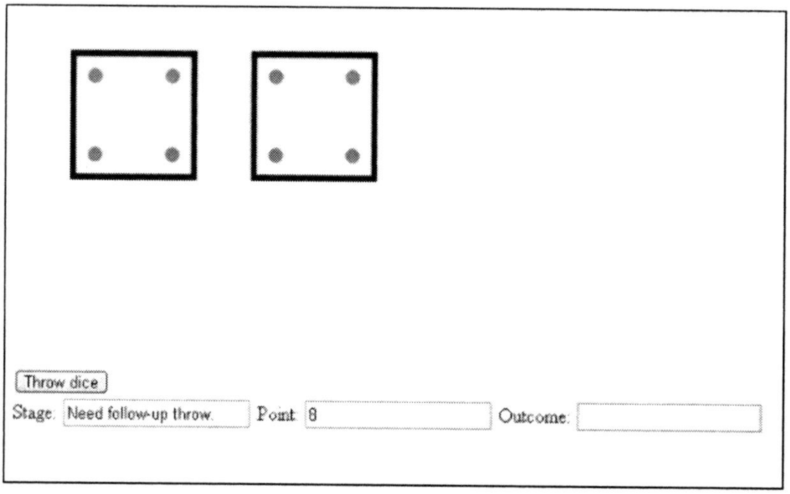

Figure 2-3. An 8 means a follow-up throw with a player's point of 8 carried over.

Let's assume that the player eventually throws an 8 again, as indicated in Figure 2-4.

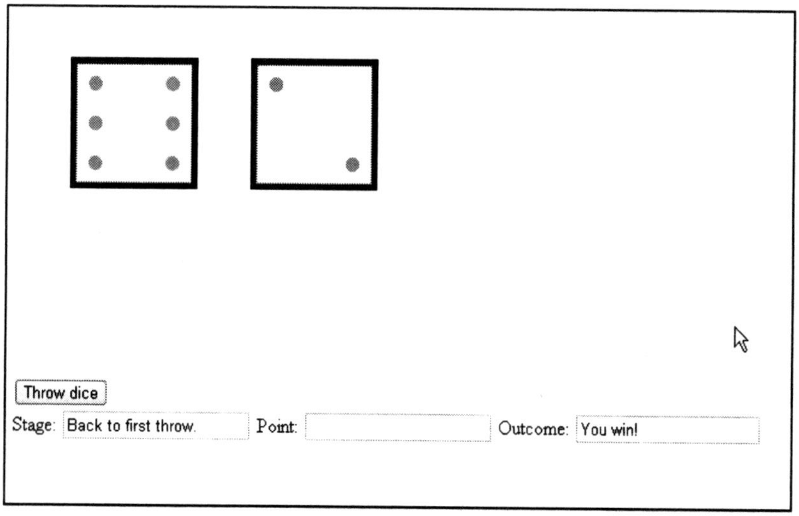

Figure 2-4. It's another throw of 8, the point value, so the player wins.

As the previous sequence shows, the only thing that counts is the sum of the values on the faces of the dice. The point value was set with two 4s, but the game was won with a 2 and a 6.

The rules indicate that a game will not always take the same number of throws of the dice. The player can win or lose on the first throw, or there may be any number of follow-up throws. It is the game builder's job is to build a game that works—and working means following the rules, even if that means play goes on and on. My students sometimes act as if their games only work if they win. In a correct implementation of the game, players will win and lose.

Critical requirements

The requirements for building the dice game begin with simulating the random throwing of dice. At first, this seems impossible since programming means specifying exactly what the computer will do. Luckily, JavaScript, like most other programming languages, has a built-in facility that produces results that appear to be random. Sometimes languages make use of the middle bits (1s and 0s) of a very long string of bits representing the time in milliseconds. The exact method isn't important to us. We will assume that the JavaScript furnished by the browser does an okay job with this, which is called pseudo-random processing.

Assuming now that we can randomly get any number from 1 to 6 and do it twice for the two die faces, we need to implement the rules of the game. This means we need a way to keep track of whether we are at a first throw or a follow-up throw. The formal name for this is the *application state*, which means the way things are right now, and is important in both games and other types of applications. Then we need to use constructs that make decisions based on conditions. Conditional constructs such as if and switch are a standard part of programming languages, and you'll soon understand why computer science teachers like me—who have never been in a casino or a back alley—really like the game of craps.

We need to give the player a way to throw the dice, so we'll implement a button on the screen to click for that. Then we need to provide information back to the player on what happened. For this application, I produced graphical feedback by drawing dice faces on the screen and also displayed information as text to indicate the stage of the game, the point value, and the result. The older term for interactions with users was *input-output (I/O),* back when that interaction mainly involved text. The term *graphical user interface (GUI)* is now commonly used to indicate the vast variety of ways that users interact with computer systems. These include using the mouse to click on a specific point on the screen or combining clicks with dragging to simulate the effect of moving an object (see the slingshot game in Chapter 4). Drawing on the screen requires the use of a coordinate system to specify points. Coordinate systems for the computer screen are implemented in similar ways in most programming languages, as I'll explain shortly.

HTML5, CSS, and JavaScript features

Let's now take a look at the specific features of HTML5, CSS, and JavaScript that provide what we need to implement the craps game.

Pseudo-random processing and mathematical expressions

Pseudo-random processing in JavaScript is performed using a built-in method called Math.random. Formally, random is a *method* of the Math *class*. The Math.random method generates a number from 0 up to, but not including 1, resulting in a decimal number, for example, 0.253012. This may not seem immediately useful for us, but it's actually a very simple process to convert that number into one we can use. We multiply that number, whatever it is, by 6, which produces a number from 0 up to but not including 6. For example, if we multiply the .253012 by 6 we get 1.518072. That's almost what we need, but not quite. The next step is to strip away the fraction and keep the whole number. To do that, we make use of another Math method, Math.floor. This method produces a whole number after removing any fractional part. As the name suggests, the floor method rounds down. In our particular case, we started with .253012, then arrived at 1.518072, so the result is the whole number 1. In general, when we multiply our random number by 6 and floor it, we'll get a number from 0 to 5. The final step is to add a 1, because our goal is to get a number from 1 to 6, over and over again, with no particular pattern.

You can use a similar approach to get whole numbers in any range. For example, if you want the numbers 1 to 13, you'd multiply the random number by 13 and then add 1. This could be useful for a card game. You'll see similar examples throughout this book.

We can combine all of these steps together into what is called an *expression*. Expressions are combinations of constants, methods, and function calls, and some things we'll explore later. We put these items together using operators, such as + for addition and * for multiplication.

Remember from Chapter 1 how tags can be combined—nesting a tag within another tag—and the one line of JavaScript code we used in the Favorite Sites application:

```
document.write(Date());
```

We can use a similar process here. Instead of having to write the `random` call and then the `floor` method as separate statements, we can pass the `random` call as an argument of the `floor` method. Take a look at this code fragment:

```
1+Math.floor(Math.random()*6)
```

This *expression* will produce a number from 1 to 6. I call it a code fragment because it isn't quite a statement. The operators + and * refer to the arithmetic operations and are the same as you'd use in normal math. The order of operations starts from the inside and works out.

- Invoke `Math.random()` to get a decimal number from 0 up to, but not quite 1.
- Multiply the result by 6.
- Take that and strip away the fraction, leaving the whole number, using `Math.floor`.
- Add 1.

You'll see a statement with this expression in our final code, but we need to cover a few other things first.

Variables and assignment statements

Like other programming languages, JavaScript has a construct called a *variable,* which is essentially a place to put a value, such as a number. It is a way of associating a name with a value. You can use the value later by referencing the name. One analogy is to office holders. In the USA, we speak of "the president." Now, in 2010, the president is Barack Obama. Before January 21, 2009, it was George W. Bush. The value held by the term "the president" changes. In programming, the value of the variable can vary as well, hence the name.

The term `var` is used to *declare* a variable.

The names of variables and functions, described in the next section, are up to the programmer. There are rules: no internal blanks and the name must start with an alphabetic character. Don't make the names too long as you don't want to type too much, but don't make them so short you forget what they are. You do need to be consistent, but you don't need to obey the rules of English spelling. For example, if you want to set up a variable to hold the sum of values and you believe that sum is spelled som, that's fine. Just make sure you use som all the time. But if you want to refer to something that's a part of JavaScript, such as `function` or `document` or `random`, you need to use the spelling that JavaScript expects.

You should avoid using the names of built-in constructs in JavaScript (such as `random` or `floor`) for your variables. Try to make the names unique, but still easily understandable. One common method of writing variable names is to use what's called camel case. This involves starting your variable name in lower case, then using a capital letter to denote when a new word starts, for example, numberOfTurns or userFirstThrow. You can see why it's called camel case—the capitals form "humps" in the word. You don't have to use this naming method, but it's a convention many programmers follow.

The line of code that will hold the pseudo-random expression explained in the previous section is a particular type of statement called an *assignment* statement. For example,

```
var ch = 1+Math.floor(Math.random()*);
```

sets the variable named ch to the value that is the result of the expression on the right-hand side of the equal sign. When used in a var statement, it also would be termed an *initialization* statement. The = symbol is used for setting initial values for variables as in this situation and in the assignment statements to be described next. I chose to use the name ch as shorthand for choice. This is meaningful for me. In general, though, if you need to choose between a short name and a longer one that you will remember, pick the longer one! Notice that the statement ends with a semi-colon. You may ask, why not a period? The answer is that a period is used in two other situations: as a decimal point and for accessing methods and properties of objects, as in document.write.

Assignment statements are the most common type of statements in programming. Here's an example of an assignment statement for a variable already defined:

```
bookname = "The Essential Guide to HTML5";
```

The use of the equal sign may be confusing. Think of it as making it true that the left-hand side equals what's produced by the right-hand side. You'll encounter many other variables and other uses of operators and assignment statements in this book.

> *Caution: The var statement defining a variable is called a declaration statement. JavaScript, unlike many other languages, allows programmers to omit declaration statements and just start to use a variable. I try to avoid doing that, but you will see it in many online examples.*

For the game of craps, we need variables that define the state of the game, namely whether it is a first throw or a follow-up throw, and what the player's point is (remember that the point is the value of the previous throw). In our implementation, these values will be held by so-called *global variables*, variables defined with var statements outside of any function definition so as to retain their value (the values of variables declared inside of functions disappear when the function stops executing).

You don't always need to use variables. For example, the first application we create here sets up variables to hold the horizontal and vertical position of the dice. I could have put literal numbers in the code because I don't change these numbers, but since I refer to these values in several different places, storing the values in variables mean that if I want to change one or both, I only need to make the change in one place.

Programmer-defined functions

JavaScript has many built-in functions and methods, but it doesn't have everything you might need. For example, as far as I know, it does not have functions specifically for simulating the throwing of dice. So JavaScript lets us define and use our own functions. These functions can take *arguments*, like the Math.floor method, or not, like Math.random. Arguments are values that may be passed to the function. Think of them as extra information. The format for a function definition is the term function followed by the name you want to give the function, followed by parentheses holding the names of any arguments, followed by an open bracket, some code, and then a closed bracket. As I note in the previous sections, the programmer chooses the name. Here's an example of a function definition that returns the product of the two arguments. As the name indicates, you could use it to compute the area of a rectangle.

```
function areaOfRectangle(wd,ln) {
    return wd * ln;
}
```

Notice the `return` keyword. This tells JavaScript to send the result of the function back to us. In our example, this lets us write something like `rect1 = areaOfRectangle(5,10)`, which would assign a value of 50 (5 × 10) to our `rect1` variable. The function definition would be written as code within the `script` element. It might or might not make sense to define this function in real life because it is pretty easy to write multiplication in the code, but it does serve as a useful example of a programmer-defined function. Once this definition is executed, which probably would be when the HTML file is loaded, other code can use the function just by calling its name, as in `areaOfRectangle(100,200)` or `areaOfRectangle(x2-x1,y2-y1)`.

The second expression assumes that x1, x2, y1, y2 refer to coordinate values that are defined elsewhere.

Functions also can be called by setting certain tag attributes. For example, the `body` tag can include a setting for the `onLoad` attribute:

```
<body onLoad="init();">
```

My JavaScript code contains the definition of a function I call `init`. Putting this into the `body` element means that JavaScript will invoke my `init` function when the browser first loads the HTML document or whenever the player clicks on the reload/refresh button. Similarly, making use of one of the new features of HTML5, I could include the button element:

```
<button onClick="throwdice();">Throw dice </button>
```

This creates a button holding the text `Throw dice`. When the player clicks it, JavaScript invokes the `throwdice` function I defined in the `script` element.

The `form` element, to be described later, could invoke a function in a similar way.

Conditional statements: *if* and *switch*

The craps game has a set of rules. One way to summarize the rules is to say, if it is a first-throw situation, we check for certain values of the dice throw. If it's not the first throw, we check for other values of the dice throw. JavaScript provides the `if` and `switch` statements for such purposes.

The `if` statement is based on *conditions,* which can be a comparison or a check for equality—for example, is a variable named `temp` greater than 85 or does the variable named `course` hold the value "Programming Games". Comparisons produce two possible logical values—true or false. So far you've seen values that are numbers and values that are strings of characters. Logical values are yet another data type. They are also called *Boolean* values, after the mathematician, George Boole. The condition and check that I mentioned would be written in code as

```
temp>85
```

and

```
course == "Programming Games"
```

Read the first expression as: Is the current value of the variable `temp` greater than 85?

and the second one as: Is the current value of the variable course the same as the string "Programming Games"?

The comparison example is easy to understand; we use > to check if one value is greater than another, and < to check the opposite. The value of the expression will be one of the two logical values true or false.

The second expression is probably a little more confusing. You may be wondering about the two equal signs and maybe also the quotation marks .The comparison operator in JavaScript (and several other programming languages) that checks for equality is this combination of two equal signs. We need two equal signs because the single equal sign is used in assignment statements and it can't do double duty. If we had written course = "Programming Games", we would have been assigning the value "Programming Games" to our course variable rather than comparing the two items. The quotation marks define a string of characters, starting with P, including the space, and ending with s.

With that under our belts, we can now take a look at how to write code that does something only if a condition is true.

```
if (condition) {
    code
}
```

If we want our code to do one thing if a condition is true and another thing if it is NOT true, the format is:

```
if (condition) {
    if true code
}
else {
    if not true code
}
```

Note that I used italics here because this is what is called *pseudo-code*, not real JavaScript that we would include in our HTML document.

Here are some real code examples. They make use of alert, a built-in function that causes a small window with the message indicated by the argument given between the parentheses to pop up in the browser. The user must click OK to continue.

```
if (temp>85) {
    alert("It is hot!");
}
if (age > 21) {
    alert("You are old enough to buy a drink.");
}
else {
    alert("You are too young to be served in a bar.");
}
```

We could write the craps application using just if statements. However, JavaScript supplies another construct that makes things easier—the switch statement. The general format is:

```
switch(x) {
case a:
```

```
    codea;
case b:
    codeb;
default: codec;
}
```

JavaScript evaluates the value of x in the first line of the switch statement and compares it to the values indicated in the cases. Once there is a hit, that is, x is determined to be equal to a or b, the code following the case label is executed. If there is no match, the code after default is executed. It's not necessary to have a default possibility. Left to its own devices, the computer would continue running through the switch statement even if it found a matching case statement. If you want it to stop when you find a match, you need to include a break statement to break out of the switch.

You can probably see already how if and switch will do what we need for the dice game. You'll read how in the next section. First, let's look at an example that determines the number of days in the month indicated by the variable mon holding three-letter abbreviations ("Jan", "Feb", etc.).

```
switch(mon) {
case "Sep":
case "Apr":
case "Jun":
case "Nov":
        alert("This month has 30 days.");
        break;
case "Feb":
        alert("This month has 28 or 29 days.");
        break;
default:
        alert("This month has 31 days.");
}
```

If the value of the variable mon is equal to "Sep", "Apr", "Jun", or "Nov", control flows to the first alert statement and then exits the switch statement because of the break. If the value of the variable mon is equal to "Feb", the alert statement mentioning 28 or 29 days executes and then the control flow exits the switch. If the value of mon is anything else, including, by the way, an invalid three-letter abbreviation, the alert mentioning 31 days is executed.

Just as HTML ignores line breaks and other white space, JavaScript does not require a specific layout for these statements. You could put everything on one line if you wished. However, make things easy on yourself and use multiple lines.

Drawing on the canvas

Now we get to one of the most powerful new features in HTML5, the canvas element. I will explain the pieces of coding that go into an application involving canvas, then show some simple examples, and finally get back to our goal of drawing dice faces on the canvas. Recall that the outline for an HTML document is

```
<html>
        <head>
                <title>… </title>
```

29

```
                    <script> …. </script>
            </head>
            <body>
            … Here is where the initial static content will go…
            </body>
</html>
```

To work with the canvas, we include the tags for canvas in the body element of the HTML document and JavaScript in the script element. I'll start by describing a standard way to write a canvas element.

```
<canvas id="canvas" width="400" height="300">
Your browser doesn't support the HTML5 element canvas.
</canvas>
```

If an HTML file with this coding is opened by a browser that does not recognize canvas, the message Your browser doesn't support the HTML5 element canvas. appears on the screen. If you were preparing web pages for all common browsers, you could choose to direct visitors to your site to something else or try another strategy. In this book, I just focus on HTML5.

The HTML canvas tag defines this element to have an id of "canvas". This could have been anything, but there's no harm in using canvas. You can have more than one canvas, however, and in that case, you would need to use distinct values for each id. That's not what we do for this application, though, so we don't have to worry about it. The attributes of width and height are set to specify the dimensions of this canvas element.

Now that we've seen the canvas in the body, let's look at the JavaScript. The first step in drawing on the canvas is to define the appropriate object in the JavaScript code. To do this, I need a variable so I set up one named ctx with the line

```
var ctx;
```

outside of any function definition. This makes it a global variable that can be accessed or set from any function. The ctx variable is something that's needed for all drawing. I chose to name my variable ctx, short for context, copying many of the examples I've seen online. I could have chosen any name.

Later in the code (you'll see all the code in the examples that follow, and you can download it from www.friendsofed.com/downloads.html), I write the code to set the value of ctx.

```
    ctx = document.getElementById('canvas').getContext('2d');
```

What this does is first get the element in the document with the id 'canvas' and then extract what is called the '2d' context. We can all anticipate that the future may bring other contexts! For now, we use the 2d one.

In the JavaScript coding, you can draw rectangles, paths including line segments and arcs, and position image files on the canvas. You can also fill in the rectangles and the paths. Before we do this, however, we need to tackle coordinate systems and radian measures.

Just as a global positioning system uses latitude and longitude to define your location on the map, we need a way to specify points on the screen. These points are called pixels, and we used them in the previous chapter to specify the width of images and the thickness of borders. The pixel is a pretty small unit of measurement, as you can see if you do any experiments. However, it's not enough for everyone to agree on the linear unit. We also need to agree on the point from which we are measuring, just as GPS systems use the Greenwich Meridian and the equator. For the two-dimensional rectangle that is the canvas, this goes by the name *origin* or *registration point.* The origin is the upper left corner of the canvas element. Note that in Chapter 6, when we describe the quiz show by creating and positioning elements in the HTML document and not in a canvas element, the coordinate system is similar. The origin is still the upper left corner of the window.

This is different from what you may recall from analytical geometry or from making graphs. The horizontal numbers increase in value moving from left to right. The vertical numbers increase in value moving *down* the screen. The standard way to write coordinates is to put the horizontal value first, followed by the vertical value. In some situations, the horizontal value is referred to as the x value and the vertical, the y value. In other situations, the horizontal value is the left (think of it as from the left) and the vertical value is the top (think of it as from the top).

Figure 2-5 shows the layout of a browser window 900 pixels wide by 600 high. The numbers indicate the coordinate values of the corners and the middle.

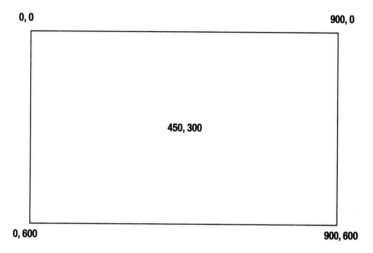

Figure 2-5. Coordinate system for browser window.

Now we'll look at several statements for drawing, and then put them together to draw simple shapes (see Figures 2-6 through 2-10). After that we'll see how to draw the dots and rectangles to represent die faces.

Here's the HTML5 JavaScript code for drawing a rectangle:

```
ctx.strokeRect(100,50,200,300);
```

This draws a hollow rectangle, with its top left corner 100 pixels from the left side and 50 pixels down from the top. The rectangle has width 200, and height 300. This statement would use whatever the current settings are for line width and for color.

The next piece of code demonstrates setting the line width to 5 and the color of the stroke, that is, the outline to the indicated RGB value, namely red. The rectangle is drawn using the values in the variables x, y, w, and h.

```
ctx.lineWidth = 5;
ctx.strokeStyle = "rgb(255,0,0)";
ctx.strokeRect(x,y,w,h);
```

This snippet

```
ctx.fillStyle = "rgb(0,0,255)";
ctx.fillRect(x,y,w,h);
```

draws a solid blue rectangle at the indicated position and dimensions. If you want to draw a blue rectangle with a red outline, you use two lines of code:

```
ctx.fillRect(x,y,w,h);
ctx.strokeRect(x,y,w,h);
```

HTML5 lets you draw so-called paths consisting of arcs and line segments. Line segments are drawn using a combination of `ctx.moveTo` and `ctx.lineTo`. I'll cover them in a number of chapters: for the slingshot game in Chapter 4, the memory game using polygons in Chapter 5, and Hangman in Chapter 9. In the cannon ball game in Chapter 4, I'll also show you how to tilt a rectangle, and the Hangman game in Chapter 9 demonstrates how to draw ovals. In this chapter, I'll focus on the arcs.

You start a path using

```
ctx.beginPath();
```

and end it, with the path being drawn, with either

```
ctx.closePath();
ctx.stroke();
```

or

```
ctx.closePath();
ctx.fill();
```

An arc can be a whole circle or part of a circle. In the dice applications, we draw only whole circles to represent the pips on the face of each die, but I'll explain how arcs work in general to make the code less mysterious. The method for drawing arcs has the following format:

```
ctx.arc(cx, cy, radius, start_angle, end_angle, direction);
```

where `cx`, `cy`, and `radius` are the center horizontal and vertical coordinates and the radius of the circle. To explain the next two parameters requires discussing ways to measure angles. You're familiar with the degree unit for angles: we speak of making a 180-degree turn, meaning a u-turn, and a 90-degree angle is produced by two perpendicular lines. But most computer programming languages use another system, called *radians*. Here's one way to visualize radians—think of taking the radius of a circle and laying it on the circle itself. You can dig into your memory and realize that it won't be a neat fit, because there are 2* PI radians around the circle, somewhat more than 6. So if we want to draw an arc that is a whole circle, we specify a starting angle of 0 and an end angle of 2*PI. Luckily, the `Math` class furnishes a constant `Math.PI` that is the value of PI (to as much accuracy, as many decimal places, as necessary), so in the code, we write 2*Math.PI. If we want to specify an arc that is half a circle, we use `Math.PI`, while a right-angle (90 degrees) will be .5*Math.PI.

The arc method requires one more argument, direction. How are we drawing these arcs? Think of the movement of the hands on a clock face. In HTML 5, clockwise is the false direction and counterclockwise is the true direction. (Don't ask why. That's just the way it's specified in HTML5.) I use the built-in JavaScript values `true` and `false`. This will be important when we need to draw arcs that are not whole circles. The nature of the particular problem dictates how you define the angles if you need to draw arcs that are not full circles.

Here are some examples, with the complete code, for you to create (using TextPad or TextWrangler) and then vary to test your understanding. The first one draws an arc, representing a smile.

```
<html>
<head>
<title>Smile</title>
<script>
function init() {
        var ctx =document.getElementById("canvas").getContext('2d');
        ctx.beginPath();
        ctx.strokeStyle = "rgb(200,0,0)";
        ctx.arc(200, 200,50,0,Math.PI, false);
        ctx.stroke();
}
</script>
</head>
<body>
<body onLoad="init();">
<canvas id="canvas" width="400" height="300">
Your browser doesn't support the HTML5 element canvas.
</canvas>
</body>
</html>
```

Figure 2-6 shows a portion of the screen with the arc produced by this code.

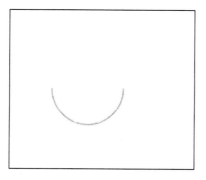

Figure 2-6. The "smile" produced by the expression `ctx.arc(200,200,50,0,Math.PI, false);`

You can look ahead to Figures 2-11, 2-12 and 2-13 in which I captured more of the screen to see the positioning of the drawing. Please vary the numbers in your own example so you can gain an understanding of how the coordinate system works and how big a pixel actually is.

Before going on to see a frown, try making the arc wider or taller or changing the color. Then try moving the whole arc up, down, left, and right. Hint: you need to change the line

`ctx.arc(200, 200,50,0,Math.PI, false);`

Change the `200,200` to reset the center of the circle and the `50` to change the radius.

Now, let's go on with other variations. Do take each one and experiment with it. Changing the last parameter of the arc method to true:

```
ctx.arc(200,200,50,0,Math.PI,true);
```

makes the arc go in a counterclockwise direction. The complete code is:

```
<html>
        <head>
                  <title>Frown</title>
<script type="text/javascript">
function init() {
        var ctx =document.getElementById("canvas").getContext('2d');
        ctx.beginPath();
        ctx.strokeStyle = "rgb(200,0,0)";
        ctx.arc(200, 200,50,0,Math.PI, true);
        ctx.stroke();
}
</script>
</head>

<body>
<body onLoad="init();">
<canvas id="canvas" width="400" height="300">
Your browser doesn't support the HTML5 element canvas.
</canvas>

</body>
</html>
```

Notice that I also changed the title. This code produces the screen shown in Figure 2-7.

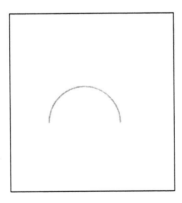

Figure 2-7. The "frown" produced by the expression ctx.arc(200,200,50,0,Math.PI, true);

Putting in the statement to close the path before the stroke:

```
ctx.closePath();
ctx.stroke();
```

in the frown example, will "finish off" the arc. The complete code is

```html
<html>
        <head>
                <title>Frown</title>
<script type="text/javascript">
function init() {
        var ctx =document.getElementById("canvas").getContext('2d');
        ctx.beginPath();
        ctx.strokeStyle = "rgb(200,0,0)";
        ctx.arc(200, 200,50,0,Math.PI, true);
        ctx.closePath();
        ctx.stroke();
}
</script>
</head>

<body>
<body onLoad="init();">
<canvas id="canvas" width="400" height="300">
Your browser doesn't support the HTML5 element canvas.
</canvas>

</body>
</html>
```

This produces the screen show in Figure 2-8.

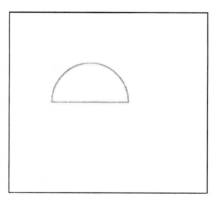

Figure 2-8. The frown becomes a half-circle by adding `ctx.closePath();` before `ctx.stroke();`

The `closePath` command is not always necessary, but it's good practice to include it. Experiment here and also look ahead to the drawing of the slingshot in Chapter 5 and the drawing of the hangman figure in Chapter 9. If you want the path filled in, you use `ctx.fill()` in place of `ctx.stroke()`, which produces a black, filled-in shape as shown in Figure 2-9. The complete code is

```html
<html>
        <head>
```

```
              <title>Smile</title>
<script type="text/javascript">
function init() {
        var ctx =document.getElementById("canvas").getContext('2d');
        ctx.beginPath();
        ctx.strokeStyle = "rgb(200,0,0)";
        ctx.arc(200, 200,50,0,Math.PI, false);
        ctx.closePath();
        ctx.fill();
}
</script>
</head>

<body>
<body onLoad="init();">
<canvas id="canvas" width="400" height="300">
Your browser doesn't support the HTML5 element canvas.
</canvas>

</body>
</html>
```

Black is the default color.

Figure 2-9. Filling in the half circle using `ctx.fill()`

If you want a shape to be filled and have a distinct outline, you use both the `fill` and the `stroke` commands and specify different colors using the `fillStyle` and `strokeStyle` properties. The color scheme is based on the same red/green/blue codes introduced in Chapter 1. You can experiment or use a tool such as Photoshop or Paint Shop Pro to get the colors you want. Here is the complete code:

```
<html>
        <head>
                <title>Smile</title>
<script type="text/javascript">
function init() {
        var ctx =document.getElementById("canvas").getContext('2d');
        ctx.beginPath();
        ctx.strokeStyle = "rgb(200,0,0)";
        ctx.arc(200, 200,50,0,Math.PI, false);
        ctx.fillStyle = "rgb(200,0,200)";
        ctx.closePath();
        ctx.fill();
        ctx.strokeStyle="rgb(255,0,0)";
```

```
        ctx.lineWidth=5;
        ctx.stroke();
}
</script>
</head>

<body>
<body onLoad="init();">
<canvas id="canvas" width="400" height="300">
Your browser doesn't support the HTML5 element canvas.
</canvas>

</body>
</html>
```

This code produces a half circle filled in with purple (a combination of red and blue), with a stroke, that is, an outline of pure red as shown in Figure 2-10. The coding specifies a path, then draws the path as a fill, and then draws the path as a stroke.

Figure 2-10. Using fill and stroke with different colors

A full circle is produced by many different commands, including:

```
ctx.arc(200,200,50,0, 2*Math.PI, true);
ctx.arc(200,200,50, 0, 2*Math.PI, false);
ctx.arc(200,200,50, .5*Math.PI, 2.5*Math.PI, false);
```

You may as well stick with the first one—it's as good as any other. Note that I still use the closePath command. A circle may be a closed figure in geometric terms, but that doesn't matter in terms of JavaScript.

If you think of the canvas element as a canvas on which you put some ink or paint, you realize you'll need to erase the canvas or the appropriate part of it to draw something new. To do this, HTML5 supplies the command

```
ctx.clearRect(x,y,width,height);
```

Later examples show how to draw a slingshot (Chapter 4), polygons for the memory/concentration game (Chapter 5), walls for a maze (Chapter 7), and the stick figure in Hangman (Chapter 9). Now let's get back to what we need for the dice game.

Displaying text output using a form

It is possible to write text on the canvas (see Chapter 5), but for the craps application, I chose to use a `form`, an element in both the older and current versions of HTML. I don't use the form for input from the player. I do use it for outputting information on the results of the throw of the dice. The HTML5 specification indicates new ways to set up forms, including checking or *validating* the type and range of input. The application in the next chapter demonstrates validation.

I used the following HTML to produce the form for the dice game:

```
<form name="f">
Stage: <input name="stage" value="First Throw"/>
Point: <input name="pv" value="   "/>
Outcome: <input name="outcome" value="     "/>
</form>
```

The form starts with a `name` attribute. The text `Stage:`, `Point:`, and `Outcome:` appear next to the input fields. The input tags—notice these are singleton tags—have both name and value fields. These names will be used by the JavaScript code. You can put any HTML within a form and a form within any HTML.

Because the dice game uses the new `button` element, I just added the `form` element with the fields used for displaying information to the player, without including an input element of type `submit`. Alternatively, I could have used a standard form with a `submit` input field (eliminating the need for the new button element) with the following code:

```
<form name="f" onSubmit="throwdice();">
Stage: <input type="text" name="stage" value="First Throw"/>
Point: <input type="text" name="pv" value="   "/>
Outcome: <input type="text" name="outcome" value="     "/>
<input type="submit" value="THROW DICE"/>
</form>
```

The input element of type `submit` produces a button on the screen. These are all the concepts we need to build the craps application. We can now go ahead and code it.

Building the application and making it your own

You may have already tried using the HTML5, CSS, and JavaScript constructs described in this chapter in small examples. Hint: please do. The only way to learn is to make your own examples. As a way to build up to the craps application, we will now look at three applications:

- throwing a single die and reloading to throw again
- throwing two dice by using a button
- the complete game of craps

Figure 2-11 shows a possible opening screen for the first application. I say possible because it won't always be a 4. I deliberately captured this screenshot to show practically all of the window so you can see where the drawing is located on the screen.

Figure 2-11. The single die application

Figure 2-12 shows the opening screen of the application for throwing a pair of dice. All that appears is the button.

Figure 2-12. The opening screen of the pair of dice application

Lastly, Figure 2-13 shows the screen after the player clicks on the button.

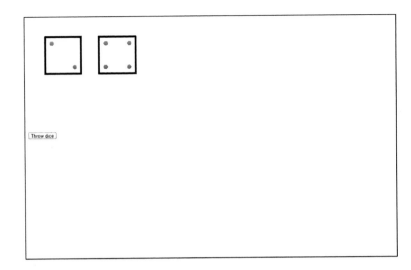

Figure 2-13. Clicking the button to throw the pair of dice

It is good technique to build your application in incremental steps. These applications are built using a text editor, such as TextPad or TextWrangler. Remember to save the file as type .html— and do this early and often. You don't have to finish before saving. When you complete the first application and have saved and tested it, you can save it once more using a new name and then make the modifications to this new copy to be the second application. Do the same for the third application.

Throwing a single die

The purpose of this first application is to display a random die face on the canvas, with circles laid out in the standard way.

For any application, there are generally many approaches that would work. I realized that I could get double duty out of some of the coding, because the pattern for the 3 die face could be made by combining the 2 and 1 patterns. Similarly, the pattern for 5 is a combination of 4 and 1. The pattern for 6 is a combination of the one for 4 and something unique. I could have put all the coding into the `init` function or used a single `drawface` function. In any case, this made sense to me and I programmed and debugged it fairly fast. Table 2-1 lists all the functions and indicates what calls what. Table 2-2 shows the complete code, explaining what each line does.

Table 2-1. Functions in the Singe Die Throw Application

Function	Invoked By / Called By	Calls
Init	invoked by action of the `onLoad` in the `<body>` tag	`drawface`
drawface	called by `init`	`draw1, draw2, draw4, draw6, draw2mid`
draw1	called by `drawface` in 3 places for 1, 3 and 5	

draw2	called by `drawface` in 2 faces for 2 and 3	
draw4	called by `drawface` in 3 places for 4, 5 and 6	
draw2mid	called by `drawface` in 1 place for 6	

Table 2-2. The Complete Code for the Throwing a Single Die Application

Code	Explanation
`<html>`	Opening `html` tag
`<head>`	Opening `head` tag
`<title>Throwing 1 die</title>`	Full `title` element
`<script>`	Opening `script` tag
`    var cwidth = 400;`	Variable holding the width of the canvas; also used to erase the canvas to prepare for redrawing
`    var cheight = 300;`	Variable holding the height of the canvas; also used to erase the canvas to prepare for redrawing
`    var dicex = 50;`	Variable holding the horizontal position of the single die
`    var dicey = 50;`	Variable holding the vertical position of the single die
`    var dicewidth = 100;`	Variable holding the width of a die face
`    var diceheight = 100;`	Variable holding the height of a die face
`    var dotrad = 6;`	Variable holding the radius of a dot
`    var ctx;`	Variable holding the canvas context, used in all the draw commands
`function init() {`	Start of the function definition for the `init` function, which is invoked `onLoad` of the document

`var ch = 1+Math.floor(Math.↪` `random()*6);`	Declare and set the value of the `ch` variable to randomly be the number 1, 2, 3, 4, 5, or 6
`drawface(ch);`	Invoke the `drawface` function with the parameter `ch`
`}`	End function definition
`function drawface(n) {`	Start of the function definition for the `drawface` function, whose argument is the number of dots
`ctx = document.getElementById('canvas').↪` `getContext('2d');`	Obtain the object that is used to draw on the canvas
`ctx.lineWidth = 5;`	Set the line width to 5
`ctx.clearRect(dicex,dicey,dicewidth,↪` `diceheight);`	Clear the space where the die face may have been drawn. This has no effect the very first time.
`ctx.strokeRect(dicex,dicey,dicewidth,↪` `diceheight)`	Draw the outline of the die face
`ctx.fillStyle = "#009966";`	Set the color for the circles. I used a graphics program to determine this value. You can do this, or experiment.
`switch(n) {`	Start `switch` using the number of dots
`case 1:`	If it is 1
`Draw1();`	Call the `draw1` function
`break;`	Break out of the switch
`case 2:`	If it is 2
`Draw2();`	Call the `draw2` function
`break;`	Break out of the switch
`case 3:`	If it is 3
`draw2();`	First call `draw2` and then
`draw1();`	Call `draw1`

`break;`	Break out of the switch
`case 4:`	If it is 4
`draw4();`	Call the draw4 function
`break;`	Break out of the switch
`case 5:`	If it is 5
`draw4();`	Call the draw4 function and then
`draw1();`	Call the draw1 function
`break;`	Break out of the switch
`case 6:`	If it is 6
`draw4();`	Call the draw4 function and then
`draw2mid();`	Call the draw2mid function
`break;`	Break out of the switch (not strictly necessary)
`}`	Close the switch statement
`}`	Close the drawface function
`function draw1() {`	Start of the definition of draw1
`var dotx;`	Variable to be used for the horizontal position for drawing the single dot
`var doty;`	Variable to be used for the vertical position for drawing the single dot
`ctx.beginPath();`	Start a path
`dotx = dicex + .5*dicewidth;`	Set the center of this dot to be at the center of the die face horizontally and
`doty = dicey + .5*diceheight;`	... vertically
`ctx.arc(dotx,doty,dotrad,0,Math.PI*2,true);`	Construct a circle (which is drawn with the fill command)

`ctx.closePath();`	Close the path
`ctx.fill();`	Draw the path, that is, fill the circle
`}`	Close draw1
`function draw2() {`	Start of draw2 function
`var dotx;`	Variable to be used for the horizontal position for drawing the two dots
`var doty;`	Variable to be used for the vertical position for drawing the two dots
`ctx.beginPath();`	Start a path
`dotx = dicex + 3*dotrad;`	Set the center of this dot to be 3 radius lengths over from the upper corner of the die face, horizontally and
`doty = dicey + 3*dotrad;`	… vertically
`ctx.arc(dotx,doty,dotrad,0,Math.PI*2,true);`	Construct the first dot
`dotx = dicex+dicewidth-3*dotrad;`	Set the center of this dot to be 3 radius lengths in from the lower corner of the die face, horizontally and
`doty = dicey+diceheight-3*dotrad;`	… vertically
`ctx.arc(dotx,doty,dotrad,0,Math.PI*2,true);`	Construct the second dot
`ctx.closePath();`	Close the path
`ctx.fill();`	Draw both dots
`}`	Close draw2
`function draw4() {`	Start of draw4 function
`var dotx;`	Variable to be used for the horizontal position for drawing the dots.
`var doty;`	Variable to be used for the vertical position for drawing the dots

`ctx.beginPath();`	Begin path
`dotx = dicex + 3*dotrad;`	Position the first dot inside the upper left corner, horizontally and
`doty = dicey + 3*dotrad;`	...vertically
`ctx.arc(dotx,doty,dotrad,0,Math.PI*2,true);`	Construct the circle
`dotx = dicex+dicewidth-3*dotrad;`	Position the second dot to be inside the lower right corner, horizontally and
`doty = dicey+diceheight-3*dotrad;`	... vertically
`ctx.arc(dotx,doty,dotrad,0,Math.`↪ `PI*2,true);`	Construct dots
`ctx.closePath();`	Close path
`ctx.fill();`	Draw 2 dots
`ctx.beginPath();`	Begin path
`dotx = dicex + 3*dotrad;`	Position this dot inside the lower left corner, horizontally and
`doty = dicey + diceheight-3*dotrad;`	... vertically. (note that this is the same y value just used)
`ctx.arc(dotx,doty,dotrad,0,Math.`↪ `PI*2,true);`	Construct circle
`dotx = dicex+dicewidth-3*dotrad;`	Position this dot just inside the upper left corner, horizontally and
`doty = dicey+ 3*dotrad;`	... vertically
`ctx.arc(dotx,doty,dotrad,0,Math.`↪ `PI*2,true);`	Construct circle
`ctx.closePath();`	Close path
`ctx.fill();`	Draw 2 dots
`}`	Close `draw4` function

`function draw2mid() {`	Start `draw2mid` function
`var dotx;`	Variable to be used for the horizontal position for drawing the two dots
`var doty;`	Variable to be used for the vertical position for drawing the two dots
`ctx.beginPath();`	Begin path
`dotx = dicex + 3*dotrad;`	Position the dots to be just inside horizontally
`doty = dicey + .5*diceheight;`	And midway vertically
`ctx.arc(dotx,doty,dotrad,0,Math.↪` `PI*2,true);`	Construct circle
`dotx = dicex+dicewidth-3*dotrad;`	Position this dot to be just inside the right border
`doty = dicey + .5*diceheight; //no change`	Position y midway
`ctx.arc(dotx,doty,dotrad,0,Math.↪` `PI*2,true);`	Construct circle
`ctx.closePath();`	Close path
`ctx.fill();`	Draw dots
`}`	Close `draw2mid` function
`</script>`	Close `script` element
`</head>`	Close head element
`<body onLoad="init();">`	Starting body tag, with `onLoad` attribute set to invoke the `init()` function

`<canvas id="canvas" width="400"`
`height="300">`
`Your browser doesn't support the HTML5↪`
`element canvas.`
`</canvas>`
	Set up canvas and provide notice if browser doesn't accept `canvas` element

`</body>` `</html>`	Close body and close `html` elements.

If you like, you can put comments in your code. Comments are pieces of text that are ignored by the browser but are there to remind you and, perhaps, others who will look at this program later, what is going on. One form of comment starts with two slashes on a line. Everything to the right of the slashes is ignored. For larger comments, you use a slash and an asterisk to start the comment and an asterisk and a slash to end it.

```
/*
This is a comment.
*/
```

This is a case of do as I say, not as I do. Since I'm using tables to put comments on every line and you can consider the whole chapter a comment, I haven't included comments in the code. You should, however.

HINT: when I was developing this code (and any code involving a random effect, I did not want to have to do the initial testing with the random coding. So, right after the line

```
var ch = 1+Math.floor(Math.random()*6);
```

I put the line

```
ch  = 1;
```

and tested it, then I changed it to

```
ch = 2;
```

and so on. I removed this line (or commented it out using //) when I was done with this phase of testing. This falls under general advice, to avoid having to play a game, in all its complexity, while developing it.

Throwing two dice

The next application makes use of a button to give the player something to do, rather than just reloading the webpage, and it also simulates the throwing of a pair of dice. Before looking at the code, think about what you can carry over from the first application. The answer is: most of it. This second application will need to do something about the positioning of the two die faces, using two more variables for this, dx and dy. It also needs to repeat the code using Math.random and calling drawface twice to produce both die faces. And there needs to be a change in what invokes a throw. Table 2-3, which describes the functions calling and being called is essentially the same as Table 2-1, except now there's a function called throwdice, which is invoked by an action set up by the onClick attribute of the button tag. Table 2-4 contains the full HTML document for the application of throwing two dice.

Table 2-3. Functions in the Two-Dice Application

Function	Invoked By / Called By	Calls
throwdice	invoked by action of the onClick in the <button> tag	drawface
drawface	called by init	draw1, draw2, draw4, draw6, draw2mid
draw1	called by drawface in 3 places for 1, 3 and 5	

draw2	called by drawface in 2 faces for 2 and 3
draw4	called by drawface in 3 places for 4, 5 and 6
draw2mid	called by drawface in 1 place for 6

Table 2-4. The Complete Two-Dice Application

Code	Explanation
`<html>`	Opening html tag
`<head>`	Opening head tag
`<title>Throwing dice</title>`	Full title element
`<script>`	Opening script tag
`    var cwidth = 400;`	Variable holding the width of the canvas
`    var cheight = 300;`	Variable holding the height of the canvas; also used to erase the canvas to prepare for redrawing
`    var dicex = 50;`	Variable holding the horizontal position of the single die; also used to erase the canvas to prepare for redrawing
`    var dicey = 50;`	Variable holding the vertical position of the single die
`    var dicewidth = 100;`	Variable holding the width of a die face
`    var diceheight = 100;`	Variable holding the height of a die face
`    var dotrad = 6;`	Variable holding the radius of a dot
`    var ctx;`	Variable holding the canvas context, used in all the draw commands
`    var dx;`	Variable used for horizontal positioning and changed for each of the two die faces

Code	Explanation
`    var dy;`	Variable used for vertical positioning. It is the same for both die faces.
`function throwdice() {`	Start of the `throwdice` function
`    var ch = 1+Math.floor(Math.random()*6);`	Declare the variable `ch` and then set it with a random value.
`    dx = dicex;`	Set `dx` for the first die face.
`    dy = dicey;`	Set `dy` for the second die face.
`    drawface(ch);`	Invoke `drawface` with `ch` as the number of dots.
`    dx = dicex + 150;`	Adjust `dx` for the second die face.
`    ch=1 + Math.floor(Math.random()*6);`	Reset `ch` with a random value.
`    drawface(ch);`	Invoke `drawface` with `ch` as the number of dots.
`}`	Close `throwdice` function.
`function drawface(n) {`	Start of the function definition for the `drawface` function, whose argument is the number of dots.
`  ctx = document.getElementById('canvas')↪.getContext('2d');`	Obtain the object that is used to draw on the canvas.
`  ctx.lineWidth = 5;`	Set the line width to 5.
`  ctx.clearRect(dx,dy,dicewidth,diceheight);`	Clear the space where the die face may have been drawn. This has no effect the very first time.
`  ctx.strokeRect(dx,dy,dicewidth,diceheight)`	Draw the outline of the die face.
`  var dotx;`	Variable to hold horizontal position.
`  var doty;`	Variable to hold vertical position.

Code	Explanation
`ctx.fillStyle = "#009966";`	Set color.
`switch(n) {`	Start switch using the number of dots.
`case 1:`	If it is 1
`draw1();`	Call the draw1 function
`break;`	Break out of the switch
`Case 2:`	If it is 2
`draw2();`	Call the draw2 function
`break;`	Break out of the switch
`Case 3:`	If it is 3
`draw2();`	First call draw2 and then
`draw1();`	Call draw1
`break;`	Break out of the switch
`Case 4:`	If it is 4
`draw4();`	Call the draw4 function
`break;`	Break out of the switch
`Case 5:`	If it is 5
`draw4();`	Call the draw4 function and then
`draw1();`	Call the draw1 function
`break;`	Break out of the switch
`Case 6:`	If it is 6
`draw4();`	Call the draw4 function and then

Code	Explanation
`draw2mid();`	Call the `draw2mid` function
`break;`	Break out of the switch (not strictly necessary)
`}`	Close `switch` statement
`}`	Close `drawface` function
`function draw1() {`	Start of definition of `draw1`
`var dotx;`	Variable to be used for the horizontal position for drawing the single dot
`var doty;`	Variable to be used for the vertical position for drawing the single dot
`ctx.beginPath();`	Start a path
`dotx = dx + .5*dicewidth;`	Set the center of this dot to be at the center of the die face (using dx) horizontally and
`doty = dy + .5*diceheight;`	... (using dy) vertically
`ctx.arc(dotx,doty,dotrad,`↪ `0,Math.PI*2,true);`	Construct a circle (it is drawn with the fill command)
`ctx.closePath();`	Close the path
`ctx.fill();`	Draw the path, that is, the circle
`}`	Close `draw1`
`function draw2() {`	Start of `draw2` function
`var dotx;`	Variable to be used for the horizontal position for drawing the two dots.
`var doty;`	Variable to be used for the vertical position for drawing the two dots
`ctx.beginPath();`	Start a path

Code	Explanation
`dotx = dx + 3*dotrad;`	Set the center of this dot to be 3 radius lengths over from the upper corner of the die face, horizontally and
`doty = dy + 3*dotrad;`	... vertically
`ctx.arc(dotx,doty,dotrad,0,Math↪.PI*2,true);`	Construct the first dot
`dotx = dx+dicewidth-3*dotrad;`	Set the center of this dot to be 3 radius lengths in from the lower corner of the die face, horizontally and
`doty = dy+diceheight-3*dotrad;`	... vertically
`ctx.arc(dotx,doty,dotrad,0,Math.↪PI*2,true);`	Construct the second dot
`ctx.closePath();`	Close the path
`ctx.fill();`	Draw both dots
`}`	Close `draw2`
`function draw4() {`	Start of `draw4` function
`var dotx;`	Variable to be used for the horizontal position for drawing the dots
`var doty;`	Variable to be used for the vertical position for drawing the dots
`ctx.beginPath();`	Begin path
`dotx = dx + 3*dotrad;`	Position the first dot inside the upper left corner, horizontally and
`doty = dy + 3*dotrad;`	...vertically
`ctx.arc(dotx,doty,dotrad,0,Math.↪PI*2,true);`	Construct the circle

Code	Explanation
`dotx = dx+dicewidth-3*dotrad;`	Position the second dot to be inside the lower right corner, horizontally and
`doty = dy+diceheight-3*dotrad;`	… vertically
`ctx.arc(dotx,doty,dotrad,0,Math.↪` `PI*2,true);`	Construct dots
`ctx.closePath();`	Close path
`ctx.fill();`	Draw 2 dots
`ctx.beginPath();`	Begin path
`dotx = dx + 3*dotrad;`	Position this dot inside the lower left corner, horizontally and
`doty = dy + diceheight-3*dotrad;↪` `//no change`	… vertically (note that this is the same y value just used)
`ctx.arc(dotx,doty,dotrad,0,Math.↪` `PI*2,true);`	Construct circle
`dotx = dx+dicewidth-3*dotrad;`	Position this dot just inside the upper left corner, horizontally and
`doty = dy+ 3*dotrad;`	… vertically
`ctx.arc(dotx,doty,dotrad,0,Math.↪` `PI*2,true);`	Construct circle
`ctx.closePath();`	Close path
`ctx.fill();`	Draw 2 dots
`}`	Close `draw4` function
`function draw2mid() {`	Start `draw2mid` function
`var dotx;`	Variable to be used for the horizontal position for drawing the two dots

Code	Explanation
`var doty;`	Variable to be used for the vertical position for drawing the two dots
`ctx.beginPath();`	Begin path
`dotx = dx + 3*dotrad;`	Position the dots to be just inside horizontally
`doty = dy + .5*diceheight;`	and midway vertically
`ctx.arc(dotx,doty,dotrad,0,Math.↪` `PI*2,true);`	Construct circle
`dotx = dx+dicewidth-3*dotrad;`	Position this dot to be just inside the right border
`doty = dy + .5*diceheight;↪` `//no change`	Position y midway
`ctx.arc(dotx,doty,dotrad,0,Math.↪` `PI*2,true);`	Construct circle
`ctx.closePath();`	Close path
`ctx.fill();`	Draw dots
`}`	Close `draw2mid` function
`</script>`	Close `script` element
`</head>`	Close `head` element
`<body>`	Starting body tag
`<canvas id="canvas" width="400" height="300">`	Canvas tag start
`Your browser doesn't support the HTML5↪` `element canvas.`	Set up canvas and provide notice if browser doesn't accept `canvas` element
`</canvas>`	Close canvas tag
` `	Line break

Code	Explanation
`<button onClick="throwdice();">Throw`↵ `dice </button>`	Button element (note attribute `onClick` setting to invoke `throwdice`)
`</body>`	Close body tag
`</html>`	Close html tag

The complete game of craps

The third application is the complete game of craps. Again, much can be carried over from the previous application. However, now we need to add in the rules of the game. Among other things, this will mean using the conditional statements `if` and `switch`, as well as global variables, that is variables defined outside of any function definition, to keep track of whether or not it is a first turn (`firstturn`) and what is the player's point (`point`). The function table is identical to the one given for the second application (Table 2-3), so I won't repeat it. Table 2-5 holds the code for this application. The new action is all in the `throwdice` function. I will comment the new lines.

Table 2-5. The Complete Craps Application

Code	Explanation
`<html>`	
`<head>`	
`<title>Craps game</title>`	
`<script>`	
`    var cwidth = 400;`	
`    var cheight = 300;`	
`    var dicex = 50;`	
`    var dicey = 50;`	
`    var dicewidth = 100;`	
`    var diceheight = 100;`	
`    var dotrad = 6;`	

Code	Description
`var ctx;`	
`var dx;`	
`var dy;`	
`var firstturn = true;`	Global variable, initialized to the value `true`
`var point;`	Global variable, does not need to be initialized because it will be set before use
`function throwdice() {`	Start of `throwdice` function
`var sum;`	Variable to hold the sum of the values for the 2 dice
`var ch = 1+Math.floor(Math.random()*6);`	Set `ch` with the first random value
`sum = ch;`	Assign this to `sum`
`dx = dicex;`	Set `dx`
`dy = dicey;`	set `dy`
`drawface(ch);`	Draw the first die face
`dx = dicex + 150;`	Adjust the horizontal position
`ch=1 + Math.floor(Math.random()*6);`	Set `ch` with a random value. This is the one for the second die.
`sum += ch;`	Add `ch` to what is already in `sum`
`drawface(ch);`	Draw the second die
`if (firstturn) {`	Now start the implementation of the rules. Is it a first turn?
`switch(sum) {`	If it is, start a `switch` with `sum` as the condition
`case 7:`	For 7

`case 11:`	.. or 11
`document.f.outcome.value="You win!";`	Display You win!
`break;`	Exit the switch
`case 2:`	For 2,
`case 3:`	.. or 3
`case 12:`	.. or 12
`document.f.outcome.value="You lose!";`	Display You lose!
`break;`	Exit the switch
`default:`	For anything else
`point = sum;`	Save the sum in the variable point
`document.f.pv.value=point;`	Display the point value
`firstturn = false;`	Set `firstturn` to false
`document.f.stage.value="Need follow-up throw.";`	Display Need follow-up throw
`document.f.outcome.value="     ";`	Erase (clear) the outcome field
`}`	End the switch
`}`	End the if-true clause
`else {`	Else (not a first turn)
`switch(sum) {`	Start the switch, again using `sum`
`case point:`	if `sum` is equal to whatever is in `point`
`document.f.outcome.value="You win!";`	Display You win!

`document.f.stage.value="Back to first throw.";`	Display Back to first throw
`document.f.pv.value=" ";`	Clear the point value
`firstturn = true;`	Reset `firstturn` so it is again true
`break;`	Exit the switch
`case 7:`	If the sum is equal to 7
`document.f.outcome.value="You lose!";`	Display You lose!
`document.f.stage.value="Back to first throw.";`	Display Back to first throw
`document.f.pv.value=" ";`	Clear the point value
`firstturn = true;`	Reset `firstturn` so it is again true
`}`	Close the switch
`}`	Close the else clause
`}`	Close the `throwdice` function
`function drawface(n) {`	
`ctx = document.getElementById('canvas').getContext('2d');`	
`ctx.lineWidth = 5;`	
`ctx.clearRect(dx,dy,dicewidth,diceheight);`	
`ctx.strokeRect(dx,dy,dicewidth,diceheight)`	
`var dotx;`	
`var doty;`	
`ctx.fillStyle = "#009966";`	

```
switch(n) {
    case 1:
        draw1();
        break;
    case 2:
        draw2();
        break;
    case 3:
        draw2();
        draw1();
        break;
    case 4:
        draw4();
        break;
    case 5:
        draw4();
        draw1();
        break;
    case 6:
        draw4();
        draw2mid();
        break;
```

```
        }

}

function draw1() {

        var dotx;

        var doty;

        ctx.beginPath();

        dotx = dx + .5*dicewidth;

        doty = dy + .5*diceheight;

        ctx.arc(dotx,doty,dotrad,0,Math.PI*2,true);

        ctx.closePath();

        ctx.fill();

}

function draw2() {

        var dotx;

        var doty;

        ctx.beginPath();

        dotx = dx + 3*dotrad;

        doty = dy + 3*dotrad;

        ctx.arc(dotx,doty,dotrad,0,Math.PI*2,true);

        dotx = dx+dicewidth-3*dotrad;

        doty = dy+diceheight-3*dotrad;

        ctx.arc(dotx,doty,dotrad,0,Math.PI*2,true);
```

```
        ctx.closePath();

        ctx.fill();

}

function draw4() {

        var dotx;

        var doty;

        ctx.beginPath();

        dotx = dx + 3*dotrad;

        doty = dy + 3*dotrad;

        ctx.arc(dotx,doty,dotrad,0,Math.PI*2,true);

        dotx = dx+dicewidth-3*dotrad;

        doty = dy+diceheight-3*dotrad;

        ctx.arc(dotx,doty,dotrad,0,Math.PI*2,true);

        ctx.closePath();

        ctx.fill();

        ctx.beginPath();

        dotx = dx + 3*dotrad;

        doty = dy + diceheight-3*dotrad;   //no change

        ctx.arc(dotx,doty,dotrad,0,Math.PI*2,true);

        dotx = dx+dicewidth-3*dotrad;

        doty = dy+ 3*dotrad;

        ctx.arc(dotx,doty,dotrad,0,Math.PI*2,true);
```

```
        ctx.closePath();

        ctx.fill();

}

function draw2mid() {

        var dotx;

        var doty;

        ctx.beginPath();

        dotx = dx + 3*dotrad;

        doty = dy + .5*diceheight;

        ctx.arc(dotx,doty,dotrad,0,Math.PI*2,true);

        dotx = dx+dicewidth-3*dotrad;

        doty = dy + .5*diceheight; //no change

        ctx.arc(dotx,doty,dotrad,0,Math.PI*2,true);

        ctx.closePath();

        ctx.fill();

}

</script>

</head>

<body>

<canvas id="canvas" width="400" height="300">

Your browser doesn't support the HTML5 element canvas.

</canvas>
```

` `	
`<button onClick="throwdice();">Throw dice </button>`	
`<form name="f">`	Start a form named f
`Stage: <input name="stage" value="First Throw"/>`	With the text Stage: right before it, set up an input field named stage
`Point: <input name="pv" value="    "/>`	With the text Point: right before it, set up an input field named pv
`Outcome: <input name="outcome" value="      "/>`	With the text Outcome: right before it, set up an input field named outcome
`</form>`	Close the form
`</body>`	Close body
`</html>`	Close html

Making the application your own

Making this application your own is not as straightforward as with the favorite sites application, because the rules of craps are the rules of craps. However, there are many things you can do. Change the size and color of the dice faces, using fillRect and setting fillStyle to different colors. Change the color and size of the whole canvas. Change the text for the outcomes to something more colorful. You also can implement other games using standard or specially made dice.

You can look ahead to the next chapter and learn about drawing images on the canvas instead of drawing each die face using arcs and rectangles. HTML5 provides a way to bring in external image files. The drawback to this approach is that you do have to keep track of these separate files.

You can develop coding for keeping score. For a gambling game, you can start the player with a fixed amount of money, say 100 of whatever the currency unit is, and deduct some amount, say 10, for playing a game, and add some amount, say 20, if and only if the player wins. You can add this bankroll information as part of the form element in the body:

```
<form name="f" id="f">
Stage: <input name="stage" value="First Throw"/>
Point: <input name="pv" value="    "/>
Outcome: <input name="outcome" value="      "/>
Bank roll: <input name="bank" value="100"/>
</form>
```

JavaScript (and other programming languages) distinguish between numbers and strings of characters representing numbers. That is, the value "100" is a string of characters, "1","0", and "0". The value 100 is a number. In either case, however, the value of a variable is stored as a sequence of 1s and 0s. For numbers, this will be the number represented as a binary number. For strings of characters, each character will be represented using a standard coding system, such as ASCII or UNICODE. In some situations, JavaScript will make the conversion from one data type to the other, but don't depend on it. The coding I suggest uses the built-in functions `String` and `Number` to do these conversions.

In the `throwdice` function, before the `if(firstturn)` statement, add the code in Table 2-6 (or something like it).

Table 2-6. Adding a Bank for the Player

Code	Explanation
`var bank = Number(document.f.bank.value);`	Sets a new variable bank to be the number represented by the value in the bank input field.
`if (bank<10) {`	Compare bank to 10.
`        alert("You ran out of money! Add some more and try again.");`	If bank is less than 10, put out an alert.
`        Return;`	Exit the function without doing anything.
`    }`	Close the if true clause.
`bank = bank - 10;`	Decrease bank by 10. This line is reached only when bank was greater than 10.
`document.f.bank.value = String(bank);`	Put the string representation of that value in the bank field.

Then in each place where the player wins (in the `switch` statement for a first turn after the 7 and 11 cases, or in the `switch` statement for a follow-up turn, after the point case, add the code in Table 2-7.

Table 2-7. Increasing the Value of the Bank

Code	Explanation
`bank = Number(document.f.bank.value);`	Set bank to be the number represented by the value in the bank input field. Setting bank again allows for the possibility of the player re-setting the bank amount in the middle of a game.

`bank +=20;`	Use the += operator to increase the value of bank by 20
`document.f.bank.value = String(bank);`	Put the string representation of the bank amount in the bank field

When the player loses, or when it is a follow-up turn, you don't add any code. The bank value goes down before each new game.

Testing and uploading the application

These applications are complete in the HTML file. No other files, such as image files, are used. Instead, the dice faces are drawn on the canvas. (For your information, my versions of dice games written in the older HTML used one or two `img` elements. To make these fixed `img` elements display different images, I wrote code that changed the `src` attribute to be a different external image file. When I uploaded the application, I had to upload all the image files.)

Open up the HTML file in the browser. The first application needs to be reloaded to get a new (single) die. The second and third applications (the third one being the craps game) use a button to roll the dice.

I repeat what I wrote earlier. To test this program, you do need to check the many cases. You are not done when you, acting as the player, win. Typical problems include

- missing or mismatched opening and closing tags
- mismatched opening and closing brackets, the { and the } surrounding functions, `switch` statements, and `if` clauses
- missing quotation marks. The color coding, as available when using TextPad and some other editors, can help here, as it will highlight keywords it recognizes.
- inconsistency in naming and use of variables and functions. These names can be anything you choose, but you need to be consistent. The function `draw2mid` will not be invoked by `drawmid2()`.

These are all, except arguably the last, mistakes in syntax, analogous to mistakes in grammar and punctuation. A mistake of semantics, that is, meaning, can be more difficult to detect. If you write the second `switch` statement to win on a 7 and lose on the point value, you may have written correct JavaScript code, but it won't be the game of craps.

It shouldn't happen here because you can copy my code, but a common mistake is to get confused about the coordinate system and think that vertical values increase going up the screen instead of down.

Summary

In this chapter, you learned how to

- declare variables and use global variables to represent application state
- write code to perform arithmetic operations
- define and use programmer-defined functions

- use several built-in features of JavaScript, including the `Math.random` and `Math.floor` methods
- use `if` and `switch` statements
- create a canvas using an HTML element
- draw rectangles and circles

This chapter introduced a key feature of HTML5, the canvas, as well as the notions of randomness and interactivity. It also presented many programming features you'll use in the examples in the rest of the book. In particular, the technique of building an application in stages is useful. The next chapter will feature the animation of a ball bouncing in a box—preparation for the real games in Chapter 4: the ballistics simulations called cannon ball and sling shot.

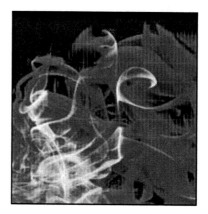

Chapter 3

Bouncing Ball

In this chapter, we will cover:

- creating programmer-defined objects
- using setInterval for animation
- drawing images
- form input and validating form input
- for loops
- drawing with gradients

Introduction

Animation, whether at the movies, using a flipbook, or generated by computer, involves displaying a sequence of still images fast enough so that we interpret what we see as movement, as life. In this chapter, I'll show you how to produce animated scenes by simulating a ball bouncing in a 2-dimensional box, with horizontal and vertical speeds that can by changed by a player. The first iteration of our program calculates new positions for the ball at fixed intervals of time and displays the result, and it also determines when there would be a virtual collision of ball and wall and how the ball would bounce off the wall. After that, we'll see how you can replace the ball with an image, and how to draw rectangles using gradients. Lastly, we'll examine the HTML5 feature for validating form input. The three examples are

- a ball bouncing in a 2-D box (Figure 3-1)
- replace the ball with an image and use a gradient for the box walls (Figure 3-2)
- validate the input (Figure 3-3)

Note: *The kind of animation we're going to produce is called computed animation, in which the position of an object is recalculated by a computer program and the object is then redisplayed. This is in contrast to cel (or frame-by-frame) animation, which uses predrawn individual static pictures. Animated gifs are examples of cel animation and can be produced in many graphics programs. The Flash authoring tool is excellent for producing and integrating computed animation and cel animation. Flash also has facilities, such as tweening, to help produce the individual static pictures.*

You'll have to imagine the animation represented by these static pictures. In Figure 3-1, notice the form with fields for setting the horizontal and vertical velocity.

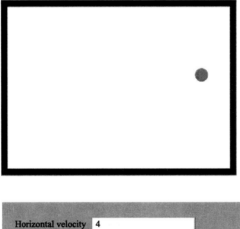

Figure 3-1. A bouncing ball

In Figure 3-2, the ball has been replaced by an image and the walls are filled in using a gradient.

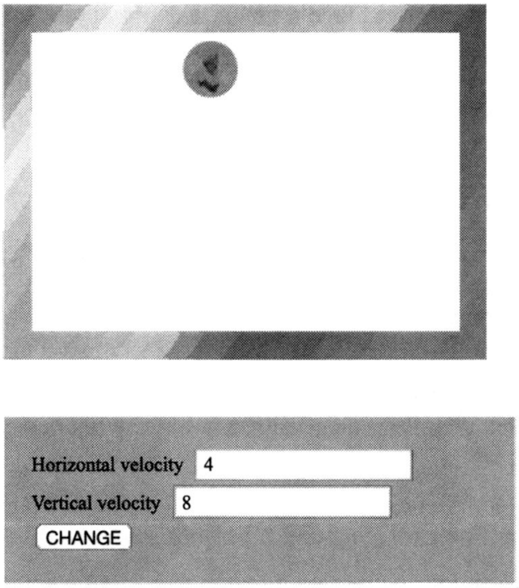

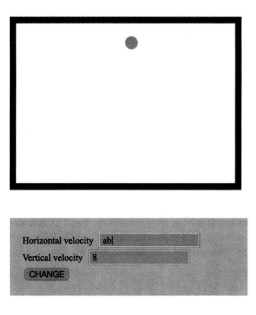

Figure 3-2. The ball is now an image from an external file.

HTML5 lets you specify what the input should be. In this example, I've specified the input should be a number and indicated minimum and maximum values. I used CSS to specify that if a user makes an invalid entry, the color of the field turns red. This is shown in Figure 3-3.

Figure 3-3. A form showing bad input

This set of applications demonstrates substantial programming but it's not really a game, though people enjoy seeing heads or other images bouncing in a box. Think about how to make it a game. You can also use ideas learned here to draw something besides a ball bouncing around in a box. The box can have different dimensions and the walls can be much fancier. The next chapter builds on this one and describes how to build simulations of a cannonball and a slingshot.

Critical requirements

It is important for this application and, indeed, for all programming, to define the requirements before you begin writing any code. The application requires things I demonstrated in previous chapters: drawing shapes on a canvas element and using a form. For this example, we will actually use the form fields for input. In the dice game described in Chapter 2, they were used strictly for output.

In Chapter 1, the HTML document made use of external image files. In Chapter 2, we drew the faces of the dice entirely with coding. In this chapter, I'll demonstrate both: a bouncing circle drawn with code and a bouncing image from an image file.

To accomplish this, we need some code that will be able to do something—right now, it doesn't matter what—at fixed intervals of time. The intervals need to be short enough that the result looks like motion.

In this case, the something-to-be-done is to reposition the ball. In addition, the code needs to determine if the ball would hit any wall. Now, there isn't a ball and there aren't any walls. It is all virtual, so it is all coding. We'll write code to perform a calculation on the virtual position of the ball versus the virtual position of each of the walls. If there is a virtual hit, the code adjusts the horizontal or vertical displacement values so the ball bounces off the wall.

To calculate the repositioning, we use either the initial values or any new values typed into the input fields of the form. However, the goal is to produce a robust system that will not act on bad input from the player. Bad input would be an entry that wasn't a number or a number outside of the specified range. We could just not act on the bad input. However, we want to give feedback to the player that the input was bad, so we'll make the input boxes change color, as Figure 3-3 shows.

HTML5, CSS, JavaScript features

Let's take a look at the specific features of HTML5, CSS, and JavaScript we need to implement the bouncing ball applications. We'll build on material covered in previous chapters, specifically the general structure of an HTML document, using a canvas element, programmer-defined and built-in functions, and a form element.

Drawing a ball, image, and gradient

As described in Chapter 2, drawing anything on the canvas, such as a circle to represent the ball, requires including the canvas element in the body section of the HTML document. Next we need to define a variable, ctx, and add code that sets up the value of this variable so we can use JavaScript. Here's the statement to implement this:

```
ctx = document.getElementById('canvas').getContext('2d');
```

As we saw in Chapter 2, a circle is created by drawing an arc as part of a path. The following lines of code start the path, set the color for the fill, specify the arc, and then use the fill method to draw a closed, filled-in path. Notice that the `arc` method uses variables to specify the coordinates of the center of the circle and the radius. The parameters 0 and `Math.PI*2` represent angles, in this case 0 to Math.PI*2, making a complete circle. The `true` parameter indicates counterclockwise, though in this particular case, `false` would produce the same effect.

```
ctx.beginPath();
ctx.fillStyle ="rgb(200,0,50)";
ctx.arc(ballx, bally, ballrad,0,Math.PI*2,true);
ctx.fill();
```

For the first version of the bouncing ball, the box is drawn as a rectangle outline. The width of the outline, termed the stroke, is set using

```
ctx.lineWidth = ballrad;
```

You can experiment with the line width. Keep in mind that if you make the width small and set the ball to travel fast, the ball can bounce past the wall in one step.

The statement that draws the rectangle is

```
ctx.strokeRect(boxx,boxy,boxwidth,boxheight);
```

I put the code for the ball before the code for the rectangle so the rectangle would be on top. I thought this looked better for the bouncing.

The second version of the program displays an image for the ball. This requires code to set up an img object using the `new` operator with a call to `Image()`, assigning that to a variable, and giving the `src` property a value. In the application, we do all this in a single statement, but let's take a look at the individual parts.

You read about `var` statements in Chapter 2. Such statements define, or *declare*, a variable. It is okay to use the name *img* for our `var` here; there's no conflict with the HTML img element. The `new` operator is well-named: it creates a new object, in this case of the built-in type `Image`. The `Image` function does not take any arguments, so there are just opening and closing parentheses.

Image objects have attributes, just like HTML elements such as `img` do. The particular image used is indicated by the value of the `src` attribute. Here, "pearl.jpg" is the name of an image file located in the same folder as the HTML document. The following two statements set up the `img` variable and set its `src` (source) to the address, the URL, of the image file.

```
var img = new Image();
img.src="pearl.jpg";
```

For your application, use the name of an image file you've chosen. It can be of type JPG, PNG, or GIF, and be sure to either put it in the same folder as your HTML document or include the entire path. Be careful about matching the case both in the name and the extension.

To draw this image on the canvas, we need a single line of code specifying the image object, the location for the upper left corner of the image, and the width and length to be used in the display of the image. As was the case with the rectangles, this code is a call of a method of a context object, so I use the variable `ctx` defined in the init function. I need to adjust the `ballx` and `bally` values I used for the center of the circle to indicate this upper corner. I use 2 times the ball radius for both the width and the length. The statement is

```
ctx.drawImage(img,ballx-ballrad,bally-ballrad,2*ballrad,2*ballrad);
```

Let's take a break now. It's your turn, dear reader, to do some work. Consider the following HTML document:

```
<html>
<head>
<title>The Origami Frog</title>
<script>
var img = new Image();
img.src = "frogface.gif";
var ctx;
function init() {
        ctx =document.getElementById("canvas").getContext('2d');
        ctx.drawImage(img,10,20,100,100);

}
</script>
</head>
<body>
<body onLoad="init();">
<canvas id="canvas" width="400" height="300">
Your browser doesn't support the HTML5 element canvas.
</canvas>
</body>
</html>
```

Find your own image file and use its name in place of frogface.gif. Change the title to something appropriate. Experiment with the line

```
ctx.drawImage(img,10,20,100,100);
```

That is, change the 10, 20 to reposition the image, and change the 100,100 to change the width and the height. Make the changes and see if the program responds as you intended. Remember that as you specify the width and height, you could be changing the shape—the *aspect ratio*—of the picture.

Now try another exercise: drawing two images on the canvas. You'll need to have two different variables in place of img. For this task, give the variables distinctive names. If you are emulating Dr. Seuss, you can use thing1 and thing2; otherwise, choose something meaningful to you!

Now, on to more drawing!

Let's see how to use gradients for this version of the program. You can use gradients to set the fillStyle property. I didn't want to have the ball on top of a filled in rectangle, so I needed to figure out how to draw the four walls separately.

A gradient is a type of object in HTML5. There are linear gradients and radial gradients. In this application we use a linear gradient. The code defines a variable to be a gradient object, using a method of a canvas context that we defined earlier with the variable ctx. The code for the gradient looks like this:

```
var grad;
grad=ctx.createLinearGradient(boxx,boxy,boxx+boxwidth,boxy+boxheight);
```

The gradient stretches out over a rectangle shape.

Gradients involve sets of colors. A typical practice is to write code to set what are called the color stops, such as to make the gradient be a rainbow. For this, I set up an array of arrays in a variable named hue.

You can think of an array as a holder for a collection of values. Whereas a variable can hold only one value, an array can hold many. In the next chapter, you'll read about an array named everything that will hold all the objects to be drawn on the screen. In Chapter 9, which describes the Hangman game, the word list is an array of words. You'll read about many applications of arrays in this book. Here's a concrete example. The following var statement sets up a variable to be a specific array:

```
var family = ["Daniel","Aviva", "Allison", "Grant", "Liam"];
```

The variable family is an array. Its data type is array. It consists of a list of people in my family (for pictures, see the memory game described in Chapter 5). To access or to set the first element of this array, you'd use family[0]. The values to specify specific members of an array are called index values or indices. Array indexing starts with zero. The expression family[0] would produce Daniel. The expression family[4] would produce Liam. If the value of a variable relative was 2, then family[relative] would produce Allison. To determine the number of elements in the array, you'd use family.length. In this case, the length is 5.

The individual items in an array can be of any type, including arrays. For example, I could modify the family array to provide more information:

```
var family  = [["Daniel","college teacher"],
  ["Aviva", "congressional staff"],
  ["Allison","graduate student"],
  ["Grant","kid"],
  ["Liam","kid"]
 ];
```

The formatting, with the line breaks and indents, is not required, but it's good practice.

The expression family[2][1] produces "graduate student". Remember: array indexing starts at 0 so the index value 2 for the array, sometimes termed the outer array in this type of example, produces ["Allison","graduate student"] and the array 1, the index for the inner array, produces "graduate student".

These inner arrays do not have to be the same length. Consider the example:

```
var family  = [["Daniel","college teacher"],
  ["Aviva", "congressional staff"],
  ["Allison","graduate student"],
  ["Grant"],
  ["Liam"]
 ];
```

The code would check the length of the array and if it was 2 instead of 1, the second item would be the profession of the individual. If the length of the inner array was 1, it would be assumed that the individual does not have a profession.

Arrays of arrays can be very useful for product names and costs. The following statement specifies the very limited inventory of a store:

```
var inventory = [
                  ["toaster",25.99],
                  ["blender",74.99],
```

```
        ["dish",10.50],
        ["rug",599.99]
        ];
```

This store has 4 items, with the cheapest being the dish, represented in the position at index 2, and the most expensive the rug at index 3.

Now, let's see how we can use these concepts for defining a gradient. We'll use an array whose individual elements are also arrays.

Each inner array holds the RGB values for a color, namely red, yellow, green, cyan, blue, magenta.

```
var hue = [
    [255,   0,   0 ],
    [255, 255,   0 ],
    [  0, 255,   0 ],
    [  0, 255, 255 ],
    [  0,   0, 255 ],
    [255,   0, 255 ]
] ;
```

These values represent colors ranging from red (RGB 255,0,0) to magenta (RGB 255,0,255), with four colors specified in between. The gradient feature in JavaScript fills in the colors to produce the rainbow pattern shown in Figure 3-3. Gradients are defined by specifying points along an interval from 0 to 1. You can specify a gradient other than a rainbow. For example, you can use a graphics program to select a set of RGB values to be the so-called stop-points, and JavaScript will fill in values to blend from one to the next.

The array numeric values are not quite what we need, so we will have to manipulate them to produce what JavaScript demands.

Manipulation of arrays often requires doing something to each member of the array. One construct for doing this, present in many programming languages, is the `for` loop, which uses a variable called an indexing variable. The structure of the `for` loop is

```
for (initial value for indexing variable; condition for continuing; change for↪
    indexing variable) {
        code to be done every time. The code usually references the indexing variable
}
```

This says: start with this initial value; keep doing the loop as long as this condition holds; and change the index value in this specified way. A typical expression for the change will use operators such as ++. The ++ operator increments the indicated variable by 1. A typical `for` header statement is

```
for (n=0;n<10;n++)
```

This `for` loop uses a variable named n, with n initialized to 0. If the value of n is less than 10, the statements inside the loop are executed. After each iteration, the value of n is increased by 1. In this case, the loop code will be executed 10 times, with n holding values 0, 1, 2, all the way up to 9.

Here's one more example, a common one to demonstrate arrays. Let the `grades` variable be set up to hold a set of grades for a student:

```
var grades = [4.0, 3.7, 3, 2.3, 3];
```

Depending on the institution, this could indicate grades of A, A-, B, C+, and B. The following snippet computes the grade-point average and stores it in the variable named gpa. Notice that we need to initialize the variable named sum to start with a value of 0. The += operator adds to the value held in sum the value in the grades array at index value g.

```
var sum = 0;
for (g=0;g<grades.length;g++) {
 sum += grades[g];
}
var gpa;
gpa = sum/grades.length;
```

To produce what we need to build the gradient, the code extracts values from the hue array and uses them to produce character strings indicating RGB values. We use the hue array along with a variable called color to set the color stops to define the gradient. The color stops are set at any point between 0 and 1, using a for loop that sets color to be a character string of the required format, namely starting with "rgb(", and including the three values.

```
for (h=0;h<hue.length;h++) {
 color = 'rgb('+hue[h][0]+','+hue[h][1]+','+hue[h][2]+')';
 grad.addColorStop(h*1/hue.length,color);
}
```

The assignment statement setting color may seem strange to you: there's a lot going on—and what are those plus signs doing? Remember, our task is to generate the character strings indicating certain RGB values. The plus signs do *not* indicate addition of numbers here but concatenation of strings of characters. This means that the values are stuck together rather than mathematically added, so while 5+5 yields 10, '5'+'5' would give 55. Because the 5s in the second example are enclosed by quote marks, they are strings rather than numbers. The square brackets are pulling out members of the array. JavaScript converts the numbers to the character string equivalent and then combines them. Remember that it's looking at arrays within arrays, so the first number within square brackets (in this case, provided by our variable h) gives us the first array, and the second number within square brackets gives us our number within that array. Let's look at a quick example. The first time our loop runs, the value of h will be 0, which gives us the first entry within the hue array. We then look up the separate parts of that entry in order to build our final color.

After all that, our code has set up the variable grad to be used to indicate a fill pattern. Instead of setting fillStyle to be a color, the code sets it to be the variable grad.

```
ctx.fillStyle = grad;
```

Drawing the rectangles is the same as before, but now with the indicated fill. These are four narrow walls at the left, right, top, and bottom of the original rectangle. I make the walls as thick as the radius of the ball. This thickness is the width in the case of the vertical walls and the height in the case of the horizontal walls.

```
ctx.fillRect(boxx,boxy,ballrad,boxheight);
ctx.fillRect(boxx+boxwidth-ballrad,boxy,ballrad,boxheight);
ctx.fillRect(boxx,boxy,boxwidth,ballrad);
ctx.fillRect(boxx,boxy+boxheight-ballrad,boxwidth,ballrad);
```

An important point to note here is that since the code is drawing or painting the canvas, to produce the effect of a moving ball, we also need code to erase everything and then redraw everything with the ball in a new spot. The statement to erase everything is:

```
ctx.clearRect(box,boxy,boxwidth,boxheight);
```

It might be possible to erase (clear) just parts of the canvas, but I chose to erase and then redraw everything. In each situation, you need to decide what makes sense.

Setting up a timing event

Setting up timing events in HTML5 is actually similar to the way it's done in the older versions of HTML. There are two built-in functions: `setInterval` and `setTimeout`. We'll look at `setInterval` here and at `setTimeout` in the memory game in Chapter 5. Each of these functions takes two arguments. Remember that arguments are extra pieces of information included in function or method calls. Back in Chapter 1, we saw that `document.write` took as its single argument what was to be written out on the screen.

I'll describe the second argument first. The second argument specifies an amount of time, in milliseconds. There are 1000 milliseconds to a second. This may seem like a very short unit to work with, but it turns out to be just what we want for games. A second (1000 milliseconds) is quite long for a computer game.

The first argument specifies what is to be done at the intervals specified by the second argument. The first argument can be the name of a function. For this application, the `init` function definition contains the following line:

```
setInterval(moveball,100);
```

This tells the `JavaScript engine` to invoke the function `moveball` every 100 milliseconds (10 times per second). `moveball` is the name of a function that will be defined in this HTML document; it is the *event handler* for the *timing interval event*. Don't be concerned if you write this line of code before writing the code to define the function. What counts is what exists when the application is run.

JavaScript also provides a way other than a function name for the event handler. You could write

```
setInterval("moveball();",100);
```

for the same effect. Putting it another way, for simple cases, when the action is the call of a function without parameters, the name of the function will do. For more complex cases (as described in the Aside note), you can write a string to specify code. The string can be a full function call, or something like this:

```
setInterval("positionx = positionx+speed;",100);
```

That is, the complete response to the event can be written in the first argument. Using a function is the way to go in most situations.

> *Note: Here is a more complex example. Suppose I had a function named `slide` that itself took one argument, and I wanted this function to be called with a value 10 times the value of the variable `d`, and I wanted this to happen every one and one-half seconds, I would code*
>
> `setInterval("slide(10*d);",1500);`

It is often the case that you want to indicate the passage of time on the screen. The following example will display 0, 1, ... etc. with the number changing every second.

```
<html>
<head>
<title>elapsed</title>
<script>
function init() {
        setInterval(increase,1000);
}
function increase() {
        document.f.secs.value = String(1+Number(document.f.secs.value));
}
</script>
</head>
<body onLoad="init();">
<form name="f">
<input type="text" name="secs" value="0"/>
</form>
</body>
</html>
```

This is a good example for you to take the time to write and run, both because it showcases timing events and also because it will make you appreciate how long a second lasts. The code takes the value out of the secs input field in the form named f, converts that value to a number, adds 1 to that number, and then converts it back to a string to assign as the value of the secs element. Try replacing the single statement inside the increase function with the statement

```
document.f.secs.value = 1+document.f.secs.value;
```

and see what happens. This is a lesson in the difference between numbers and character strings. Please play around with this little example. If you want to make the numbers go up in smaller increments, change the 1000 to 250 and the 1 to .25. This makes the script show quarter-second changes.

If you want to allow your code to stop a particular event, you can set up a global variable (one that's outside of any function). I use a variable named tev, my shorthand for timing event.

```
var tev;
```

You would then modify the setInterval call to be:

```
tev = setInterval(moveball,100);
```

When you wanted to stop this event, you'd include this code:

```
clearInterval(tev);
```

To reiterate, the setInterval function sets up a timing event that keeps occurring until it is cleared. If you know you want an event to happen just once, the setTimeout method sets up exactly one event. You can use either method to produce the same results, but JavaScript furnishes both to make things easier.

For the bouncing ball application, the moveball function calculates a new position for the ball, does the calculations to check for collisions and when they occur, redirects the ball and draws a new display. This is done over and over—the calls to moveball keep happening because we used setInterval.

Calculating a new position and collision detection

Now that we know how to draw, and how to clear and redraw, and we know how to do something at fixed intervals, the challenge is how to calculate the new positions and how to do collision detection. We'll do this by declaring variables `ballx` and `bally` to hold the x and y coordinates of the ball's center; `ballvx` and `ballvy` to hold the amount by which the ball position is to be changed, and `ballboundx`, `inboxboundx`, `ballboundy` and `inboxboundy` to indicate a box slightly smaller than the actual box for the collision calculation. The amounts by which the ball position is to be changed are initialized to 4 and 8 (totally arbitrarily) and are changed if and when a player makes a valid change (see next section) and clicks on the change button. These amounts are termed displacements or deltas and, less formally, velocities or speeds.

The change in direction is pretty simple in this situation. If the ball "hits" a vertical wall, the horizontal displacement must change sign; i.e., if the ball was moving 4 units to the right and we hit a wall, we add -4 to its position, which starts it moving to the left. The vertical displacement stays the same. The hit is determined by comparing the *next* horizontal value with the boundary. Similarly, if the ball "hits" a horizontal wall as determined by comparing the vertical position with the appropriate boundary, the vertical displacement changes sign while the horizontal displacement remains the same. The change is for the next iteration. The check for collisions is done four times, that is, for each of the 4 walls. The calculation consists of comparing the proposed new x or y value, as appropriate, with the boundary condition for the particular wall. The tentative new position is adjusted if the ball center goes past one of the four walls to be exactly at the boundary. This has the effect of making the ball go slightly behind each wall or appear to be squeezed by each wall. The boundary values are set up to be just inside the box with the upper corner at `boxx`, `boxy`, a width of `boxwidth`, and a height of `boxheight`. I could use a more complex calculation to compare any point on the circle with any point on the walls. However, there is a more fundamental principle involved here. There are no walls and no ball. This is a simulation based on calculations. The calculations are done at intervals. If the ball is moving fast enough and the walls are thin enough, thinner than the `ballrad` specified here, the ball can escape the box. This is why I do the calculation in terms of the next move and a slightly smaller box.

```
var boxboundx = boxwidth+boxx-ballrad;
var boxboundy = boxheight+boxy-ballrad;
var inboxboundx = boxx+ballrad;
var inboxboundy = boxy+ballrad;
```

Here is the code for the `moveandcheck` function, the function that checks for collisions and reposition the ball:

```
function moveandcheck() {
    var nballx = ballx + ballvx;
    var nbally = bally +ballvy;
    if (nballx > boxboundx) {
        ballvx =-ballvx;
        nballx = boxboundx;
    }
    if (nballx < inboxboundx) {
        nballx = inboxboundx
        ballvx = -ballvx;
    }
    if (nbally > boxboundy) {
        nbally = boxboundy;
```

```
        ballvy =-ballvy;
    }
    if (nbally < inboxboundy) {
        nbally = inboxboundy;
        ballvy = -ballvy;
    }
    ballx = nballx;
    bally = nbally;
}
```

You might say that not much actually happens here and you'd be correct. The variables `ballx` and `bally` are modified to be used later when things get drawn to the canvas.

It is not obvious from this code, but do keep in mind that vertical values (y values) increase going down the screen and horizontal values (x values) increase going from left to right.

Validation

Caution: As of this writing, some validation works in Chrome, and perhaps other browsers, but not in Firefox.

HTML5 provides new facilities for validating form input. The creator of a form can specify that an input field is of type `number` as opposed to `text`, and HTML5 will immediately check that the user/player entered a number. Similarly, we can specify `max` and `min` values. The code for the form is

```
<form name="f" id="f" onSubmit="return change();">
  Horizontal velocity <input name="hv" id="hv" value="4" type="number" min="-10"
max="10" />
<br>
  Vertical velocity <input name="vv" id="vv" value="8" type="number" min="-10"
max="10"/>
<input type="submit" value="CHANGE"/>
</form>
```

The input is still text, that is, a string of characters, but the values are to be text that can be interpreted as a number in the indicated range.

Other types of input include "email" and "URL" and it is very handy to have HTML5 check these. Of course, you can check any character string to see if it's a number using `isNumber` and more complicated coding, including *regular expressions* (patterns of characters that can be matched against), to check for valid e-mail addresses and URLs. One common tactic for checking an e-mail address is to make the user type it in twice so you can compare the two and make sure the user hasn't made any mistakes.

We want to take advantage of the work HTML5 will do for us, but we also want to let the user/player know if something is wrong. You can use HTML5 and CSS to do this, by specifying a style for valid and invalid input.

```
input:valid {background:green;}
input:invalid {background:red;}
```

HTML5 validation is not fully operational in all browsers, so I won't spend a lot of time on it. If you're using a compliant browser, such as Chrome, you can test out the example given in the next section. Notice that the ball keeps bouncing even if an invalid value, say "abc" is entered where a number was specified, because the program continues to use the current settings.

> Tip: Validating input and generating appropriate feedback to users is important in any application. Among the new features HTML5 provides is a pattern attribute in the input element in which a special language called regular expressions can be used to specify valid input. Put **HTML5 regular expressions** into a search field to find up-to-date information.

HTML page reload

Before continuing, I want to mention some issues that may cause unexpected problems. Browsers come with reload/refresh buttons. The document is reloaded when the button is clicked. We made use of this in the simple die throw application in Chapter 2. However, at times you may want to prevent a reload and, in such cases, you can put a `return (false);` in functions that don't have anything to return to keep the page from reloading.

When a document has a form, reloading does not always reinitialize the form input. You may need to leave the page and then reload it using the full URL.

Lastly, browsers try to use files previously downloaded to the client (user) computer rather than requesting files from a server based on inspection of the date and time. The files on the client computer are stored in what is called the cache. If you think you made a change but the browser isn't displaying the latest version, you may need to take steps such as clearing the cache.

Building the application and making it your own

I will now explain the code for the basic bouncing ball application; the application that uses an image for the ball and gradients for the walls; and the one that validates the input. Table 3-1 shows all the function calls and what is being called. This is the same for all three applications.

Table 3-1. Functions in the Bouncing Ball Applications

Function	Invoked By/Called By	Calls
init	Action of onLoad in the body tag	moveball
moveball	Invoked directly by init and by action of setInterval	moveandcheck
moveandcheck	Invoked by moveball	
change	Invoked by action of onSubmit in the form tag	

The moveandcheck code could be part of the moveball function. I chose to separate it because it is a good practice to define functions that perform specific actions. Generally, more, smaller functions are better than fewer, larger ones when you're developing applications. By the way, when doing your own programming, don't forget to put comments in the code as described in Chapter 2. And add blank lines to make the code more readable. Table 3-2 shows the code for the basic bouncing ball application and explains what each line does.

Table 3-2. The Bouncing Ball Application

Code	Explanation
`<html>`	Start html
`<head>`	Start head
`<title>Bouncing Ball↪` `with inputs</title>`	Complete title element
`<style>`	Start style
`form {`	Start form styling
`width:330px;`	Set up width
`margin:20px;`	Set margin
`background-color:brown;`	Set color
`padding:20px;`	Set internal padding
`}`	Close this style
`</style>`	Close style element
`<script type="text/javascript">`	Start script element. (The type is not required. I show it here just to let you know what you'll see in many examples online.)
`var boxx = 20;`	x location of upper corner of box
`var boxy = 30;`	y location of upper corner of box
`var boxwidth = 350;`	Box width
`var boxheight = 250;`	Box height
`var ballrad = 10;`	Radius of ball

Code	Explanation
`var boxboundx =↪` `boxwidth+boxx-ballrad;`	Right boundary
`var boxboundy =↪` `boxheight+boxy-ballrad;`	Bottom boundary
`var inboxboundx =↪` `boxx+ballrad;`	Left boundary
`var inboxboundy =↪` `boxy+ballrad;`	Top boundary
`var ballx = 50;`	Initial x position of ball
`var bally = 60;`	Initial y position of ball
`var ctx;`	Variable holding canvas context
`var ballvx = 4;`	Initial horizontal displacement
`var ballvy = 8;`	Initial vertical displacement
`function init() {`	Start of `init` function
`ctx = document.getElementById↪` `('canvas').getContext('2d');`	Set the `ctx` variable
`  ctx.linewidth = ballrad;`	Set line width
`ctx.fillStyle ="rgb(200,0,50)";`	Set fill style
`  moveball();`	Invoke `moveball` function the first time to move, check, and display the ball
`setInterval(moveball,100);`	Set up timing event
`}`	Close of `init` function
`function moveball(){`	Start of `moveball` function
`  ctx.clearRect(boxx,boxy,↪` `boxwidth,boxheight);`	Clear (erase) box (including any paint from a ball)

Code	Explanation
`moveandcheck();`	Do the check and the move the ball
`ctx.beginPath();`	Start path
`ctx.arc(ballx, bally,` `ballrad,0,Math.PI*2,true);`	Set up to draw of circle at current location of ball
`ctx.fill();`	Fill in the path; that is, draw a filled circle
`ctx.strokeRect(boxx,boxy,↪` `boxwidth,boxheight);`	Draw rectangle outline
`}`	Close `moveball`
`function moveandcheck() {`	Start of `moveandcheck`
`var nballx = ballx + ballvx;`	Set tentative next x position
`var nbally = bally +ballvy;`	Set tentative next y position
`if (nballx > boxboundx) {`	Is this x value beyond the right wall?
`ballvx =-ballvx;`	If so, change vertical displacement
`nballx = boxboundx;`	Set the next x to be exactly at this boundary.
`}`	Close clause
`if (nballx < inboxboundx) {`	Is this x value less than the right boundary?
`nballx = inboxboundx`	If so, set the x value to be exactly at the boundary
`ballvx = -ballvx;`	Change the vertical displacement
`}`	Close clause
`if (nbally > boxboundy) {`	Is the y value beyond the bottom boundary?
`nbally = boxboundy;`	If so, set the y value to be exactly at the boundary
`ballvy =-ballvy;`	Change the horizontal displacement

Code	Explanation
`}`	Close clause
`if (nbally < inboxboundy) {`	Is the y value less than the top boundary?
`nbally = inboxboundy;`	If so, set the y value to be exactly the boundary
`ballvy = -ballvy;`	Change the vertical displacement
`}`	Close clause
`ballx = nballx;`	Set the x position to `nballx`
`bally = nbally;`	Set the y position to `nbally`
`}`	Close `moveandcheck` function
`function change() {`	Start of `change` function
`ballvx = Number(f.hv.value);`	Convert input to number and assign to `ballvx`
`ballvy = Number(f.vv.value);`	Convert input to number and assign to `ballvy`
`return false;`	Return `false` to make sure there isn't a page reload
`}`	Close function
`</script>`	Close script
`</head>`	Close head
`<body onLoad="init();">`	Start body element. Set up call to `init` function
`<canvas id="canvas" width=➥ "400" height="300">`	Start of `canvas` element
`Your browser doesn't support the➥ HTML5 element canvas.`	Message for non-compliant browsers
`</canvas>`	Close `canvas` element
` `	Line break

Code	Explanation
`<form name="f" id="f" onSubmit=➥` `"return change();">`	Start of form. Give name and id (may need for some browsers). Set up action on submit button.

`  Horizontal velocity <input name="hv"➥`
`id="hv" value="4" type="number"➥`
`min="-10" max="10" />`
	Label an input field for horizontal velocity

` `	Line break

`  Vertical velocity <input name=➥`
`"vv" id="vv" value="8" type="number"➥`
`min="-10" max="10"/>`
	Label an input field for vertical velocity

`<input type="submit" value="CHANGE"/>`	Submit button
`</form>`	Close `form`
`</body>`	Close `body`
`</html>`	Close `html`

The application that uses an image as the ball and the gradient-filled walls is very similar. Table 3-3 shows all the code—but I just comment the code that is different. I'm not being lazy; the idea is to let you see how each application is built on the previous one.

Table 3-3. The Second Application, with an Image as the Ball and Gradient-Filled Walls

Code	Explanation
`<html>`	
`<head>`	
`   <title>Bouncing Ball with inputs</title>`	
`   <style>`	
`   form {`	
`     width:330px;`	
`     margin:20px;`	

Code	Explanation
`background-color:#b10515;`	
`padding:20px;`	
`}`	
`</style>`	
`<script type="text/javascript">`	
`var boxx = 20;`	
`var boxy = 30;`	
`var boxwidth = 350;`	
`var boxheight = 250;`	
`var ballrad = 20;`	This isn't a substantial change, but the picture required a bigger radius.
`var boxboundx = boxwidth+boxx-ballrad;`	
`var boxboundy = boxheight+boxy-ballrad;`	
`var inboxboundx = boxx+ballrad;`	
`var inboxboundy = boxy+ballrad;`	
`var ballx = 50;`	
`var bally = 60;`	
`var ballvx = 4;`	
`var ballvy = 8;`	
`var img = new Image();`	Defining the img variable as an Image object. This is what the new operator and the call to the Image function do.

Code	Explanation
`img.src="pearl.jpg";`	Set the `src` for this image to be the "pearl.jpg" file.
`var ctx;`	
`var grad;`	Set `grad` as a variable. It will be assigned a value in the `init` function.
`var color;`	Used in setting up the gradient `grad`
`var hue = [`	Used in setting up the gradient `grad`. This is an array of arrays, each inner array supplying RGB values.
`[255,   0,   0 ],`	Red
`[255, 255,   0 ],`	Yellow
`[  0, 255,   0 ],`	Green
`[  0, 255, 255 ],`	Cyan
`[  0,   0, 255 ],`	Blue
`[255,   0, 255 ]`	Purple (magenta)
`];`	Close array
`function init(){`	Used to set up the gradient
`var h;`	
`ctx = document.getElementById('canvas').↪getContext('2d');`	
`grad = ctx.createLinearGradient(boxx,boxy,↪boxx+boxwidth,boxy+boxheight);`	Create and assign a gradient value.
`for (h=0;h<hue.length;h++) {`	Start of for loop

Code	Explanation
`color = 'rgb('+hue[h][0]+','`↪ `+hue[h][1]+','+hue[h][2]+')';`	Set up `color` as a character string that indicates an RGB value.
`grad.addColorStop(h*1/6,color);`	Set up the color stop to define the gradient.
`}`	Close for loop
`ctx.fillStyle = grad;`	Set the fill to be `grad`
`ctx.lineWidth = ballrad;`	
`moveball();`	
`setInterval(moveball,100);`	
`}`	
`function moveball(){`	
`ctx.clearRect(boxx,boxy,boxwidth,boxheight);`	
`moveandcheck();`	
`ctx.drawImage(img,ballx-ballrad,`↪ `bally-ballrad,2*ballrad,2*ballrad);`	Draw an image
`ctx.fillRect(boxx,boxy,ballrad,boxheight);`	Draw the left wall
`ctx.fillRect(boxx+boxwidth-` `ballrad,boxy,ballrad,boxheight);`	Draw the right wall
`ctx.fillRect(boxx,boxy,boxwidth,ballrad);`	Draw the top wall
`ctx.fillRect(boxx,boxy+boxheight-` `ballrad,boxwidth,ballrad);`	Draw the bottom wall
`}`	
`function moveandcheck() {`	

Code	Explanation
`var nballx = ballx + ballvx;`	
`var nbally = bally +ballvy;`	
`if (nballx > boxboundx) {`	
`    ballvx =-ballvx;`	
`    nballx = boxboundx;`	
`}`	
`if (nballx < inboxboundx) {`	
`    nballx = inboxboundx`	
`    ballvx = -ballvx;`	
`}`	
`if (nbally > boxboundy) {`	
`    nbally = boxboundy;`	
`    ballvy =-ballvy;`	
`}`	
`if (nbally < inboxboundy) {`	
`  nbally = inboxboundy;`	
`    ballvy = -ballvy;`	
`}`	
`ballx = nballx;`	
`bally = nbally;`	

Code	Explanation
`}`	
`function change() {`	
`    ballvx = Number(f.hv.value);`	
`    ballvy = Number(f.vv.value);`	
`    return false;`	
`}`	
`</script>`	
`</head>`	
`<body onLoad="init();">`	
`<canvas id="canvas" width=`↪ `"400" height="300">`	
`This browser doesn't support`↪ ` the HTML5 canvas element.`	
`</canvas>`	
` `	
`<form name="f" id="f" onSubmit=`↪ `"return change();">`	
`  Horizontal velocity <input name=`↪ `"hv" id="hv" value="4" type=`↪ `"number" min="-10" max="10" />`	
` `	
`  Vertical velocity <input name=`↪ `"vv" id="vv" value="8" type=`↪ `"number" min="-10" max="10"/>`	
`<input type="submit" value="CHANGE"/>`	

Code	Explanation
`</form>`	
`</body>`	
`</html>`	

I chose to put the modest change of the style information in the first application. Table 3-4 shows the third bouncing ball application, with form validation. Again, I have only commented the new code, but I include all the code for completeness sake.

Table 3-4. The Third Bouncing Ball Application, with Form Validation

Code	Explanation
`<html>`	
`<head>`	
`    <title>Bouncing Ball with inputs</title>`	
`    <style>`	
`      form {`	
`      width:330px;`	
`      margin:20px;`	
`      background-color:brown;`	
`      padding:20px;`	
`}`	
`input:valid {background:green;}`	Set up feedback for valid input
`input:invalid {background:red;}`	Set up feedback for invalid input
`    </style>`	
`    <script type="text/javascript">`	

Code	Explanation
`var cwidth = 400;`	
`var cheight = 300;`	
`var ballrad = 10;`	
`var boxx = 20;`	
`var boxy = 30;`	
`var boxwidth = 350;`	
`var boxheight = 250;`	
`var boxboundx = boxwidth+boxx-ballrad;`	
`var boxboundy = boxheight+boxy-ballrad;`	
`var inboxboundx = boxx+ballrad;`	
`var inboxboundy = boxy+ballrad;`	
`var ballx = 50;`	
`var bally = 60;`	
`var ctx;`	
`var ballvx = 4;`	
`var ballvy = 8;`	
`function init(){`	
`ctx = document.getElementById('canvas').`↪ `getContext('2d');`	
`ctx.lineWidth = ballrad;`	
`  moveball();`	

Code	Explanation
`  setInterval(moveball,100);`	
`}`	
`function moveball(){`	
`  ctx.clearRect(boxx,boxy,boxwidth,boxheight);`	
`  moveandcheck();`	
`  ctx.beginPath();`	
`  ctx.fillStyle ="rgb(200,0,50)";`	
`  ctx.arc(ballx, bally, ballrad,0,Math.PI*2,true);`	
`  ctx.fill();`	
`   ctx.strokeRect(boxx,boxy,boxwidth,boxheight);`	
`}`	
`function moveandcheck() {`	
`     var nballx = ballx + ballvx;`	
`     var nbally = bally +ballvy;`	
`  if (nballx > boxboundx) {`	
`     ballvx =-ballvx;`	
`     nballx = boxboundx;`	
`  }`	
`  if (nballx < inboxboundx) {`	

Code	Explanation
`    nballx = inboxboundx`	
`     ballvx = -ballvx;`	
`  }`	
` if (nbally > boxboundy) {`	
`    nbally = boxboundy;`	
`    ballvy =-ballvy;`	
`  }`	
` if (nbally < inboxboundy) {`	
`   nbally = inboxboundy;`	
`    ballvy = -ballvy;`	
`  }`	
` ballx = nballx;`	
` bally = nbally;`	
`}`	
`function change() {`	
`    ballvx = Number(f.hv.value);`	
`    ballvy = Number(f.vv.value);`	
`    return false;`	
`}`	
`</script>`	
`</head>`	

Code	Explanation
`<body onLoad="init();">`	
`<canvas id="canvas" width="400" height="300">`	
`Your browser doesn't support the HTML5 element canvas.`	
`</canvas>`	
` `	
`<form name="f" id="f" onSubmit="return change();">`	
`  Horizontal velocity <input name="hv" id=↵` `"hv" value="4" type="number" min="-10" max="10" />`	
` `	
`  Vertical velocity <input name="vv" id=↵` `"vv" value="8" type="number" min="-10" max="10"/>`	
`<input type="submit" value="CHANGE"/>`	
`</form>`	
`</body>`	
`</html>`	

There are many ways you can make this application your own. You can select your own image for the ball and experiment with the colors for the walls, with or without the gradients. You can change the position and the dimensions of each wall. You can add text and HTML markup to the page. You can change the look of the form.

You can include more than one ball, keeping track of the positions of each. If you decide to use two balls, you need two sets of variables and two lines of code for each one line you had before. One systematic way to do this is to use the search function in the editor to find all instances of ball and, for each line, substitute two lines, so in place of ballx, you have ball1x and ball2x, and in place of the var ballx = 50; use

```
var ball1x = 50;
var ball2x = 250;
```

This puts the second ball 200 pixels over on the canvas.

You would also need a second set of all the comparisons for the walls.

If you want to use more than two balls, you may want to consider using arrays. Subsequent chapters will show you how to handle sets of objects.

You also can try writing code that slows the ball each time it hits a wall. This is a nice effect and does simulate a real physical result. In each of the places in the code where the direction is changed by changing the sign of the appropriate variable, add in a factor to decrease the absolute value. For example, if I chose to decrease the value by 10%, I would write

```
if (nballx > boxboundx) {
      ballvx =-ballvx *.9;
      nballx = boxboundx;
}
```

This means that the incremental change in the vertical direction would go down to 90% of what it was.

Testing and uploading the application

The first and third applications are complete in the HTML documents. The second application requires the image file to be present in the same folder. You can access files anywhere on the Web, but you need to make sure you include the correct address. For example, if you upload the HTML document to a folder called mygames and upload pearl.jpg to a subfolder of mygames named images, the line indicating this must be

```
img.src = "images/pearl.jpg";
```

You must also use accurate file extensions, such as JPG, that indicate the correct file type. Some browsers are forgiving but many are not. You can try to submit bad data and see the response using different browsers.

Summary

In this chapter, you learned how to create an application with animation that changes based on input from the user. We covered a number of programming and HTML5 features, including

- setInterval to set up a timing event for the animation
- validation of form input
- programmer-defined functions to reposition a circle or an image horizontally and vertically to simulate a bouncing ball
- tests to check for virtual collisions
- drawing rectangles, images and circles, including gradients for the coloring

The next chapter describes the cannonball and slingshot games in which the player attempts to hit targets. These applications use the same programming and HTML5 features we used to produce the animation, but take them a step further. You will also see an example of animation in the rock-paper-scissors implementation in Chapter 8.

Chapter 4

Cannonball and Slingshot

In this chapter, you will learn techniques for

- maintaining a list of objects to draw on the screen
- rotating objects drawn on the screen
- mouse drag and drop operations
- calculations to simulate ballistic motion (effects of gravity) and collisions

Introduction

This chapter demonstrates another example of animation, in this case simulation of ballistics, also called projectile motion. A ball or ball-like object maintains a constant horizontal (x) displacement, with the vertical displacement changing as it would due to gravity. The resulting motion is an arc. The ball stops when it (virtually) hits the ground or the target. The code you'll see produces the animation using the same technique demonstrated for the ball bouncing in a box. The code repositions the ball and redraws the scene at fixed intervals. We will look at three examples.

- A very simple ballistics simulation: a ball taking off and traveling in an arc before hitting a target or the ground. The parameters of flight are horizontal and initial vertical speeds, which are set by the player using form input fields. The ball simply stops when it hits the target or the ground.
- An improved cannonball, with a rectangle representing the cannon tilted at an angle. The parameters of flight are the speed out of the cannon and the angle of the cannon. Again, these are set by the player using form input fields. The program calculates the initial horizontal and vertical displacement values.

- A slingshot. The parameters of flight are determined by the player dragging, then releasing a ball shape tethered to a stick drawing representing a slingshot. The speed is determined by the distance from the ball to a place on the slingshot. The angle is the angle from the horizontal of this part of the slingshot.

Figure 4-1 shows the simple (no cannon) application.

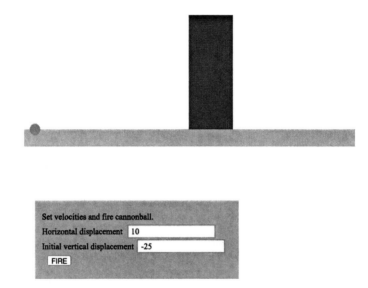

Figure 4-1. The ball lands on the ground.

Figure 4-2 shows the opening screen for the second application. The target is an Image and the rectangle representing the cannon can be rotated. Notice the controls refer to an angle and an initial velocity

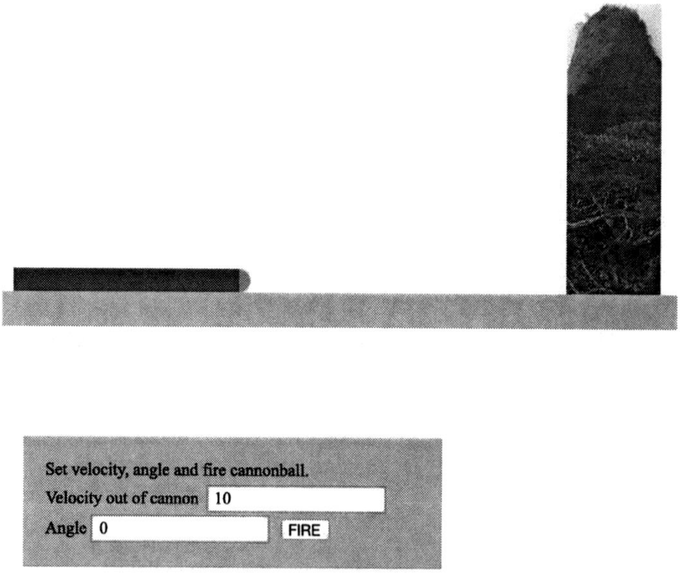

Figure 4-2. Rotating cannon with image as target

Figure 4-3 shows the scene after a successful hit. Notice that the cannon is rotated and the original image for the target has been replaced with a new image.

Figure 4-3. After firing the cannon and hitting target

The opening screen of the slingshot application is shown in Figure 4-4. This application is similar to the cannon, but the parameters of flight are set by the player using a mouse to drag on the ball and the target is now a chicken.

Figure 4-4. Opening screen of the slingshot application

For the slingshot, I decided I wanted the ball to keep going until it hit the ground. However, if the chicken was hit, I wanted it to be replaced by feathers, as shown in Figure 4-5. Notice that the strings of the slingshot remain where they were when the mouse button was released and the ball took flight. I found I needed more time looking at the strings in order to plan my next shot. If you want, you can change the game so that the strings snap back to their original position or create a new-game button. In my example, the game is replayed by reloading the HTML file.

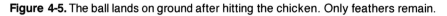

Figure 4-5. The ball lands on ground after hitting the chicken. Only feathers remain.

The programming for these applications uses many of the same techniques demonstrated in the bouncing ball applications. The repositioning of the ball in flight is only as different as it needs to be to simulate the effects of the vertical displacement changing because of gravity. The slingshot application provides a new way for the player to interact with the application, using drag and drop actions with the mouse.

The cannonball with cannon and the slingshot use drawing features for the cannon and slingshot and external image files for the original targets and hit targets. If you want to change the targets, you'll need to find image files and upload them with the application. The complete applications are available at `www.friendsofed.com/downloads.html`.

Critical requirements

Our first requirement is to produce animation by setting up an event to occur at fixed intervals of time, and then setting up a function to handle the event by repositioning the ball and checking for collisions. We covered this in the previous chapter on the bouncing ball application. What's new here is the calculation for simulating gravity. The calculation indicated by a simple physics model works out a new vertical displacement based on changing the vertical displacement by a constant amount and then computing the average of the old and new displacements to compute the new position.

- The horizontal displacement (held by variable dx) is the horizontal velocity (horvelocity) and does not change. In code: dx = horvelocity;

- The vertical velocity at the start of the interval is `verticalvel1`
- The vertical velocity at end of the interval is `verticalvel1` plus the acceleration amount (gravity). In code: `verticalvel2 = verticalvel1 + gravity;`
- The vertical displacement for the interval (dy) is the average of `verticalvel1` and `verticalvel2`. In code: `dy = (verticalvel1 + verticalvel2)*.5;`

This is a standard way of simulating gravity or any other constant acceleration.

> Note: I made up my value for gravity to produce a pleasing arc. You can use a standard value, but you'll need to do research to assign realistic values for the starting velocity out of the mouth of the cannon and for a slingshot. You also need to determine the mapping between pixels and distances. The factor would be different for the cannonball and the slingshot.

The second version of the program must rotate the cannon based on either the initial values or the player's input for the velocity out of the mouth of the cannon and the cannon angle and calculate the horizontal and vertical values based on these values.

The third version of the program, the slingshot, must allow the player to press and hold the mouse button and drag the ball along with the strings of the slingshot, then let the mouse button up to release the ball. The motion parameters are calculated based on the angle and the distance of the ball from the top of the slingshot.

Both the second and third versions of the program require a way to replace the target image with another image.

HTML5, CSS, and JavaScript features

Now let's look at the specific features of HTML5 and JavaScript that provide what we need to implement the ballistics simulation applications. Luckily, we can build on material covered in previous chapters, specifically the general structure of an HTML document, using a `canvas` element, programmer-defined and built-in functions, a `form` element, and variables. Let's start with programmer-defined objects and using arrays.

Arrays and programmer-defined objects

HTML5 lets you draw on a canvas, but once something is drawn, it's as if paint or ink were laid down; the thing drawn doesn't retain its individual identity. HTML5 is not like Flash in which objects are positioned on a Stage and can be individually moved and rotated. However, we can still produce the same effects, including rotation of individual objects.

Because these applications have a somewhat more complicated display, I decided to develop a more systematic approach to drawing and redrawing different things on the canvas. To that end, I created an array called `everything` that holds the list of objects to be drawn on the canvas. Think of an array as a set, or more accurately, a sequence of items. In previous chapters, we discussed variables set up to hold values such as numbers or character strings. An array is another type of value. My `everything` array will serve as a to-do list of what needs to be drawn on the canvas.

I am using the term *objects* in both the English and the programming sense. In programming terms, an object consists of *properties* and *methods*, that is, data and coding or behavior. In the annotated links example described in the first chapter, I demonstrated the write method of the document object. I used the variable ctx, which is of type 2D context of a canvas object, methods such as fillRect, and properties such as fillStyle. These were built-in; that is, they were already defined objects in HTML5's version of JavaScript. For the ballistics applications, I defined my own objects, specifically Ball, Picture, Myrectangle, and Sling. Each of these different objects includes the definition of a draw method as well as properties indicating position and dimensions. I did this so I can draw each of a list of things. The appropriate draw method accesses the properties to determine what and where to draw. I also included a way to rotate individual objects.

Defining an object is straightforward: I simply define a function called the *constructor* function for Ball, Picture, and Myrectangle, and use these functions with the operator new to assign the values to variables. I can then write code using the familiar dot notation to access or assign the properties and to invoke methods I've set up in the constructor function. Here is the constructor function for a Ball object:

```
function Ball(sx,sy,rad,stylestring) {
   this.sx = sx;
   this.sy = sy;
   this.rad = rad;
   this.draw = drawball;
   this.moveit = moveball;
   this.fillstyle = stylestring;
}
```

The term this refers to the object that's created when this function is used with the keyword new. The fact that this.draw and this.moveit are assigned the names of functions is not obvious from looking at the code, but that's what happens. The definitions of those two functions follow. Notice that they each use the term this to get at the properties necessary to draw and move the object.

```
function drawball() {
        ctx.fillStyle=this.fillstyle;
        ctx.beginPath();

        ctx.arc(this.sx,this.sy,this.rad,0,Math.PI*2,true);
        ctx.fill();
}
```

The drawball function draws a filled-in circle, a complete arc, on the canvas. The color of the circle is the color set when this Ball object was created.

The function moveball doesn't move anything immediately. Looking at the issue abstractly, moveball changes where the application positions the object. The function changes the values of the sx and sy properties of the object and when it is displayed next, these new values are used to make the drawing.

```
function moveball(dx,dy) {
        this.sx +=dx;
        this.sy +=dy;
}
```

The next statement, declaring the variable cball, builds a new object of type Ball by using the operator new and the function Ball. The parameters to the function are based on set values for the cannon because I want the ball to appear at the mouth of the cannon to start out.

```
var cball = new
Ball(cannonx+cannonlength,cannony+cannonht*.5,ballrad,"rgb(250,0,0)");
```

The Picture, Myrectangle, and Slingshot functions are similar and will be explained below. They each specify a draw method. For this application, I only use moveit for cball, but I defined moveit for the other objects just in case I later want to build on this application. The variables cannon and ground will be set to hold a new Myrectangle, and the variables target and htarget will be set to hold a new Picture.

> Tip: Names made up by programmers are arbitrary, but it's a good idea to be consistent in both spelling and case. HTML5 appears to disregard case, in contrast to a version of HTML called XHTML. Many languages treat upper- and lowercase as different letters. I generally use lowercase, but I capitalized the first letter of Ball, Picture, Slingshot, and Myrectangle because the convention is that functions intended to be constructors of objects should start with capital letters.

Each of the variables will be added to the everything array using the array method push, which adds a new element to the end of the array.

Rotations and translations for drawing

HTML5 lets us translate and rotate drawings. Take a look at the following code. I urge you to create this example and then experiment with it to improve your understanding. The code draws a large red rectangle on the canvas with the upper corner at (50,50) and a tiny blue, square on top of it.

```html
<html>
<head>
    <title>Rectangle</title>
    <script type="text/javascript">
        var ctx;
function init(){
   ctx = document.getElementById('canvas').getContext('2d');
        ctx.fillStyle = "rgb(250,0,0)";
        ctx.fillRect(50,50,100,200);
ctx.fillStyle = "rgb(0,0,250)";
        ctx.fillRect(50,50,5,5);
}
</script>
</head>
<body onLoad="init();">
<canvas id="canvas" width="400" height="300">
Your browser doesn't support the HTML5 element canvas.
</canvas>
</body>
</html>
```

The result is shown in Figure 4-6.

Figure 4-6. Rectangle (no rotation)

In this exercise, the goal is to rotate the large rectangle, pivoting on the upper-left corner where the small blue square is. I want the rotation to be counterclockwise.

One slight complication, common to most programming languages, is that the angle input for rotations as well as the trigonometry functions must be in *radians*, not degrees. Radians were explained in Chapter 2, but here's a reminder. Instead of 360 degrees in a full circle, the measurement is based on two times the mathematical constant pi radians in a circle. Fortunately, we can use the built-in feature of JavaScript, Math.PI. One pi radians is equivalent to 180 degrees and pi divided by 2 is equivalent to a right angle, 90 degrees. To specify a rotation of 30 degrees, we use pi divided by 6 or, in coding, Math.PI/6. To change the init function given previously to do a rotation, I put in a rotation of negative pi divided by 6 (equivalent to 30 degrees going counterclockwise), draw the red rectangle, and then rotate back, undo the rotation, to draw the blue square:

```
function init(){
    ctx = document.getElementById('canvas').getContext('2d');
    ctx.fillStyle = "rgb(250,0,0)";
    ctx.rotate(-Math.PI/6);
    ctx.fillRect(50,50,100,200);
    ctx.rotate(Math.PI/6);
    ctx.fillStyle = "rgb(0,0,250)";
    ctx.fillRect(50,50,5,5);
}
```

Unfortunately, the drawing in Figure 4-7 is not what I wanted.

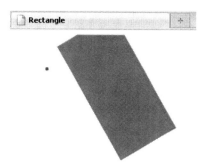

Figure 4-7. Drawing and rotating a rectangle

The problem is the rotation point is at the origin, (0,0) and not at the corner of the red rectangle. So, I need to write code to perform a translation, then the rotation, then a translation back in order to draw at the correct place. I can do this using features of HTML5. All drawing on the canvas is done in terms of a coordinate system, and I can use the save and restore operations to save the current coordinate system—the position and orientation of the axes—and then restore it to make follow-on drawings. Here's the code.

```
function init(){
    ctx = document.getElementById('canvas').getContext('2d');
    ctx.fillStyle = "rgb(250,0,0)";
    ctx.save();
    ctx.translate(50,50);
    ctx.rotate(-Math.PI/6);
    ctx.translate(-50,-50);
    ctx.fillRect(50,50,100,200);
    ctx.restore();
    ctx.fillStyle = "rgb(0,0,250)";
    ctx.fillRect(50,50,5,5);
}
```

The rotate method expects an angle in radian units and clockwise is the positive direction. So my code is rotating 30 degrees counterclockwise, producing what I had in mind, as shown in Figure 4-8.

Figure 4-8. Save, translate, rotate, translate, restore

By the way, we can't expect our players to put in angles using radians. They, and we, are too accustomed to degrees (90 degrees is a right angle, 180 degrees is your arc when you make a u-turn, etc.). The program must do the work. The conversion from degrees to radians is to multiply by pi/180.

> Note: Most programming languages use radians for angles in trig functions. Flash uses degrees in certain situations and radians in others, so in some ways JavaScript is less confusing by only using radians.

With this background, I add to the information in the `everything` array indications as to whether there is to be a rotation and, if so, the required translation point. This is my idea. It has nothing to do with HTML5 or JavaScript, and it could have been done differently. The underlying task is to create and maintain information on objects in the simulated scene. The canvas feature of HTML5 provides a way to draw pictures and display images, but it does not retain information on objects!

The items in the `everything` array for the second and third applications are themselves arrays. The first (0th index) value points to the object. The second (1st index) is `true` or `false`. A value of true means that a rotation angle value and x and y values for translation follow. In practice, this means that the inner arrays have either two values, with the last one being false, or five values.

> Note: At this point, you may be thinking: she set up a general system just to rotate the cannon. Why not put in something just for the cannon? The answer is we could, but the general system does work and something just for the cannon might have had just as much coding.

The first application uses horizontal and vertical displacement values picked up from the form. The player must think of the two separate values. For the second application, the player inputs two values again, but they are different. One is the speed out of the mouth of the cannon and the other is the angle of the cannon. The program does the rest. The initial and unchanging horizontal displacement and the initial vertical displacement are calculated from the player's input: the velocity out of the cannon and an angle. The calculation is based on standard trigonometry. Luckily, JavaScript provides the trig functions as part of the Math class of built-in methods.

Figure 4-9 shows the calculation of the displacement values from the out of cannon and angle values specified by the player. The minus sign for the vertical is due to the way JavaScript screen coordinates have y values increasing going down the screen.

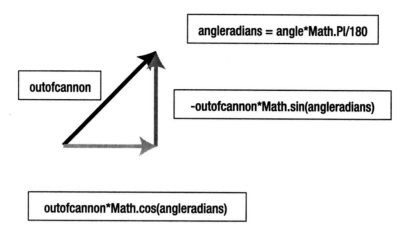

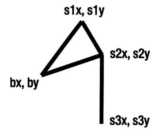

Figure 4-9. Calculating horizontal * vertical displacements

At this point, you may want to skip ahead to read about the implementation of the cannonball applications. You can then come back to read about what is required for the slingshot.

Drawing line segments

For the slingshot application, I have added a new object type by defining two functions, Sling and drawsling. My idealized slingshot is represented by 4 positions, as shown in Figure 4-10. Please understand that we could have done this in a number of different ways.

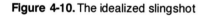

Figure 4-10. The idealized slingshot

Drawing the slingshot consists of drawing four line segments based on the four points. The bx,by point will change as I'll describe in the next section. HTML5 lets us draw line segments as part of a path. We've already used paths for drawing circles. You can draw a path as a stroke or as a fill. For the circles, we used the fill method, but for the slingshot, I just want lines. Drawing a line may involve two steps: move to one end of the line and then draw it. HTML5 provides the moveTo and lineTo methods. The path is not drawn until the stroke or fill method is invoked. The drawsling function is a good illustration of line drawing.

```
function drawsling() {
   ctx.strokeStyle = this.strokeStyle;
   ctx.lineWidth = 4;
   ctx.beginPath();
```

```
    ctx.moveTo(this.bx,this.by);
    ctx.lineTo(this.s1x,this.s1y);
    ctx.moveTo(this.bx,this.by);
    ctx.lineTo(this.s2x,this.s2y);
    ctx.moveTo(this.s1x,this.s1y);
    ctx.lineTo(this.s2x,this.s2y);
    ctx.lineTo(this.s3x,this.s3y);
    ctx.stroke();
}
```

It does the following:

- adds to path a line from `bx,by` to `s1x,s1y`
- adds to path a line from `bx,by` to `s2x,s2y`
- adds to path a line from `s1x,s1y` to `s2x,s2y`
- adds to path a line from `s2x,s2y` to `s3x,s3y`

As always, the way to learn this is to experiment with your own designs. If there's no invocation of `moveTo`, the next `lineTo` draws from the destination of the last `lineTo`. Think of holding a pen in your hand and either moving it on the paper or lifting it up and moving without drawing anything. You also can connect arcs. Chapter 5 demonstrates drawing polygons.

Mouse events for pulling on the slingshot

The slingshot application replaces form input with mouse drag and drop operations. This is appealing because it's closer to the physical act of pulling back on a slingshot.

When the player presses down on the mouse button, it is the first of a sequence of events to be managed by the program. Here is pseudo-code for what needs to be done.

When the player presses the mouse button, check if the mouse is on top of the ball. If not, do nothing. If so, set a variable named inmotion.

If the mouse is moving, check inmotion. If it is set, move the ball and the strings of the slingshot. Keep doing this until the mouse button is released.

When the player releases the mouse button, reset inmotion to false. Calculate the angle and initial velocity of the ball and from these calculate the horizontal velocity and the initial vertical velocity. Start the ball moving.

You can use HTML5 and JavaScript to set up event handling for pressing the standard (left) mouse button, moving the mouse, and releasing the mouse button. The code uses a method based on the canvas element directly, not the so-called context. Here is the code, which is in the `init` function:

```
canvas1 = document.getElementById('canvas');
canvas1.addEventListener('mousedown',findball,false);
canvas1.addEventListener('mousemove',moveit,false);
canvas1.addEventListener('mouseup',finish,false);
```

Now because this event is in terms of the whole canvas, the `findball` function must determine if the mouse is over the ball. The first task is to get the mouse x and y coordinates. Unfortunately, different browsers implement mouse events in different ways. The following works for Firefox, Chrome, and Safari.

When other browsers, such as Internet Explorer, support HTML5, this code will need to be checked and, possibly, modified.

```
if ( ev.layerX || ev.layerX==0) {
    mx= ev.layerX;
    my = ev.layerY;
}
else if (ev.offsetX || ev.offsetX==0 ) {
    mx = ev.offsetX;
    my = ev.offsetY;
}
```

This works because if `ev.layerX` does not exist, its value will be interpreted as false. If `ev.layerX` does exist but has value 0, its value will also be interpreted as false, but `ev.layerX==0` will be true.

Think of this code as saying: is there a good `ev.layerX` value? If so, let's use it. Otherwise, let's try `ev.offsetX`. If neither of these work, `mx` and `my` will not get set and I should add another `else` clause to tell the player that the code doesn't work in his browser.

Now, the next step is to determine if the (`mx`,`my`) point is on the ball. I am repeating myself, but it is important to understand that the ball is now the equivalent of ink or paint on canvas and we can't go any further without determining whether the (`mx`,`my`) point is on top of the ball. How do we do this? We can calculate how far (`mx`,`my`) is from the center of the ball and see if that's less than the radius of the ball. There is a standard formula for distance in the plane. My code is a slight variation on this idea. It makes the determination by calculating the square of the distance and comparing it to the square of the ball's radius. I do this to avoid computing the square root.

If the mouse click was on the ball, that is, within a radius distance of the center of the ball, this function sets the global variable `inmotion` to true. The `findball` function ends with a call to `drawall()`.

Whenever the mouse moves, there's a call to the `moveit` function where we check whether `inmotion` is true. If it isn't, nothing happens. If it is, the same code as before is used to get the mouse coordinates and the ball's center, and the `bx`,`by` values for the slingshot are set to the mouse coordinates. This has the effect of dragging the ball and stretching the slingshot strings.

When the mouse button is released, we call the `finish` function, which doesn't do anything if `inmotion` is not true. When would this happen? If the player is moving the mouse around *not* on the ball and pressing and releasing the button.

If `inmotion` is true, the function immediately sets it to false and does the calculations to determine the flight of the ball, generating the information that in the earlier cannonball application was entered by the player using a form. The information is the angle with the horizontal and the distance of the ball to the straight part of the slingshot. This is the angle formed by (`bx`,`by`) to (`s1x`, `s1y`), and the horizontal and the distance from (`bx`,`by`) to (`s1x`, `s1y`), more precisely, the square of the distance.

I use `Math.atan2` to do these calculations: calculating an angle from change in x and change in y. This is a variant of the arctangent function.

I use the `distsq` function to determine the square of the distance from (`bx`,`by`) to (`s1x`, `s1y`). I want to make the velocity dependent on this value. Pulling the strings back farther would mean a faster flight. I did some experiments and decided that using the square and dividing by 700 produced a nice arc.

The last step is to put in a call first to drawall() and then to setInterval to set up the timing event. Again, finish does an analogous job to fire in the first and second applications. In the first application, our player entered the horizontal and initial vertical values. In the second application, the player entered an angle (in degrees) and a velocity out of the mouth of the cannon, and the program did the rest. In slingshot, we did away with a form and numbers and provided a way for the player to pull back, or virtually pull back, on a slingshot. The program had more to do, both in terms of responding to mouse events and calculations.

Changing the list of items displayed using array splice

The last task to explain is the replacement of the target image with another picture. Since I wanted two different effects, I used different approaches. For the second application, I wanted the ball to disappear along with the original target and display what I set up in the variable htarget. What I do is keep track of where the original target was placed on the everything array and remove it and substitute htarget. Similarly, I remove the ball from the everything array. For the slingshot operation, I don't remove the target but change its img property to be feathers. Please note that in the code, chicken and feathers are Image objects. Each has a src property that points to a file.

```
var chicken = new Image();
chicken.src = "chicken.jpg";
var feathers = new Image();
feathers.src = "feathers.gif";
```

For both of these operations, I use the array method splice. It has two forms: you can just remove any number of elements or you can remove and then insert elements. The general form of splice is

arrayname.splice(index where splice is to occur, number of iterms to be removed, new item(s) to be added)

If more than one item is to be added, there are more arguments. In my code, I add a single item, which is itself an array. My representation of objects in the everything array uses an array for each object. The second argument of the array indicates if there is any rotation.

The following two lines of code do what I need: remove the target, stick in htarget with no rotation, and then remove the ball.

```
everything.splice(targetindex,1,[htarget,false]);
everything.splice(ballindex,1);
```

By the way, if I simply wanted to remove the last item in an array, I could use the method pop. In this situation, however, the target may be somewhere in the middle of the everything array, so I need to write code to keep track of its index value.

Distance between points

There are two places in the slingshot program in which I use the distance between points or, more accurately, the square of the distance. I need to find out if the mouse cursor is on top of the ball and I want to make the initial velocity—the equivalent of the velocity out of the cannon— depending on the stretch, so to speak, of the slingshot, the distance (bx,by) to (s1x, s1y). The formula for the distance between two points x1,y1 and x2,y2 is the square root of the sum of the squares of (x1-x2) and (y1-y2). I decided to avoid the computation of taking a square root by just computing the sum of the squares. This provides the same test for the mouse cursor being on top of the ball. For the other task, I decided it was okay to use the square of the distance for the initial velocity. I experimented with some numbers and, as I mentioned earlier, 700 seemed to work.

Building the application and making it your own

Let's now take a look at the code for the basic firing of a cannonball, without a cannon, based on horizontal and initial vertical speeds; the firing of a cannonball from a cannon, based on angle and initial speed out of the cannon; and the slingshot, based on angle and initial speed determined from the position of the mouse. As in previous chapters, I'll present the functions and what they call or are called by for each application. In this case, the tables are similar, though not identical, for all three applications. The calling is more varied than previous examples in that there are situations in which functions are invoked because they are named as methods of a programmer-defined object or as part of a declaration (var) statement. This is a characteristic of *object-oriented, event-driven programming*. I'll also present the complete code for each application in its own table, along with an explanation of what each line does. Table 4-1 shows the functions for the basic cannonball application.

Table 4-1. Functions in the Simplest Cannonball Application

Function	Invoked By / Called By	Calls
init	Action of the onLoad in body tag	drawall
drawall	Invoked directly by init, fire, change	Calls the draw method of all objects in the everything array. These are the functions drawball, drawrects.
fire	Invoked by action of the onSubmit attribute in form	drawall
change	Invoked by action of the setInterval function called in fire	drawall, calls the moveit method of cball, which is moveball
Ball	Invoked directly by code in a var statement	
Myrectangle	Invoked directly by code in a var statement	
drawball	Invoked by call of the draw method for the one Ball object	
drawrects	Invoked by call of the draw method for the target object	
moveball	Invoked by call of the moveit method for the one Ball object	

Table 4-2 shows the complete code for the simplest application, with the ball moving in an arc and no actual cannon.

Table 4-2. The First Cannonball Application

Code	Explanation
`<html>`	Opening `html` tag
`<head>`	Opening `head` tag
`<title>Cannonball</title>`	Complete `title` element
`<style>`	Opening `style` tag
`form {`	Style for the form
`width:330px;`	`Width`
`margin:20px;`	External `margin`
`background-color:brown;`	`Color`
`padding:20px;`	Internal `padding`
`}`	Close this style
`</style>`	Close `style` element
`<script>`	Opening `script` tag
`var cwidth = 600;`	Set value for width of canvas, used for clearing
`var cheight = 400;`	Set value for height of canvas, used for clearing
`var ctx;`	Variable to hold canvas context
`var everything = [];`	Array to hold all objects to be drawn. Initialized as an empty array
`var tid;`	Variable to hold identifier for the timing event
`var horvelocity;`	Variable to hold the horizontal velocity (aka displacement)

Code	Explanation
`var verticalvel1;`	Variable to hold vertical displacement at start of interval
`var verticalvel2;`	Variable to hold vertical displacement at end of interval, after change by gravity
`var gravity = 2;`	Amount of change in vertical displacement. Arbitrary. Makes for a nice arc.
`var iballx = 20;`	Initial horizontal coordinate for the ball
`var ibally = 300;`	Initial vertical coordinate for the ball
`function Ball(sx,sy,rad,stylestring) {`	Start of function to define a `Ball`. object. Use the parameters to set the properties.
`this.sx = sx;`	Set the `sx` property of THIS object
`this.sy = sy;`	…`sy`
`this.rad = rad;`	…`rad`
`this.draw = drawball;`	…`draw`. Since `drawball` is the name of a function, this makes `draw` a method that can be invoked
`this.moveit = moveball;`	…`moveit` set to the function `moveball`
`this.fillstyle = stylestring;`	…`fillstyle`
`}`	Close the `Ball` function
`function drawball() {`	Header for the `drawball` function
`ctx.fillStyle=this.fillstyle;`	Set up the `fillStyle` using the property of this object
`ctx.beginPath();`	Start a path
`ctx.arc(this.sx,this.sy`↪`,this.rad,0,Math.PI*2,true);`	Set up to draw a circle
`ctx.fill();`	Draw the path as a filled path

Code	Explanation
`}`	Close the function
`function moveball(dx,dy) {`	Header for the `moveball` function
`this.sx +=dx;`	Increment the `sx` property by `dx`
`this.sy +=dy;`	Increment the `sy` property by `dy`
`}`	Close function
`var cball = new Ball(iballx,ibally,↪` `10,"rgb(250,0,0)");`	Create a new `Ball` object at the indicated position, radius, and color. Assign it to the variable `cball`. Note that nothing is drawn at this time. The information is just set up for later use.
`function Myrectangle(sx,sy,swidth,↪` `sheight,stylestring) {`	Header for function to construct a `Myrectangle` object
`this.sx = sx;`	Sets the `sx` property of THIS object
`this.sy = sy;`	...`sy`
`this.swidth = swidth;`	...`swidth`
`this.sheight = sheight;`	...`sheight`
`this.fillstyle = stylestring;`	...`stylestring`
`this.draw = drawrects;`	... `draw`. This sets up a method that can be invoked.
`this.moveit = moveball;`	....`moveit`. This sets up a method that can be invoked. It is not used in this program.
`}`	Close `Myrectangle` function
`function drawrects() {`	Header for `drawrects` function
`ctx.fillStyle = this.fillstyle;`	Set the `fillStyle`
`ctx.fillRect(this.sx,this.sy,↪` `this.swidth,this.sheight);`	Draw the rectangle using the object properties
`}`	Close function

Code	Explanation
`var target = new Myrectangle(300,100,`↵ `80,200,"rgb(0,5,90)");`	Build a `Myrectangle` object and assign to target
`var ground = new Myrectangle(0,300,`↵ `600,30,"rgb(10,250,0)");`	Build a `Myrectangle` object and assign to ground
`everything.push(target);`	Add target to `everything`
`everything.push(ground);`	Add ground
`everything.push(cball);`	Add `cball` (which will be drawn last, so on top of other stuff
`function init(){`	Header for `init` function
`    ctx = document.getElementById`↵ `('canvas').getContext('2d');`	Set up `ctx` in order to draw on the canvas
`  drawall();`	Draw everything
`}`	Close `init`
`function fire() {`	Head for `fire` function
`  cball.sx = iballx;`	Reposition `cball` in x
`  cball.sy = ibally;`	Reposition `cball` in y
`  horvelocity =  Number(document.`↵ `f.hv.value);`	Set horizontal velocity from form. Make a number
`  verticalvel1 = Number(document.`↵ `f.vv.value);`	Set initial vertical velocity from form
`      drawall();`	Draw everything
`      tid = setInterval`↵ `(change,100);`	Start timing event
`      return false;`	Return `false` to prevent refresh of HTML page
`}`	Close function

Code	Explanation
`function drawall() {`	Function header for `drawall`
`    ctx.clearRect➥` `(0,0,cwidth,cheight);`	Erase canvas
`    var i;`	Declare `var i` for the for loop
`for (i=0;i<everything.length;i++)➥` `  {`	For each item in `everything` array...
`        everything[i].draw();}`	...invoke the object's `draw` method. Close for loop.
`}`	Close function
`function change() {`	Header for `change` function
`    var dx = horvelocity;`	Set `dx` to be `horvelocity`
`    verticalvel2 =➥` `verticalvel1 + gravity;`	Compute new vertical velocity (add gravity)
`    var dy = (verticalvel1 +➥` `verticalvel2)*.5;`	Compute average velocity for the time interval
`    verticalvel1 = verticalvel2;`	Now set old to be new
`    cball.moveit(dx,dy);`	Move `cball` computed amount
`    var bx = cball.sx;`	Set `bx` to simplify the `if`
`    var by = cball.sy;`	... and `by`
`    if ((bx>=target.sx)&&(bx<=➥` `(target.sx+target.swidth))&&`	Is the ball within the target horizontally...
`    (by>=target.sy)&&(by<=➥` `(target.sy+target.sheight))) {`	and vertically?
`        clearInterval(tid);`	If so, stop motion
`    }`	Close if true clause
`    if (by>=ground.sy) {`	Is the ball beyond ground?

Code	Explanation
`clearInterval(tid);`	If so, stop motion
`}`	Close if true clause
`drawall();`	Draw everything
`}`	Close change function
`</script>`	Close script element
`</head>`	Close head element
`<body onLoad="init();">`	Open body and set call to init
`<canvas id="canvas" width=↪` `"600" height="400">`	Define canvas
`Your browser doesn't support↪` `the HTML5 element canvas.`	Warning to users of non-compliant browsers
`</canvas>`	Close canvas
` `	Line break
`<form name="f" id="f"↪` `onSubmit="return fire();">`	Starting form tag, with name and id. This sets up call to fire.
`Set velocities and fire↪` `cannonball.  `	Label and line break

`Horizontal displacement <input name=↪`
`"hv" id="hv" value="10" type=↪`
`"number" min="-100" max="100" />`
	Label and specification of input field

` `	Line break

`Initial vertical displacement <input↪`
`name="vv" id="vv" value="-25"↪`
`type="number" min="-100" max="100"/>`
	Label and specification of input field

`<input type="submit" value="FIRE"/>`	Submit input element
`</form>`	Close form element

Code	Explanation
`</body>`	Close `body` element
`</html>`	Close `html` element

You certainly can make improvements to this application, but it probably makes more sense to first make sure you understand it as is and then move on to the next.

Cannonball: with cannon, angle, and speed

Our next application adds a rectangle to represent the cannon, a picture for the original target instead of the simple rectangle used in the first application, and a second picture for the hit target. The cannon rotates as specified by input in the form. I made the everything array an array of arrays because I needed a way to add the rotation and translation information. I also decided to make the result more dramatic when the cannonball hits the target. This means the code in the change function for checking for a collision is the same, but the code in the if-true clause removes the old target, puts in the hit target, and removes the ball. Now, having said all this, most of the coding is the same. Table 4-3, which shows the functions, has two additional lines for Picture and drawAnImage.

Table 4-3. Functions in the Second Cannonball Application

Function	Invoked By / Called By	Calls
`init`	Action of the `onLoad` in body tag	`drawall`
`drawall`	Invoked directly by `init`, `fire`, `change`	Calls the `draw` method of all objects in the `everything` array. These are the functions drawball, drawrects.
`fire`	Invoked by action of the `onSubmit` attribute in form	`drawall`
`change`	Invoked by action of the `setInterval` function called in `fire`	`drawall`, calls the `moveit` method of `cball`, which is `moveball`
`Ball`	Invoked directly by code in a `var` statement	
`Myrectangle`	Invoked directly by code in a `var` statement	
`drawball`	Invoked by call of the `draw` method for the one `Ball` object	
`drawrects`	Invoked by call of the `draw` method for the `target` object	

Function	Invoked By / Called By	Calls
moveball	Invoked by call of the moveit method for the one Ball object	
Picture	Invoked directly by code in var statements	
drawAnImage	Invoked by call of the draw method for a Picture object	

Table 4-4 shows the complete code for the second application, but only the changed lines have comments.

Table 4-4. The Second Cannonball Application

Code	Explanation
`<html>`	
`<head>`	
`    <title>Cannonball</title>`	
`    <style>`	
`        form {`	
`        width:330px;`	
`        margin:20px;`	
`        background-color:brown;`	
`        padding:20px;`	
`}`	
`    </style>`	
`    <script type="text/javascript">`	
`        var cwidth = 600;`	

Code	Explanation
`var cheight = 400;`	
`var ctx;`	
`var everything = [];`	
`var tid;`	
`var horvelocity;`	
`var verticalvel1;`	
`var verticalvel2;`	
`var gravity = 2;`	
`var cannonx = 10;`	x location of cannon
`var cannony = 280;`	y location of cannon
`var cannonlength = 200;`	Cannon length (i.e., width)
`var cannonht = 20;`	Cannon height
`var ballrad = 10;`	
`var targetx = 500;`	x position of target
`var targety = 50;`	y position of target
`var targetw = 85;`	Target width
`var targeth = 280;`	Target height
`var htargetx = 450;`	x position of the hit target
`var htargety = 220;`	y position of the hit target
`var htargetw = 355;`	Hit target width
`var htargeth = 96;`	Hit target height

Code	Explanation
`function Ball(sx,sy,rad,stylestring) {`	
`  this.sx = sx;`	
`  this.sy = sy;`	
`  this.rad = rad;`	
`  this.draw = drawball;`	
`  this.moveit = moveball;`	
`  this.fillstyle = stylestring;`	
`}`	
`function drawball() {`	
`    ctx.fillStyle=this.fillstyle;`	
`    ctx.beginPath();`	
`    //ctx.fillStyle= rgb(0,0,0);`	
`    ctx.arc(this.sx,this.sy,this.rad,↵` `0,Math.PI*2,true);`	
`    ctx.fill();`	
`}`	
`function moveball(dx,dy) {`	
`    this.sx +=dx;`	
`    this.sy +=dy;`	
`}`	
`var cball = new Ball(cannonx+cannonlength,↵` `cannony+cannonht*.5,ballrad,"rgb(250,0,0)");`	

Code	Explanation
`function Myrectangle(sx,sy,swidth,sheight,↵` `stylestring) {`	
`    this.sx = sx;`	
`    this.sy = sy;`	
`    this.swidth = swidth;`	
`    this.sheight = sheight;`	
`    this.fillstyle = stylestring;`	
`    this.draw = drawrects;`	
`    this.moveit = moveball;`	
`}`	
`function drawrects() {`	
`    ctx.fillStyle = this.fillstyle;`	
`    ctx.fillRect(this.sx,this.sy,↵` `this.swidth,this.sheight);`	
`}`	
`function Picture (sx,sy,swidth,↵` `sheight,filen) {`	Header for function to set up `Picture` object
`    var imga = new Image();`	Create an `Image` object
`    imga.src=filen;`	Set the file name
`    this.sx = sx;`	Set the `sx` property
`    this.sy = sy;`	... `sy`
`    this.img = imga;`	Set the `img` property to `imga`
`    this.swidth = swidth;`	... `swidth`

Code	Explanation
`        this.sheight = sheight;`	... `sheight`
`        this.draw = drawAnImage;`	... `draw`. This will be the `draw` method for objects of this type.
`     this.moveit = moveball;`	... This will be the `moveit` method. Not used.
`}`	Close `Picture` function
`function drawAnImage() {`	Header for `drawAnImage` function
`     ctx.drawImage(this.img,this.sx,`↪ `this.sy,this.swidth,this.sheight);`	Draw image using properties of this object
`}`	Closes function
`var target = new Picture(targetx,targety,`↪ `targetw,targeth,"hill.jpg");`	Construct new `Picture` object and assign to `target` variable
`var htarget = new Picture(htargetx,`↪ ` htargety, htargetw, htargeth, "plateau.jpg");`	Construct new `Picture` object and assign to `htarget` variable
`var ground = new Myrectangle(0,300,`↪ `600,30,"rgb(10,250,0)");`	Construct new `Myrectangle` object and assign to `ground`
`var cannon = new Myrectangle(cannonx,`↪ `cannony,cannonlength,cannonht,"rgb(40,40,0)");`	Construct new `Myrectangle` object and assign to `cannon`
`var targetindex = everything.length;`	Save what will be the index for `target`
`everything.push([target,false]);`	Add `target` to `everything`
`everything.push([ground,false]);`	Add `ground` to `everything`
`var ballindex = everything.length;`	Save what will be the index for `cball`
`everything.push([cball,false]);`	Add `cball` to `everything`
`var cannonindex = everything.length;`	Save what will be the index for `cannon`
`everything.push([cannon,true,0,`↪ `cannonx,cannony+cannonht*.5]);`	Add `cannon` to `everything`; reserve space for rotation

Code	Explanation
`function init(){`	
`    ctx = document.getElementById`↪`('canvas').getContext('2d');`	
`  drawall();`	
`}`	
`function fire() {`	
`   var angle = Number(document.f`↪`.ang.value);`	Extract angle from form, convert to number
`   var outofcannon = Number`↪`(document.f.vo.value);`	Extract velocity out of cannon from form, convert to number
`   var angleradians = angle*Math`↪`.PI/180;`	Convert to radians
`   horvelocity =  outofcannon*Math`↪`.cos(angleradians);`	Compute horizontal velocity
`   verticalvel1 = - outofcannon*Math`↪`.sin(angleradians);`	Compute initial vertical velocity
`   everything[cannonindex][2]=`↪`  - angleradians;`	Set information to rotate cannon
`   cball.sx = cannonx +`↪`cannonlength*Math.cos(angleradians);`	Set x for cball at mouth of what will be rotated cannon
`   cball.sy = cannony+cannonht*.5`↪`  - cannonlength*Math.sin(angleradians);`	Set y for cball at mouth of what will be rotated cannon
`       drawall();`	
`       tid = setInterval(change,100);`	
`       return false;`	

Code	Explanation
`}`	
`function drawall() {`	
`ctx.clearRect(0,0,cwidth,cheight);`	
`var i;`	
`for (i=0;i<everything.length;i++) {`	
`var ob = everything[i];`	Extract array for object
`if (ob[1]) {`	Need to translate and rotate?
`ctx.save();`	Save original axes
`ctx.translate(ob[3],ob[4]);`	Do indicated translation
`ctx.rotate(ob[2]);`	Do indicated rotation
`ctx.translate(-ob[3],-ob[4]);`	Translate back
`ob[0].draw();`	Draw object
`ctx.restore(); }`	Restore axes
`else {`	Else (no rotation)
`ob[0].draw();}`	Do drawing
`}`	Close for loop
`}`	Close function
`function change() {`	
`var dx = horvelocity;`	
`verticalvel2 =verticalvel1 + gravity;`	
`var dy=(verticalvel1 + verticalvel2)*.5;`	

Code	Explanation
`verticalvel1 = verticalvel2;`	
`cball.moveit(dx,dy);`	
`var bx = cball.sx;`	
`var by = cball.sy;`	
`if ((bx>=target.sx)&&(bx<=(target↪` `.sx+target.swidth))&&`	
`(by>=target.sy)&&(by<=(target↪` `.sy+target.sheight))) {`	
`clearInterval(tid);`	
`everything.splice↪` `(targetindex,1,[htarget,false]);`	Remove target and insert htarget
`everything.splice↪` `(ballindex,1);`	Remove the ball
`drawall();`	
`}`	
`if (by>=ground.sy) {`	
`clearInterval(tid);`	
`}`	
`drawall();`	
`}`	
`</script>`	
`</head>`	
`<body onLoad="init();">`	

Code	Explanation
`<canvas id="canvas" width="600"↪` `height="400">`	
`Your browser doesn't support the↪` `HTML5 element canvas.`	
`</canvas>`	
` `	
`<form name="f" id="f" onSubmit=↪` `"return fire();">`	
`Set velocity, angle and fire↪` `cannonball.  `	
`Velocity out of cannon <input name=↪` `"vo" id="vo" value="10" type=↪` `"number" min="-100" max="100" />`	Label indicating that this is the velocity out of mouth of cannon
` `	
`Angle <input name="ang" id="ang"↪` `value="0" type="number" min=↪` `"0" max="80"/>`	Label indicating that this is the angle of the cannon
`<input type="submit" value="FIRE"/>`	
`</form>`	
`</body>`	
`</html>`	

This application provides many possibilities for you to make it your own. You can change the cannon, the ball, the ground, and the target. If you don't want to use images, you can use drawings for the target and the hit target. You can draw other things on the canvas. You just need to make sure that the cannonball (or whatever you set your projectile to be) is on top or wherever you want it to be. You could, for example, make the ground cover up the ball. You can use an animated gif for any Image object, including the `htarget`. You could also use images for the cannon and the ball. One possibility is to use an animated gif file to represent a spinning cannonball. Remember that all image files referenced in the code must be in the same folder as the uploaded HTML file. If they are in a different place on the Web, make sure the reference is correct.

The support for audio and video in HTML5 varies across the browsers. You can look ahead to the presentation of video as a reward for completing the quiz in Chapter 6, and to the audio presented as part of the rock-paper-scissors game in Chapter 8. If you want to tackle this subject, it would be great to have a sound when the cannonball hits the target and a video clip showing the target exploding.

Moving away from the look of the game, you can invent a scoring system, perhaps keeping track of attempts versus hits.

Slingshot: using a mouse to set parameters of flight

The slingshot application is built on the cannonball application. There are differences, but much is the same. Reviewing and understanding how more complicated applications are built on simpler ones will help you to create your own work.

Creating the slingshot application involves designing the slingshot, and implementing the mouse events to move the ball and parts of the slingshot, and then fire the ball. The form is absent because the player's moves are just the mouse actions. In addition, I used a somewhat different approach for what to do when the target was hit. I check for the ball to intersect with an area within the target by 40 pixels. That is, I require the ball to hit the middle of the chicken! When there's a hit, I change the target.src value to be another Image element, going from a picture of a chicken to a picture of feathers. Moreover, I don't stop the animation, so the ball only stops when it hits the ground. As I indicated earlier, I don't have the slingshot slings return to their original position, as I wanted to see the position to plan my next attempt.

Table 4-5 shows the functions calling and being called in the slingshot application. This table is quite similar to the one for the cannonball applications.

Table 4-5. Functions in the Slingshot Application

Function	Invoked By / Called By	Calls
init	Action of the onLoad in body tag	drawall
drawall	Invoked directly by init, fire, change	Calls the draw method of all objects in the everything array. These are the functions drawball, drawrects.
findball	Invoked by action of addEventListener in init for the mousedown event	drawall
distsq	Called by findball	
moveit	Invoked by action of addEventListener in init for the mousemove event	drawall
finish	Invoked by action of the addEventListener in init for the mouseup event	drawall

Function	Invoked By / Called By	Calls
change	Invoked by action of the setInterval function called in finish	drawall, calls the moveit method of cball, which is moveball.
Ball	Invoked directly by code in a var statement	
Myrectangle	Invoked directly by code in a var statement	
drawball	Invoked by call of the draw method for the one Ball object	
drawrects	Invoked by call of the draw method for the target object	
moveball	Invoked by call of the moveit method for the one Ball object	
Picture	Invoked directly by code in var statements	
drawAnImage	Invoked by call of the draw method for a picture object	
Sling	Invoked directly by code in var statements	
drawsling	Invoked by call of the draw method for mysling	

Table 4-6 shows the code for the slingshot application, with the new or changed lines commented. Notice that the form is absent from the body element. Before looking at the code, try to identify what parts will be the same as in the cannonball application and what would be different.

Table 4-6. The Slingshot Application

Code	Explanation
`<html>`	
`<head>`	
`    <title>Slingshot pulling back</title>`	
`    <script type="text/javascript">`	
`        var cwidth = 1200;`	

Code	Explanation
`var cheight = 600;`	
`var ctx;`	
`var canvas1;`	
`var everything = [];`	
`var tid;`	
`var startrockx = 100;`	Starting position x
`var startrocky = 240;`	Starting position y
`var ballx = startrockx;`	Set ballx
`var bally = startrocky;`	Set bally
`var ballrad = 10;`	
`var ballradsq = ballrad*ballrad;`	Save this value
`var inmotion = false;`	
`var horvelocity;`	
`var verticalvel1;`	
`var verticalvel2;`	
`var gravity = 2;`	
`var chicken = new Image();`	Name of original target
`chicken.src = "chicken.jpg";`	Set image file
`var feathers = new Image();`	Name of hit target
`feathers.src = "feathers.gif";`	Set image file
`function Sling(bx,by,s1x,s1y,s2x,s2y,`↪ `s3x,s3y,stylestring) {`	Function defining a slingshot based on the four points plus a color

Code	Explanation
`    this.bx = bx;`	Set property bx
`    this.by = by;`	... by
`    this.s1x = s1x;`	... s1x
`    this.s1y = s1y;`	... s1y
`    this.s2x = s2x;`	... s2x
`    this.s2y = s2y;`	... s2y
`    this.s3x = s3x;`	... s3x
`    this.s3y = s3y;`	... s3y
`    this.strokeStyle = stylestring;`	... strokeStyle
`    this.draw = drawsling;`	Set the draw method
`    this.moveit = movesling;`	Set the move method (not used)
`}`	Close function
`function drawsling() {`	Function header for drawsling
`    ctx.strokeStyle = this.strokeStyle;`	Set this style
`    ctx.lineWidth = 4;`	Set line width
`    ctx.beginPath();`	Start the path
`    ctx.moveTo(this.bx,this.by);`	Move to bx,by
`    ctx.lineTo(this.s1x,this.s1y);`	Set up to draw to s1x,s1y
`    ctx.moveTo(this.bx,this.by);`	Move to bx,by
`    ctx.lineTo(this.s2x,this.s2y);`	Set up to draw to s2x,s2y
`    ctx.moveTo(this.s1x,this.s1y);`	Move to s1x,s1y

Code	Explanation
`    ctx.lineTo(this.s2x,this.s2y);`	Set up to draw to s2x,s2y
`    ctx.lineTo(this.s3x,this.s3y);`	Draw to s3x,s3y
`    ctx.stroke();`	Now draw the path
`}`	Close function
`function movesling(dx,dy) {`	Header for movesling
`    this.bx +=dx;`	Add dx to bx
`    this.by +=dy;`	Add dy to by
`    this.s1x +=dx;`	Add dx to s1x
`    this.s1y +=dy;`	Add dy to s1y
`    this.s2x +=dx;`	Add dx to s2x
`    this.s2y +=dy;`	Add dy to s2y
`    this.s3x +=dx;`	Add dx to s3x
`    this.s3y +=dy;`	Add dy to s3y
`}`	Close function

`var mysling= new`
`Sling(startrockx,startrocky,➥`
`startrockx+80,startrocky-10,startrockx+80,➥`
` startrocky+10,startrockx+70,➥`
`startrocky+180,"rgb(120,20,10)");`
	Build new Sling and assign it to the mysling variable

`function Ball(sx,sy,rad,stylestring) {`	
`  this.sx = sx;`	
`  this.sy = sy;`	
`  this.rad = rad;`	
`  this.draw = drawball;`	

Code	Explanation
`  this.moveit = moveball;`	
`  this.fillstyle = stylestring;`	
`}`	
`function drawball() {`	
`      ctx.fillStyle=this.fillstyle;`	
`      ctx.beginPath();`	
`      ctx.arc(this.sx,this.sy,this.rad,↪` `0,Math.PI*2,true);`	
`      ctx.fill();`	
`}`	
`function moveball(dx,dy) {`	
`      this.sx +=dx;`	
`      this.sy +=dy;`	
`}`	
`var cball = new Ball(startrockx,startrocky,↪` `ballrad,"rgb(250,0,0)");`	
`function myrectangle(sx,sy,swidth,↪` `sheight,stylestring) {`	
`      this.sx = sx;`	
`      this.sy = sy;`	

Code	Explanation
this.swidth = swidth;	
this.sheight = sheight;	
this.fillstyle = stylestring;	
this.draw = drawrects;	
this.moveit = moveball;	
}	
function drawrects() {	
ctx.fillStyle = this.fillstyle;	
ctx.fillRect(this.sx,this.sy,➥ this.swidth,this.sheight);	
}	
function Picture (sx,sy,swidth,➥ sheight,imga) {	
this.sx = sx;	
this.sy = sy;	
this.img = imga;	
this.swidth = swidth;	
this.sheight = sheight;	
this.draw = drawAnImage;	
this.moveit = moveball;	
}	
function drawAnImage() {	

Code	Explanation
`        ctx.drawImage(this.img,this.sx,this.↪` `sy,this.swidth,this.sheight);`	
`}`	
`var target = new Picture(700,210,209,↪` `179,chicken);`	Build new `Picture` object and assign it to `target`
`var ground = new myrectangle(0,370,↪` `1200,30,"rgb(10,250,0)");`	
`everything.push(target);`	
`everything.push(ground);`	Put the ground on top of the chickens' feet
`everything.push(mysling);`	
`everything.push(cball);`	
`function init(){`	
`   ctx = document.getElementById↪` `('canvas').getContext('2d');`	
`   canvas1 = document.getElementById↪` `('canvas');`	
`   canvas1.addEventListener('mousedown',↪` `findball,false);`	Set up event handling for the `mousedown` event
`   canvas1.addEventListener('mousemove',↪` `moveit,false);`	Set up event handling for the `mousemove` event
`   canvas1.addEventListener('mouseup',↪` `finish,false);`	Set up event handling for the `mouseup` event
`  drawall();`	
`}`	
`function findball(ev) {`	Function header for `mousedown` event
`     var mx;`	Variable to hold mouse x

Code	Explanation
`var my;`	Variable to hold mouse y
`if ( ev.layerX ||  ev.layerX↪` `== 0) {`	`ev.layerX` is okay
`mx= ev.layerX;`	Use it for `mx`
`my = ev.layerY; }`	Use `layerY` for `my`
`else if (ev.offsetX || ev.offsetX↪` `== 0) {`	Else try offset
`mx = ev.offsetX;`	Set `mx`
`my = ev.offsetY; }`	Set `my`
`if (distsq(mx,my, cball.sx,↪` `cball.sy)<ballradsq) {`	Is mouse over ball?
`inmotion = true;`	Set `inmotion`
`drawall();`	Draw everything
`}`	Close if over ball
`}`	Close function
`function distsq(x1,y1,x2,y2) {`	Header for `distsq`
`return (x1-x2)*(x1-x2)+(y1-y2)*↪` `(y1-y2);`	Return distance squared
`}`	Close function
`function moveit(ev) {`	Function header for `mousemove` event
`var mx;`	For mouse x
`var my;`	For mouse y
`if (inmotion) {`	in motion?
`if ( ev.layerX ||  ev.layerX == 0) {`	Does `layerX` work?
`mx= ev.layerX;`	Use it for `mx`

Code	Explanation
`my = ev.layerY;`	`ev.layerY` for `my`
`} else if (ev.offsetX || ev.offsetX == 0) {`	Does `offsetX` work?
`mx = ev.offsetX;`	Use it for `mx`
`my = ev.offsetY;`	Use `offsetY` for `my`
`}`	Close if true
`cball.sx = mx;`	Position ball x
`cball.sy = my;`	...and y
`mysling.bx = mx;`	Position `sling` bx
`mysling.by = my;`	... and by
`drawall();`	Draw everything
`}`	Close if in motion
`}`	Close function
`function finish(ev) {`	Function for `mousedown`
`if (inmotion) {`	In motion?
`inmotion = false;`	Reset `inmotion`
`var outofcannon = distsq(mysling.bx,mysling.by,↬ mysling.s1x,mysling.s1y)/700;`	Base `outofcannon` proportional to square of `bx`,`by` to `s1x`,`s1y`
`var angleradians = -Math.atan2↬ (mysling.s1y-mysling.by,↬ mysling.s1x-mysling.bx);`	Compute angle
`horvelocity = outofcannon*Math.cos↬ (angleradians);`	
`verticalvel1 = - outofcannon*Math.sin↬ (angleradians);`	

Code	Explanation
`        drawall();`	
`        tid = setInterval(change,100);`	
`    }`	
`}`	
`function drawall() {`	
`    ctx.clearRect(0,0,cwidth,cheight);`	
`    var i;`	
`    for (i=0;i<everything.length;i++) {`	
`            everything[i].draw();`	
`    }`	
`}`	
`function change() {`	
`    var dx = horvelocity;`	
`    verticalvel2 = verticalvel1 + gravity;`	
`    var dy = (verticalvel1 + ↪` `verticalvel2)*.5;`	
`    verticalvel1 = verticalvel2;`	
`    cball.moveit(dx,dy);`	
`    var bx = cball.sx;`	
`    var by = cball.sy;`	

`    if ((bx>=target.sx+40)&&(bx<=↪`
`(target.sx+target.swidth-40))&&↪`
` (by>=target.sy+40)&&(by<=↪`
`(target.sy+target.sheight-40))) {`
	Check for inside of target (40 pixels)

Code	Explanation
`            target.img = feathers;`	Change target `img`
`        }`	
`        if (by>=ground.sy) {`	
`            clearInterval(tid);`	
`        }`	
`        drawall();`	
`}`	
`</script>`	
`</head>`	
`<body onLoad="init();">`	
`<canvas id="canvas" width="1200"↪` `  height="600">`	
`Your browser doesn't support the↪` `  HTML5 element canvas.`	
`</canvas>`	
` `	

`Hold mouse down and drag ball. Releasing↪`
`  the mouse button will shoot the slingshot.↪`
`   Slingshot remains at the last position.↪`
`  Reload page to try again.`
	Instructions for using mouse

`</body>`	
`</html>`	

Testing and uploading the application

These applications can be created without external image files, but using images for the target and the hit target is fun, so you remember to include those files when you upload your project. You can choose your own targets. Perhaps you feel kindly towards chickens!

You'll need to test that the program performs correctly in three situations: when the ball plops down to the left of the target, when the ball hits the target, and when the ball sails over the target. Note that I massaged the values so that the chicken needs to be hit in the middle, so it is possible for the ball to touch the head or tail and not cause the feathers to appear.

You can vary the position of the cannon and its target and hit target, and the slingshot and the chicken and the feathers, by changing the variables such as `startrockx`, and you can modify the gravity variable. If you put the slingshot closer to the target, you can have more ways to hit the chicken: pulling more to the left for a direct shot versus pulling down for more of a lob. Enjoy!

As I mentioned, you could use an animated gif for the hit target in either the cannonball or slingshot applications. This would produce a nice effect.

Summary

In this chapter, you learned how to create two ballistics applications. It is important to understand how they are the same and how they are different. The programming techniques and HTML5 features include

- programmer-defined objects
- `setInterval` to set up a timing event for the animation, as done for the bouncing ball
- building an array using the `push` method and using the array as a list of what to display
- modifying arrays using the `splice` method
- the use of trig functions with calculations to rotate the cannon and to resolve the horizontal and vertical velocities so as to simulate gravity
- using a `form` for player input
- handling mouse events (`mousedown`, `mousemove`, `mouseup`), with `addEventListener` to obtain player input
- move drawing arcs, rectangles, lines and images on a canvas

The technique of programmer-defined objects and the use of an array of objects to display will come up again in later chapters. The next chapter focuses on a familiar game known as either memory or concentration. It will use a different timing event as well as the `Date` function, introduced in Chapter 1.

Chapter 5

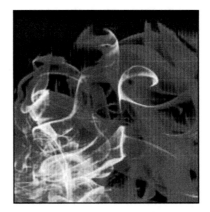

The Memory (aka Concentration) Game

In this chapter, we will cover

- drawing polygons
- placing text on the canvas
- programming techniques for representing information
- programming a pause
- calculating elapsed time
- one method of shuffling a set of card objects

Introduction

This chapter demonstrates two versions of a card game known variously as memory or concentration. Cards appear face down, and the player turns over two at a time (by clicking on them) in an attempt to find matched pairs. The program removes matches from the board but [virtually] flips back cards that do not match. When players make all the matches, the game shows the elapsed time.

The first version of the game I describe uses polygons for the face cards; the second uses family photos. You'll notice other differences, which were made to illustrate several HTML5 features, but I also urge you to think about what the versions have in common.

Figure 5-1 shows the opening screen of version one. When a player completes the game, the form that keeps track of matches also shows the elapsed time.

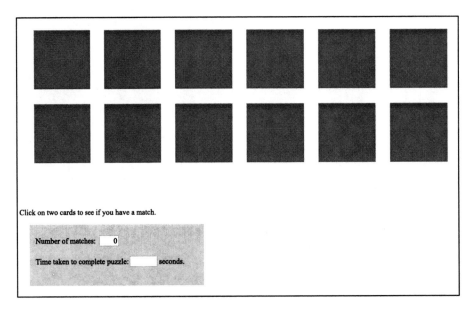

Figure 5-1. Opening screen of the memory game, version one

Figure 5-2 displays the result after a player has clicked on two cards (the purple squares). The depicted polygons don't match, so after a pause the program replaces them with images of the card backs, making the cards appear to have flipped over.

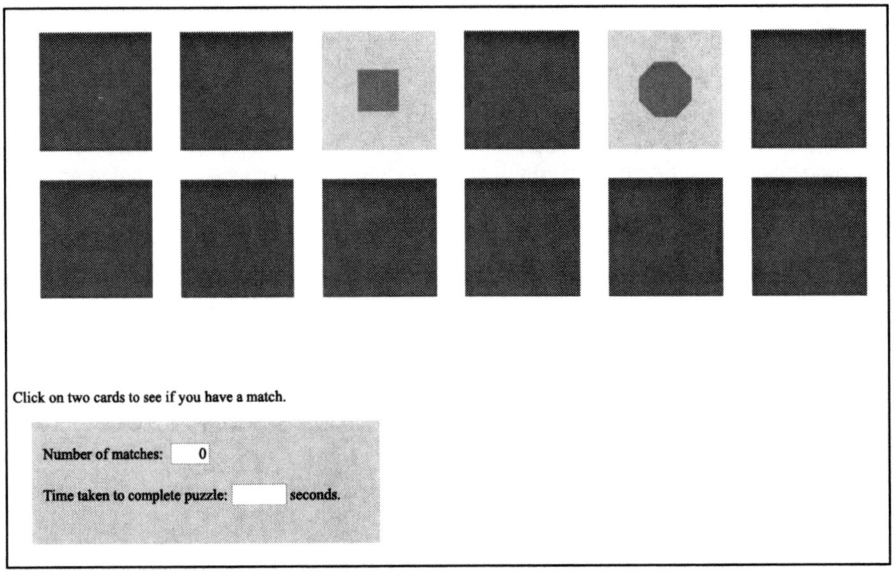

Figure 5-2. Two card fronts: no match

When two cards match, the application removes them and notes the match in the form (Figure 5-3).

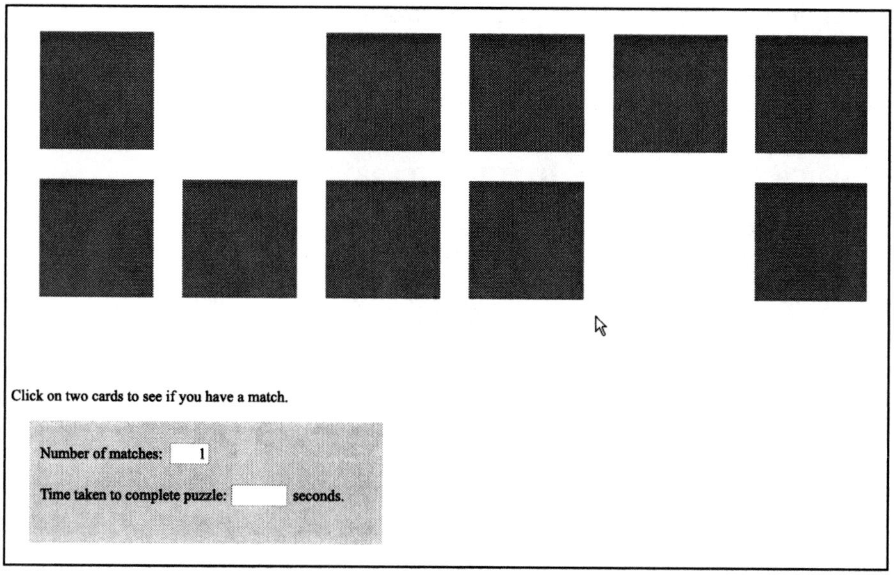

Figure 5-3. The application has removed the two cards that matched.

As illustrated in Figure 5-4, the game displays the result—in this case, 6 matches in 36 seconds—when the player finishes.

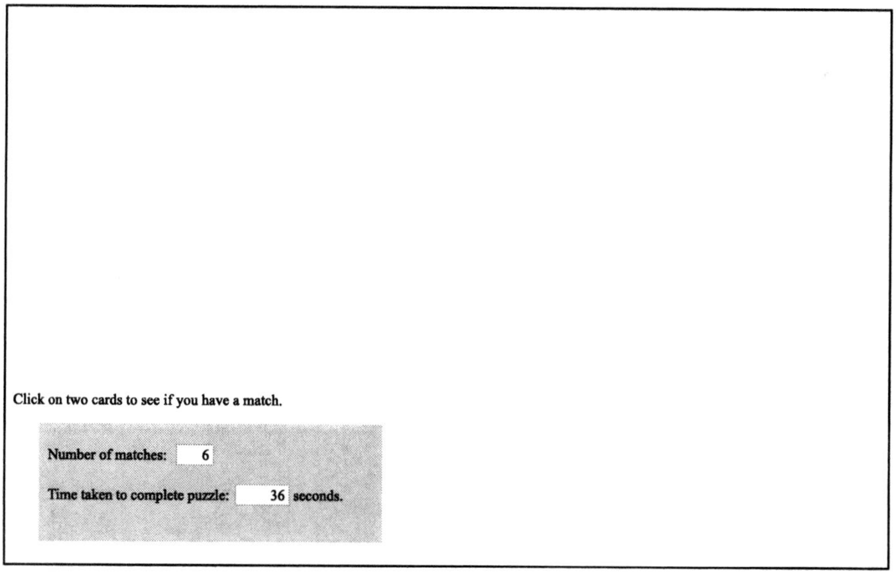

Figure 5-4. Version one of the game after the player has completed it.

In version two of the game, the card fronts display photographs of people rather than polygons. And note that although many memory games consider images to be the same only if they're completely identical, this one is similar to a 2 of Hearts matching a 2 of Diamonds in a deck of playing cards. To illustrate a programming point, we'll define a match as the same person, even in differing pictures. This requires a method of encoding the information we use to determine matching states. Version two of the game also demonstrates writing text on the canvas, as you can see in Figure 5-5, which depicts the opening screen.

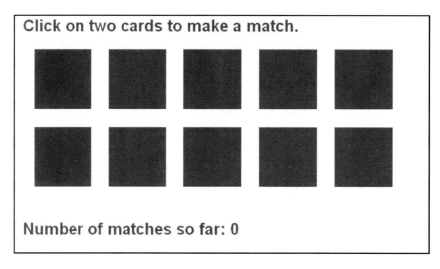

Figure 5-5. The memory game, version two, opening screen

To see one possible result of clicking on two cards in our new game, look at Figure 5-6.

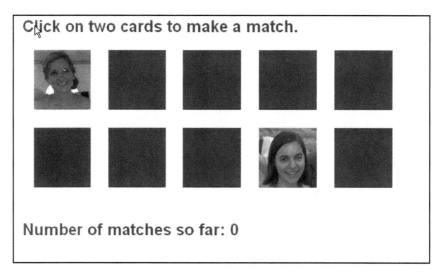

Figure 5-6. This screen shows non-matching photos.

Because the result shows two different people—after pausing to let the player view both pictures—the application flips the cards over and lets the player try again. Figure 5-7 shows a successful selection—two images of the same person (albeit in different pictures).

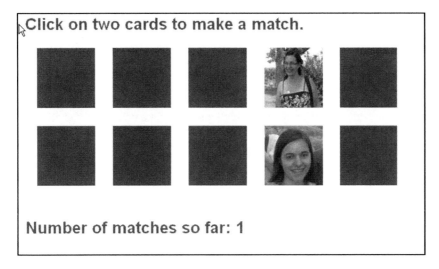

Figure 5-7. This screenshot shows a match (different scenes, but the same person).

The application removes matched images from the board. When all cards are removed, the time taken to complete the game appears along with instructions on how to play again, as shown in Figure 5-8.

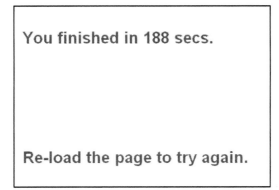

Figure 5-8. The final screen of the game (photo version). All images have been matched, so no cards appear.

You can play the game using photos available for download from the book's page on the Friends of ED web site (www.friendsofed.com/), but it's more fun to use your own. You can start with a small number—say two or three pairs of images—then work up to images of the whole family, class, or club. And for version one of the game, you can replace the polygons with your own designs.

Critical requirements

The digital versions of the games require ways to represent the card backs (which are all the same) and the fronts with their distinct polygons or photos. The applications must also be able to tell which cards match and where cards are on the board. Additionally, players require feedback. In the real-world game, participants flip over two cards and look for a match (which takes a few moments). If there's none, they flip the cards face down again.

The computer program must show the faces of the selected cards and pause after revealing the second card so players have time to see the two faces. This pause is an example of something required for a computer implementation that occurs more-or-less naturally when people play the game. The application should also display the current number of pairs found and, when the game is complete, the length of time participants took to find them all. The polygon and photo versions of the program use different approaches to accomplish these tasks.

Here's a summary of what the two game versions must do:

- Draw the card backs.
- Shuffle the cards before a player makes an initial selection so the same array of choices doesn't appear every time.
- Detect when a player clicks on a card, and distinguish between a first and a second click.
- On detecting a click, show the appropriate card face by: drawing polygons in the case of game version one or displaying the correct photograph for version two.
- Remove pairs that match.
- Operate appropriately even if those pesky players do the unexpected, such as clicking on the same card twice or on an empty space formerly occupied by a card.

HTML5, CSS, JavaScript features

Let's go over the specific HTML5 and JavaScript features that provide what we need to implement the games. We'll build on material covered previously: the general structure of HTML documents; how to draw rectangles, images, and paths made up of line segments on a canvas element; programmer-defined and built-in functions; programmer objects; the form element; and arrays.

New HTML5 and JavaScript features include the time out event, the use of Date objects for the calculation of elapsed time, writing and drawing text on the canvas, and several useful programming techniques that you'll find valuable in future applications.

As in the previous chapters, this section describes the HTML5 features and programming techniques in general terms. You can see all the code in context in the "Building the Application" section. If you like, you can skip to that section to see the code, then return here for explanations of how the features work.

Representing cards

When we hold a physical card in our hands, we can see what it is. There's a card face and back, and the backs are all the same. We can clearly determine the cards' positions on the game board and whether their faces or backs show. To implement a computer game, we must represent—*encode*—all that information. Encoding is an essential part of creating many computer applications, not just games.

In this chapter (and throughout the book), I describe one way to accomplish the task. Keep in mind, though, that there's rarely just one way to implement a feature of an application. That said, different strategies for building an application will likely have some techniques in common.

Our approach to handling cards will employ a programmer-defined object. Creating a programmer-defined object in JavaScript involves writing the constructor function; in this case we'll call it `Card`. The advantage of using programmer-defined objects is that JavaScript provides the dot notation needed to access information and code for objects of a common type. We did this for the cannonball and slingshot games in Chapter 4.

We'll give the `Card` object properties that will hold the card's location (`sx` and `sy`) and dimensions (`swidth` and `sheight`), a pointer to a function to draw a back for the card, and for each case, the information that specifies the appropriate front (`info`).

In the case of a polygon, the value of `info` will indicate the number of sides to be drawn. (In a later section we'll discuss the code for drawing it.) For a photo card face, the value will be a reference, `img`, to an `Image` object we've created. The object will hold a specific image file along with a number (`info`) that ties together pictures that match. To draw the image for the file, we'll use the built-in `drawImage` method.

Needless to say, the cards don't exist as physical entities, with two sides. The application draws the card's face or back on the canvas where the player expects to see it. The function `flipback` draws the card's back. To give the appearance of a removed card, `flipback` effectively erases a card by drawing a rectangle that's the color of the board.

Both applications use a function named `makedeck` to prepare the deck, a process that includes creation of the `Card` objects. For the polygon version of the game, we store the number of sides (from three to eight) in the `Card` objects. The application draws no polygons during setup, though. The photos version sets up an array called `pairs`, listing the image file names for the photos. You can follow this example to create your own family or group memory game.

> Tip: If you use the online code to play the game, as noted earlier, you can download the image files. To make the game your own, you need to upload the pictures and then change the code to reference your files. The code indicates what you need to change.

The `makedeck` function creates the `Image` objects and uses the `pairs` array to set the `src` property to the image object. When the code creates `Card` objects, it puts in the index value that controls the `pairs` array so that matched photos have the same value. As in the polygon version, the application draws no image on the canvas during the creation of the deck. On the screen, the cards all appear the same; the information is different, though. These cards are in fixed positions—shuffling comes later.

The code interprets position information, the `sx` and `sy` properties, differently for `Card` and `Polygon`. In the first case, the information refers to the upper-left corner. In the second case, the value identifies the center of the polygon. You can compute one from the other, though.

Using Date for timing

We need a way to determine how long the player took to make all the matches. JavaScript provides a way to measure elapsed time. You can view the code in context in the "Building the Application section." Here I provide an explanation of how to determine the number of seconds between two distinct events in a running program.

A call to Date() generates an object with date and time information. The two lines

```
starttime = new Date();
starttime = Number(starttime.getTime());
```

store the number of milliseconds (thousands of a second) since the start of 1970 in the variable starttime. (The reason JavaScript uses 1970 doesn't matter.)

When either of our two memory programs determines the game is over, it invokes Date() again as follows:

```
var now = new Date();
var nt = Number(now.getTime());
var seconds = Math.floor(.5+(nt-starttime)/1000);
```

This code

1. creates a new Date object and stores it in the variable now.

2. extracts the time using getTime, converts it to Number, and assigns it to the variable nt. This means nt holds the number of milliseconds from the start of 1970 until the point at which the code called Date. The program then subtracts the saved starting time, starttime, from the current time, nt.

3. divides by 1,000 to get to seconds.

4. adds .5 and invokes Math.floor to round the result up or down to whole seconds.

If you need more precision than seconds provides, omit or modify the last step.

You can use this code whenever you need to calculate time elapsed between two events in a program.

Providing a pause

When we play memory using real cards, we don't consciously pause before flipping nonmatching cards face down. But as noted earlier, our computer implementation must provide a pause so players have time to see the two differing cards. You may recall from chapters 3 and 4 that the animation applications—bouncing ball, cannonball, and slingshot—used the JavaScript function setInterval to set up events at fixed time intervals. We can employ a related function, setTimeout, in our memory games. (To see the complete code in context, go to the "Building the Application" section.) Let's see how to set up the event and what happens when the pause time runs out.

The setTimeout function sets up a single event, which we can use to impose a pause. The choose function, called when a player clicks on the canvas, first checks the firstpick variable to determine if the person has made a first or second selection. In either case, the program draws the card front on the canvas in the same spot as the card back. If the click was a second choice and the two cards match, the code sets the variable matched to true or false, depending on whether the cards did or didn't match. If the application determines that the game isn't over, the code invokes

```
setTimeout(flipback,1000);
```

This leads to a call to the `flipback` function in 1,000 milliseconds (1 second). The function `flipback` then uses the `matched` variable to determine whether to redraw card backs or erase the cards by drawing rectangles with the table background color at the appropriate card locations.

You can use `setTimeout` to set up any individual timed events. You need to specify the time interval and the function you want invoked when the interval expires. Remember that the time unit is milliseconds.

Drawing text

HTML5 includes a mechanism for placing text on the canvas. This provides a much more dynamic, flexible way to present text than previous versions. You can create some good effects by combining text placement with the drawing of rectangles, lines, arcs, and images we've already demonstrated. In this section, we'll outline the steps for placing text in a canvas element, and we'll include a short example that you can try. If you want, skip ahead to the "Building the Application" section to view the complete description of the code that produces what you see in Figures 5-5 through 5-8 for the photos version of the memory game.

To put text on the canvas, we write code that sets the `font`, and then we use `fillText` to draw a string of characters starting at a specified x-y location. The following example creates words using an eclectic set of fonts (see the caution note later in the section).

```
<html>
<head>
    <title>Fonts</title>
<script type="text/javascript">
var ctx;
function init(){
   ctx = document.getElementById('canvas').getContext('2d');
   ctx.font="15px Lucida Handwriting";
   ctx.fillText("this is Lucida Handwriting", 10, 20);
   ctx.font="italic 30px HarlemNights";
   ctx.fillText("italic HarlemNights",40,80);
   ctx.font="bold 40px HarlemNights"
   ctx.fillText("HarlemNights",100,200);
   ctx.font="30px Accent";
   ctx.fillText("Accent", 200,300);
}
</script>
</head>
<body onLoad="init();">
<canvas id="canvas" width="900" height="400">
Your browser doesn't support the HTML5 element canvas.
</canvas>
</body>
</html>
```

This HTML document produces the screenshot shown in Figure 5-9.

Figure 5-9. Text in different fonts drawn on the canvas, produced using the font and fillText functions

Caution: Make sure you pick fonts that will be present on the computers of all your players. In Chapter 10 you'll learn how to use a CSS feature, called font-family, that provides a systematic way to specify a primary font and backups.

Note that although what you see appears to be text, you're actually looking at ink on the canvas—that is, bitmap images of text, not a text field that you can modify in place. This means that to change the text, we need to write code that will completely erase the current image. We do so by setting the fillStyle to the value we placed in the variable tablecolor earlier, and use fillRect at the appropriate location and with the necessary dimensions.

After creating the text image, the next step is to set fillStyle to a color other than tablecolor. We'll use the color we chose for the card backs. For the opening screen display of the photograph memory game, here's the code to set the font used for all text:

```
ctx.font="bold 20pt sans-serif";
```

Using the sans-serif font makes sense, since it's a standard font present on any computer.

Putting together what we've done to this point, here's the code to display the number of matches at a particular point in the game:

```
ctx.fillStyle= tablecolor;
ctx.fillRect(10,340,900,100);
ctx.fillStyle=backcolor;
ctx.fillText
    ("Number of matches so far: "+String(count),10,360);
```

The first two statements erase the current tally and the next two put in the updated result. The expression `"Number of matches so far: "+String(count)` deserves more explanation. It accomplishes two tasks:

- It takes the variable `count`, which is a number, and turns it into a string of characters.
- It concatenates the constant string `"Number of matches so far: "` with the result of `String(count)`.

The concatenation demonstrates that the plus sign has two meanings in JavaScript: If the operands are numbers, the sign indicates addition. If the operands are character strings, it indicates the two strings should be concatenated—put together. A fancy phrase for a single symbol having several meanings is *operator overloading*.

What will JavaScript do if one operand is a string and the other a number? The answer depends on which of the two operands is what data type. You'll see examples of code in which the programmer doesn't put in the commands to convert text to a number or vice versa, but the statement works because of the specific order of operations.

I suggest not taking chances, though. Instead, try to remember the rules that govern interpretation of the plus sign. If you notice that your program increases a number from, say, 1 to 11 to 111 when you're expecting 1, 2, 3, your code is concatenating strings instead of incrementing numbers, and you need to convert strings to numbers.

Drawing polygons

Creating polygons provides a good demonstration of HTML5's drawing facilities. To understand the code-development process used here for drawing polygons, think of the geometric figure as a wheel-like shape with spokes emanating from its center to each of its vertices. The spokes will not appear in the drawings, but are to help you, like they helped me, figure out how to draw a polygon. Figure 5-10 illustrates this with a triangle.

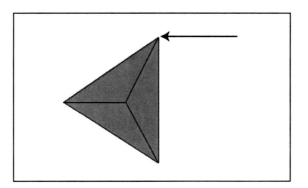

Figure 5-10. Representing a triangle as a spoked geometric shape can help clarify code development for drawing polygons. The arrow indicates the first point in the drawing path.

To determine the measure of the angle between spokes, we divide the quantity `2*Math.PI` (representing a complete circle) by the number of sides the polygon has. We use the angle value and the `moveTo` method to draw the points of the path.

The program draws the polygon as a filled-in path that starts at the point (indicated by the arrow in Figure 5-10) specified by one-half the value of `angle`. To get to the point, we use the `moveTo` method along with the radius, `Math.sin` and `Math.cos`. We then use the `lineTo` method for n-1 more points, proceeding in clockwise fashion. For the triangle, n-1 is two more points. For the octagon it would be seven more. After running through a `for` loop with the `lineTo` points, we invoke the `fill` method to produce a filled-in shape. To see the complete annotated code, go to the "Building the Application" section."

> *Note: Drawing and redrawing polygons takes time, but that doesn't cause problems with this application. If a program has a large number of intricate designs, preparing them ahead of time as pictures may make sense. That approach, however, requires users to download the files, which can take quite a while. You need to experiment to see which approach works better overall.*

Shuffling cards

As noted previously, the memory game requires the program to shuffle the cards before each round, since we don't want the cards to appear in the same position time after time. The best way to shuffle sets of values is the subject of extensive research. In Chapter 10, which describes the card game called blackjack or 21, you'll find a reference to an article that describes a technique claimed to be the most efficient way to produce a shuffled deck.

For memory/concentration, let's implement the way I played the game as a child. I and the others would lay out all the cards, then pick up and swap pairs. When we thought we had done it a sufficient number of times, we would begin to play. In this section, we'll explore a few more concepts behind this approach. (To examine the `shuffle` function, you can skip ahead to the "Building the Application" section.)

To write the JavaScript for the swap method of shuffling, we first need to define "sufficient number of times." Let's make that three times the number of cards in the deck, which we've represented in the array variable `deck`. But since there are no cards, just data representing cards, what are we swapping? The answer is the information uniquely defining each card. For the polygon memory game, this is the property `info`. For the picture game, it's `info` and `img`.

To get a random card, we use the expression `Math.floor(Math.random()*dl)`, where `dl`, standing for deck length, holds the number of cards in the deck. We do this twice to obtain the pair of cards to be (virtually) swapped. This could produce the same number, meaning a card is swapped with itself, but that's not really a concern. If it happens, this step in this process has no effect. The code mandates a large number of swaps, so one swap not doing anything is okay.

Carrying out the swap is the next challenge, and it requires some temporary storage. We'll use one variable, `holder`, for the polygon version of the game and two variables, `holderimg` and `holderinfo`, for the picture case.

Implementing clicking on a card

The next step is to explain how we implement the player moves, namely the player clicking on a card. In HTML5, we can handle the `click` event employing much the same approach that we took with the `mousedown` event (described in Chapter 4). We'll use the `addEventListener` method:

```
canvas1 = document.getElementById('canvas');
canvas1.addEventListener('click',choose,false);
```

This appears in the init function. The choose function must contain code to determine which card we choose to shuffle. The program must also return the coordinates of the mouse when the player clicks on the canvas. The methodology for obtaining mouse coordinates is also the same as that covered in Chapter 4.

Unfortunately, different browsers implement handling of mouse events in different ways. I discussed this in Chapter 4, and I repeat the explanation here. The following works in Chrome, Firefox, and Safari.

```
if ( ev.layerX || ev.layerX==0) {
    mx= ev.layerX;
    my = ev.layerY;
}
else if (ev.offsetX || ev.offsetX==0 ) {
    mx = ev.offsetX;
    my = ev.offsetY;}
```

This works because if ev.layerX doesn't exist, it will be assigned a value of false. If it does exist but has value 0, the value will also be interpreted as false, but ev.layerX==0 will be true. So if there's a good ev.layerX value, the program uses it. Otherwise, the code looks at ev.offsetX. If neither works, mx and my won't get set.

Because the cards are rectangles, going through the deck and doing compare operations is relatively easy using the mouse cursor coordinates (mx, my), the location of the upper-left corner, and the width and height of each card. Here's how we construct the if condition:

```
if ((mx>card.sx)&&(mx<card.sx+card.swidth)&&(my>card.sy)&&(my<card.sy+card.sheight))
{
```

> Note: The next chapter, which describes the way you create HTML markup at runtime, shows how to set up event handling for specific elements positioned on the screen as opposed to using the whole canvas element.

We clear the variable firstpick and initialize it as true, which indicates that this is the first of two picks by a player. The program changes the value to false after the first pick and back to true after the second. Variables like this, which flip back and forth between two values, are called *flags* or *toggles*.

Preventing certain types of cheating

Note that the specifics of this section apply just to these memory games, but the general lesson holds for building any interactive application. There are at least two ways a player can thwart the game. Clicking twice on the same card is one; clicking on a region where a card has been removed (that is, the board has been painted over) is another.

To deal with the first case, after the if-true clause that determines whether the mouse is over a certain card, insert the if statement

```
if ((firstpick) || (i!=firstcard)) break;
```

This line of code triggers an exit from the `for` statement if the index value (i) is fine, which happens when either: 1) this is a first pick or 2) this isn't a first pick and i doesn't correspond to the first card chosen.

Preventing the second problem—clicking on a "ghost" card—requires more work. When the application removes cards from the board, in addition to painting over that area of the canvas, we can assign a value (-1, say) to the `sx` property. This will mark the card as having been removed. This is part of the `flipback` function. The `choose` function contains the code that examines the `sx` property and does the checking (only if `sx` is >= 0). The function incorporates both cheating tests in the following `for` loop:

```
for (i=0;i<deck.length;i++){
    var card = deck[i];
    if (card.sx >=0)
        if
((mx>card.sx)&&(mx<card.sx+card.swidth)&&(my>card.sy)&&(my<card.sy+card.sheight)) {
        if ((firstpick)|| (i!=firstcard)) break;
        }
    }
```

In the three `if` statements, the second is the whole clause of the first. The third has the single statement `break`, which causes control to leave the `for` loop. Generally, I recommend using brackets (for example: `{` and `}`) for `if true` and `else` clauses, but here I used the stripped-down format for single statements to show you that format and also because it seemed clear enough.

Now let's move on to building our two memory games.

Building the application and making it your own

This section presents the complete code for both versions of the game. Because the applications contain multiple functions, the section provides a table for each game that tells what each function calls and is called by.

Table 5-1 is the function listing for the polygon version of the memory game. Notice that some of the invocation of functions is done based on events.

Table 5-1. Functions in the Polygon Version of the Memory Game

Function	Invoked By/Called By	Calls
init	Invoked in response to the onLoad in the body tag	makedeck shuffle
choose	Invoked in response to the addEventListener in init	Polycard drawpoly (invoked as the draw method of a polygon)
flipback	Invoked in response to the setTimeout call in choose	

Function	Invoked By/Called By	Calls
drawback	Invoked as the draw method for a card in makedeck and flipback	
Polycard	Called in choose	
shuffle	Called in init	
makedeck	Called in init	
Card	Called by makedeck	
drawpoly	Called as the draw method of Polygon in choose	

Table 5-2 shows the commented code for the complete polygon version of the application. When reviewing it, think about the similarities to applications described in other chapters. And remember that this illustrates just one way to name the application's components and program it. Other ways may work equally well.

Whatever programming choices you make, put comments in your code (using two slashes per line: //) and include blank lines. You don't need to comment every line, but doing a decent job of commenting will serve you well when you have to go back to your code to make improvements.

Table 5-2. Complete Code for the Polygon Version of the Memory Game

`<html>`	Starting html tag
`<head>`	Starting head tag
`<title>Memory game using polygons</title>`	Complete title element
`<style>`	Starting style tag
`form {`	Specify styling for the form
`width:330px;`	Set the width
`margin:20px;`	Set the external margin
`background-color:pink;`	Set the color

`Padding:20px;`	Set the internal padding
`}`	Close the style
`input {`	Set the styling for input fields
`text-align:right;`	Set right alignment— suitable for numbers
`}`	Close the style
`</style>`	Close the style element
`<script type="text/javascript">`	Start the `script` element. The `type` specification isn't necessary but is included here because you'll see it.
`var ctx;`	Variable that holds the canvas context
`var firstpick = true;`	Declare and initialize `firstpick`
`var firstcard;`	Declare a variable to hold the info defining the first pick
`var secondcard;`	Declare a variable to hold the info defining the second pick
`var frontbgcolor = "rgb(251,215,73)";`	Set the background color value for the card fronts
`var polycolor = "rgb(254,11,0)";`	Set the color value for the polygons
`var backcolor = "rgb(128,0,128)";`	Set the color value for card backs

`var tablecolor = "rgb(255,255,255)";`	Set the color value for the board (table)
`var cardrad = 30;`	Set the radius for the polygons
`var deck = [];`	Declare the deck, initially an empty array
`var firstsx = 30;`	Set the position in x of the first card
`var firstsy = 50;`	Set the position in y of the first card
`var margin = 30;`	Set the spacing between cards
`var cardwidth = 4*cardrad;`	Set the card width to four times the radius of the polygons
`var cardheight = 4*cardrad;`	Set the card height to four times the radius of the polygons
`var matched;`	This variable is set in `choose` and used in `flipback`
`var starttime;`	This variable is set in `init` and used to calculate elapsed time
`function Card(sx,sy,swidth,sheight,info) {`	Header for the `Card` function, setting up card objects
`this.sx = sx;`	Set the horizontal coordinate
`this.sy = sy;`	... vertical coordinate
`this.swidth = swidth;`	... width

`    this.sheight = sheight;`	.... height
`    this.info = info;`	... info (the number of sides)
`    this.draw = drawback;`	Specify how to draw
`}`	Close the function
`function makedeck() {`	Function header for setting up the deck
`    var i;`	Used in the for loop
`    var acard;`	Variable to hold the first of a pair of cards
`    var bcard;`	Variable to hold the second of a pair of cards
`    var cx = firstsx;`	Variable to hold the x coordinate. Start out at the first x position.
`    var cy = firstsy;`	Will hold the y coordinate. Start out at the first y position.
`    for(i=3;i<9;i++) {`	Loop to generate cards for triangles through octagons
`        acard = new Card(cx,cy,cardwidth,cardheight,i);`	Create a card and position
`        deck.push(acard);`	Add to deck
`        bcard = new Card(cx,cy+cardheight+margin,cardwidth,cardheight,i);`	Create a card with the same info, but below the previous card on screen
`        deck.push(bcard);`	Add to deck

`cx = cx+cardwidth+ margin;`	Increment to allow for card width plus margin
`acard.draw();`	Draw the card on the canvas
`bcard.draw();`	Draw the card on the canvas
`}`	Close the for loop
`Shuffle();`	Shuffle the cards
`}`	Close the function
`function shuffle() {`	Header for `shuffle` function
`var i;`	Variable to hold a reference to a card
`var k;`	Variable to hold a reference to a card
`var holder;`	Variable needed to do the swap
`var dl = deck.length`	Variable to hold the number of cards in the deck
`var nt;`	Index for the number of swaps
`for (nt=0;nt<3*dl;nt++) {`	For loop
`i = Math.floor(Math.random()*dl);`	Get a random card
`k = Mathfloor(Math.random()*dl);`	Get a random card
`holder = deck[i].info;`	Store the info for i
`deck[i].info = deck[k].info;`	Put in i info for k
`deck[k].info = holder;`	Put into k what was in k

`}`	Close `for` loop
`}`	Close function
`function Polycard(sx,sy,rad,n) {`	Function header for `Polycard`
`this.sx = sx;`	Set up the x coordinate
`this.sy = sy;`	... the y
`this.rad = rad;`	...the polygon radius
`this.draw = drawpoly;`	...how to draw
`this.n = n;`	...number of sides
`this.angle = (2*Math.PI)/n`	Compute and store the angle
`}`	Close the function
`function drawpoly() {`	Function header
`ctx.fillStyle= frontbgcolor;`	Set the front background
`ctx.fillRect(this.sx-2*this.rad,this.sy-2*this.rad,4*this.rad,4*this.rad);`	The corner of the rectangle is up and to the left of the center of the polygon
`ctx.beginPath();`	Start the path
`ctx.fillStyle=polycolor;`	Change to color for polygon
`var i;`	Index variable
`var rad = this.rad;`	Extract the radius
`ctx.moveTo(this.sx+rad*Math.cos(-.5*this.angle),this.sy+rad*Math.sin(-.5*this.angle));`	Move up to the first point

`for (i=1;i<this.n;i++) {`	For loop for the successive points
`    ctx.lineTo(this.sx+rad*Math.cos((i-` `.5)*this.angle),this.sy+rad*Math.sin((i-.5)*this.angle));`	Set up drawing of line segments
`}`	Close `for` loop
`ctx.fill();`	Fill in the path
`}`	Close function
`function drawback() {`	Function header
`ctx.fillStyle = backcolor;`	Set card back color
`ctx.fillRect(this.sx,this.sy,this.swidth,this.sheight);`	Draw rectangle
`}`	Close function
`function choose(ev) {`	Function header for `choose` (click on a card)
`var mx;`	Variable to hold mouse x
`var my;`	Variable to hold mouse y
`var pick1;`	Variable to hold reference to created `Polygon` object
`var pick2;`	Variable to hold reference to created `Polygon` object
`if ( ev.layerX || ev.layerX == 0) {`	Can we use `layerX` and `layerY`?
`mx= ev.layerX;`	Set `mx`
`my = ev.layerY;`	Set `my`

`}`	Close if true
`else if (ev.offsetX || ev.offsetX == 0) {`	Can we use `offsetX` and `offset`?
`mx = ev.offsetX;`	Set `mx`
`my = ev.offsetY;`	Set `my`
`}`	Close `else`
`var i;`	Declare variable for indexing in the `for` loop
`for (i=0;i<deck.length;i++){`	Loop through the whole deck
`var card = deck[i];`	Extract a card reference to simplify the code
`if (card.sx >=0)`	Check that card isn't marked as having been removed
`if ((mx>card.sx)&&(mx<card.sx+card.swidth)&&(my>card.sy)&&(my<card.sy+card.sheight)) {`	And then check if the mouse is over this card
`if ((firstpick)|| (i!=firstcard)) break;`	If so, check that the player isn't clicking on the first card again, and if this is true, leave the `for` loop
`}`	Close `if true` clause
	Close `for` loop
`if (i<deck.length) {`	Was the `for` loop exited early?
`if (firstpick) {`	If this is a first pick…

`firstcard = i;`	...Set `firstcard` to reference the card in the deck
`firstpick = false;`	Set `firstpick` to `false`
`pick1 = new Polycard(card.sx+cardwidth*.5,card.sy+cardheight*.5,cardrad,card.info);`	Create polygon with its coordinates at the center
`pick1.draw();`	Draw polygon
`}`	Close if first pick
`else {`	Else...
`secondcard = i;`	...Set `secondcard` to reference the card in the deck
`pick2 = new Polycard(card.sx+cardwidth*.5,card.sy+cardheight*.5,cardrad,card.info);`	Create polygon with its coordinates at the center
`pick2.draw();`	Draw polygon
`if (deck[i].info==deck[firstcard].info) {`	Check for a match
`matched = true;`	Set `matched` to true
`var nm = 1+Number(document.f.count.value);`	Increment the number of matches
`document.f.count.value = String(nm);`	Display the new count
`if (nm>= .5*deck.length) {`	Check if the game is over
`var now = new Date();`	Get new `Date` info
`var nt = Number(now.getTime());`	Extract and convert the time
`var seconds = Math.floor(.5+(nt-starttime)/1000);`	Compute the seconds elapsed

`document.f.elapsed.value = String(seconds);`	Output the time
`}`	Close if this is the end of the game
`}`	Close if there's a match
`else {`	Else...
`matched = false;`	Set matched to `false`
`}`	Close the `else` clause
`firstpick = true;`	Reset `firstpick`
`setTimeout(flipback,1000);`	Set up the pause
`}`	Close not first pick
`}`	Close good pick (click on a card—`for` loop exited early)
`}`	Close the function
`function flipback() {`	Function header—`flipback` handling after the pause
`if (!matched) {`	If no match...
`deck[firstcard].draw();`	...Draw the card back
`deck[secondcard].draw();`	...Draw the card back
`}`	...Close the clause
`else {`	Else need to remove cards
`ctx.fillStyle = tablecolor;`	Set to the table/board color

`ctx.fillRect(deck[secondcard].sx,deck[secondcard].sy,deck[secondcard].swidth,deck[secondcard].sheight);`	Draw over the card
`ctx.fillRect(deck[firstcard].sx,deck[firstcard].sy,deck[firstcard].swidth,deck[firstcard].sheight);`	Draw over the card
`deck[secondcard].sx = -1;`	Set this so the card won't be checked
`deck[firstcard].sx = -1;`	Set this so tso card won't be checked
`}`	Close if there's no match
`}`	Close the function
`function init(){`	Function header init
`ctx = document.getElementById('canvas').getContext('2d');`	Set ctx to do all the drawing
`canvas1 = document.getElementById('canvas');`	Set canvas1 for event handling
`canvas1.addEventListener('click',choose,false);`	Set up event handling
`makedeck();`	Create the deck
`document.f.count.value = "0";`	Initialize visible count
`document.f.elapsed.value = "";`	Clear any old value
`starttime = new Date();`	First step to setting starting time
`starttime = Number(starttime.getTime());`	Reuse the variable to set the milliseconds from benchmark
`shuffle();`	Shuffle the card info values

`}`	Close the function
`</script>`	Close the `script` element
`</head>`	Close `head` element
`<body onLoad="init();">`	Body tag, set up `init`
`<canvas id="canvas" width="900" height="400">`	Canvas start tag
`Your browser doesn't support the HTML5 element canvas.`	Warning message
`</canvas>`	Close `canvas` element
` `	Line break before instructions
`Click on two cards to see if you have a match.`	Instructions
`<form name="f">`	Form start tag
`Number of matches:  <input type="text" name="count" value="0" size="1"/>`	Label and input element used for output
`<p>`	Paragraph break
`Time taken to complete puzzle: <input type="text" name="elapsed" value="  " size="4"/> seconds.`	Label and input element used for output
`</form>`	Close `form`
`</body>`	Close body
`</html>`	Close html

You can change this game by changing the font, font size, color, and background color for the form. More ways to make the application your own are suggested later in this section.

The version of the memory game that uses pictures has much the same structure as the polygon version. It doesn't require a separate function to draw the picture. Table 5-3 is the function listing for this version of the game.

Table 5-3. Functions in the Photo Version of the Memory Game

Function	Invoked By/Called By	Calls
init	Invoked in response to the onLoad in the body tag	makedeck shuffle
choose	Invoked in response to the addEventListener in init	
flipback	Invoked in response to the setTimeout call in choose	
drawback	Invoked as the draw method for a card in makedeck and flipback	
shuffle	Called in init	
makedeck	Called in init	
Card	Called by makedeck	

The code for the photos version of the memory game is similar to that for the polygon version. Most of the logic is the same. But because this example demonstrates the writing of text on the canvas, the HTML document doesn't have a form element. The code follows in Table 5-4, with comments on the lines that are different. I also indicate where you would put in the names of the image files for your photographs. Before looking at this second version of the memory game, think about which parts are likely to be the same and which may be different.

Table 5-4. Complete Code for the Photo Version of the Memory Game

`<html>`	
`<head>`	
`    <title>Memory game using pictures</title>`	Complete title element
`    <script type="text/javascript">`	
`      var ctx;`	
`      var firstpick = true;`	

`var firstcard = -1;`	
`var secondcard;`	
`var backcolor = "rgb(128,0,128)";`	
`var tablecolor = "rgb(255,255,255)";`	
`var deck = [];`	
`var firstsx = 30;`	
`var firstsy = 50;`	
`var margin = 30;`	
`var cardwidth = 100;`	You may need to change this if you want your pictures to be a different width…
`var cardheight = 100;`	…and/or height
`var matched;`	
`var starttime;`	
`var count = 0;`	Needed to keep count internally
`var pairs = [`	The array of pairs of image files for the five people
`["allison1.jpg","allison2.jpg"],`	This is where you put in the names of your picture files
`[ "grant1.jpg","grant2.jpg"],`	…
`["liam1.jpg","liam2.jpg"],`	…
`["aviva1.jpg","aviva2.jpg"],`	…

`["daniel1.jpg","daniel2.jpg"]`	You can use any number of paired pictures, but notice how the array holding the last pair does not have a comma after the bracket.
`    ]`	
`function Card(sx,sy,swidth,sheight, img, info) {`	
`    this.sx = sx;`	
`    this.sy = sy;`	
`    this.swidth = swidth;`	
`    this.sheight = sheight;`	
`    this.info = info;`	Indicates matches
`    this.img = img;`	Img reference
`    this.draw = drawback;`	
`}`	
`function makedeck() {`	
`    var i;`	
`    var acard;`	
`    var bcard;`	
`    var pica;`	
`    var picb;`	
`    var cx = firstsx;`	
`    var cy = firstsy;`	
`    for(i=0;i<pairs.length;i++) {`	

Code	Comment
`pica = new Image();`	Create the Image object
`pica.src = pairs[i][0];`	Set to the first file
`acard = new Card(cx,cy,cardwidth,cardheight,pica,i);`	Create Card
`deck.push(acard);`	
`picb = new Image();`	Create the Image object
`picb.src = pairs[i][1];`	Set to second file
`bcard = new Card(cx,cy+cardheight+margin,cardwidth,cardheight,picb,i);`	Create Card
`deck.push(bcard);`	
`cx = cx+cardwidth+ margin;`	
`acard.draw();`	
`bcard.draw();`	
`    }`	
`}`	
`function shuffle() {`	
`var i;`	
`var k;`	
`var holderinfo;`	Temporary place for the swap
`var holderimg;`	Temporary place for the swap
`var dl = deck.length`	
`var nt;`	
`    for (nt=0;nt<3*dl;nt++) {   //do the swap 3 times deck.length times`	

Code	Comment
`i = Math.floor(Math.random()*dl);`	
`k = Math.floor(Math.random()*dl);`	
`holderinfo = deck[i].info;`	Save the info
`holderimg = deck[i].img;`	Save the img
`deck[i].info = deck[k].info;`	Put k's info into i
`deck[i].img = deck[k].img;`	Put k's img into i
`deck[k].info = holderinfo;`	Set to the original info
`deck[k].img = holderimg;`	Set to the original img
`    }`	
`}`	
`function drawback() {`	
`ctx.fillStyle = backcolor;`	
`ctx.fillRect(this.sx,this.sy,this.swidth,this.sheight);`	
`}`	
`function choose(ev) {`	
`    var out;`	
`    var mx;`	
`    var my;`	
`    var pick1;`	
`    var pick2;`	
`    if ( ev.layerX ||  ev.layerX == 0) {`	Reminder: This is the code for handling differences among the three browsers

`mx= ev.layerX;`	
`my = ev.layerY;`	
`} else if (ev.offsetX || ev.offsetX == 0) {`	
`mx = ev.offsetX;`	
`my = ev.offsetY;`	
`}`	
`var i;`	
`for (i=0;i<deck.length;i++){`	
`var card = deck[i];`	
`if (card.sx >=0)  //this is the way to avoid checking for clicking on this space`	
`if ((mx>card.sx)&&(mx<card.sx+card.swidth)&&(my>card.sy)&&(my<card.sy+card.sheight)) {`	
`if ((firstpick)|| (i!=firstcard)) {`	
`break;}`	
`}`	
`if (i<deck.length) {`	
`if (firstpick) {`	
`firstcard = i;`	
`firstpick = false;`	
`ctx.drawImage(card.img,card.sx,card.sy,card.swidth,card.sheight);`	Draw the photo
`}`	
`else {`	

Code	Description
`secondcard = i;`	
`ctx.drawImage(card.img,card.sx,card.sy,card.swidth,card.sheight);`	Draw the photo
`if (card.info==deck[firstcard].info) {`	Check if there's a match
`    matched = true;`	
`    count++;`	Increment count
`    ctx.fillStyle= tablecolor;`	
`              ctx.fillRect(10,340,900,100);`	Erase area where text will be
`    ctx.fillStyle=backcolor;`	Reset to the color for text
`ctx.fillText("Number of matches so far: "+String(count),10,360);`	Write out count
`if (count>= .5*deck.length) {`	
`var now = new Date();`	
`var nt = Number(now.getTime());`	
`var seconds = Math.floor(.5+(nt-starttime)/1000);`	
`    ctx.fillStyle= tablecolor;`	
`    ctx.fillRect(0,0,900,400);`	Erase the whole canvas
`    ctx.fillStyle=backcolor;`	Set for drawing
`out="You finished in "+String(seconds)+` `" secs.";`	Prepare the text
`    ctx.fillText(out,10,100);`	Write the text
`ctx.fillText("Reload the page to try again.",10,300);`	Write the text
`}`	

```
        }

    else {

            matched = false;

            }

            firstpick = true;

            setTimeout(flipback,1000);

                }

            }

    }

    function flipback() {

        var card;

        if (!matched) {

        deck[firstcard].draw();

        deck[secondcard].draw();

        }

        else {

                ctx.fillStyle = tablecolor;

ctx.fillRect(deck[secondcard].sx,deck[secondcard].sy,deck[second
card].swidth,deck[secondcard].sheight);

ctx.fillRect(deck[firstcard].sx,deck[firstcard].sy,deck[firstcar
d].swidth,deck[firstcard].sheight);

                    deck[secondcard].sx = -1;

                    deck[firstcard].sx = -1;
```

}	
}	
`function init(){`	
`ctx = document.getElementById('canvas').getContext('2d');`	
`canvas1 = document.getElementById('canvas');`	
`canvas1.addEventListener('click',choose,false);`	
`makedeck();`	
`shuffle();`	
`ctx.font="bold 20pt sans-serif";`	Set font
`ctx.fillText("Click on two cards to make a match.",10,20);`	Display instructions as text on canvas
`ctx.fillText("Number of matches so far: 0",10,360);`	Display the count
`starttime = new Date();`	
`starttime = Number(starttime.getTime());`	
}	
`</script>`	
`</head>`	
`<body onLoad="init();">`	
`<canvas id="canvas" width="900" height="400">`	
`Your browser doesn't support the HTML5 element canvas.`	
`</canvas>`	
`</body>`	
`</html>`	

Though these two programs are real games, they can be improved. For example, the player can't lose. After reviewing this material, try to figure out a way to force a loss, perhaps by limiting the number of moves or imposing a time limit.

These applications start the clock when they're loaded. Some games wait to begin timing until the player performs the first action. If you want to take this friendlier approach, you'd need to set up a logical variable initialized to `false` and create a mechanism in the `choose` function for checking whether this variable has been set to `true`. Since it may not have been, you'd have to include code for setting the starttime variable.

This is a single-player game. You can devise a way to make it a game for two. You probably need to assume that the people are taking turns properly, but the program can keep separate scores for each participant.

Some people like to set up games with levels of difficulty. To do so, you could increase the number of cards, decrease the pause time, or take other measures.

You can make this application yours by using your own pictures. You can, of course, use images of friends and family members, but you could also create an educational game with pictures that represent items or concepts such as musical-note names and symbols, countries and capitals, maps of counties and names, and more. You can change the number of pairs as well. The code refers to the `length` of the various arrays, so you don't need to go through the code changing the number of cards in the deck. You may need to adjust the values of the `cardwidth` and `cardheight` variables, though, to arrange the cards on the screen.

Another possibility, of course, is using a standard deck of 52 cards (or 54 with jokers). For an example using playing cards, skip ahead to Chapter 10, which takes you through creation of a blackjack game. For any matching game, you'll need to develop a way to represent the information defining which cards match.

Testing and uploading the application

When we, the developers, check our programs, we tend to do the same thing on each pass. Users, players, and customers, however, often do strange things. That's why getting others to test our applications is a good idea. So ask friends to test out your game. You should always have people who had no hand in building the application test it. You may discover problems you didn't identify.

The HTML document for the polygon version of the memory game contains the complete game, since the program draws and redraws the polygons on the fly. The photo version of the game requires you to upload all the images. You can vary this game by using image files from the Web (outside of your own Web page). Note that the `pairs` array needs to have the complete addresses.

Summary

In this example, you learned how to implement two versions of the game known as memory or concentration) using programming techniques and HTML5 features. These included

- examples of programmer-defined functions and programmer-defined objects
- how to draw polygons on the canvas using `moveTo` and `lineTo` along with `Math` trig methods
- guidance on how to use a form to show information to players
- a method for drawing text with a specified font on the canvas
- instructions about how to draw images on the canvas
- using `setTimeout` to force a pause
- employing `Date` objects to compute elapsed time

The applications demonstrated ways to represent information to implement two versions of a familiar game. The next chapter will temporarily depart from the use of canvas to demonstrate dynamic creation and positioning of HTML elements. It also will feature the use of HTML5's video element.

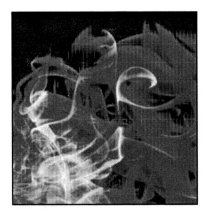

Chapter 6

Quiz

In this chapter, we will cover

- creating HTML by code
- positioning and repositioning HTML elements
- responding to clicks of the mouse
- arrays of arrays
- playing video

Introduction

This chapter demonstrates how HTML elements can be created dynamically and then positioned and repositioned on the screen. This is in contrast not only to drawing on a canvas element but also to the old way of creating static web pages. Our goal is to produce a quiz in which the player must match the names of countries and capital cities. We will use an array of arrays to hold the necessary information and build on the game to give more feedback to the player, including playing a video clip as a reward for getting the correct answers. The ability to display video directly (or *natively*) using HTML5 is a big improvement over the old system, which required using the `<object>` element and third-party plug-ins on the player's computer. In our game, the video serves only a minor role, but the fact that developers and designers can use HTML5 and JavaScript to produce a specific video at a specific point in the running of an application is very important.

The basic information for the quiz consists of country and capital city name pairs for the G20 countries. (Note: the European Union is one of the entries.) The program chooses at random four country/capital pairs and presents them in boxes on the screen. Figure 6-1 shows an opening screen.

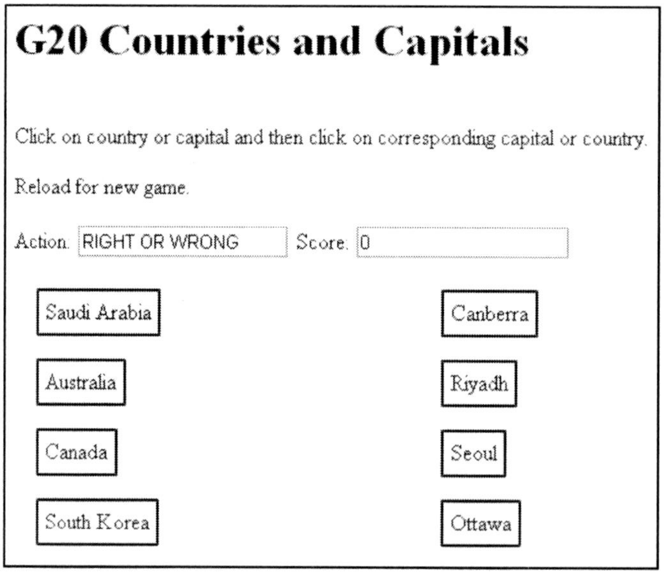

Figure 6-1. An opening screen for the quiz

Players attempt to match a country and its capital by clicking first on one and then the other, and the blocks change color to indicate success. Figure 6-2 shows the correct matching of Canada and Ottawa, and Figure 6-3 shows a second match. Notice that the blocks have been colored in and the Score goes to 1 and then to 2.

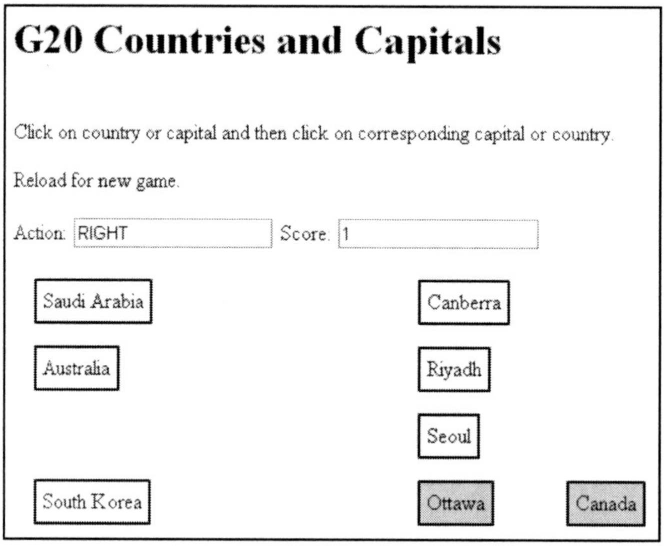

Figure 6-2. One pair correctly matched

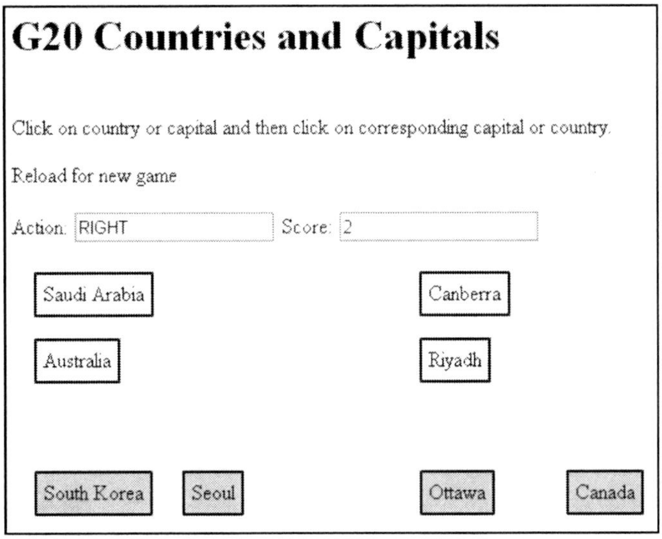

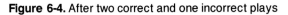

G20 Countries and Capitals

Click on country or capital and then click on corresponding capital or country.

Reload for new game

Action: RIGHT   Score: 2

Saudi Arabia   Canberra

Australia   Riyadh

South Korea   Seoul   Ottawa   Canada

Figure 6-3. A second successful match

Now the player makes a mistake by pairing Riyadh with Australia. Figure 6-4 shows the result: the program moves the Riyadh block, but the Action field indicates WRONG. The Score is still 2, and the blocks remain white.

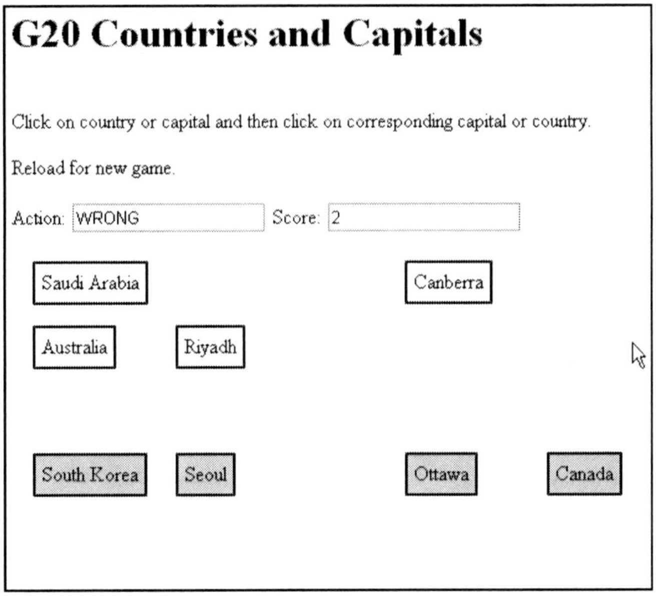

G20 Countries and Capitals

Click on country or capital and then click on corresponding capital or country.

Reload for new game.

Action: WRONG   Score: 2

Saudi Arabia   Canberra

Australia   Riyadh

South Korea   Seoul   Ottawa   Canada

Figure 6-4. After two correct and one incorrect plays

This quiz program allows the player to try again, as shown in Figure 6-5.

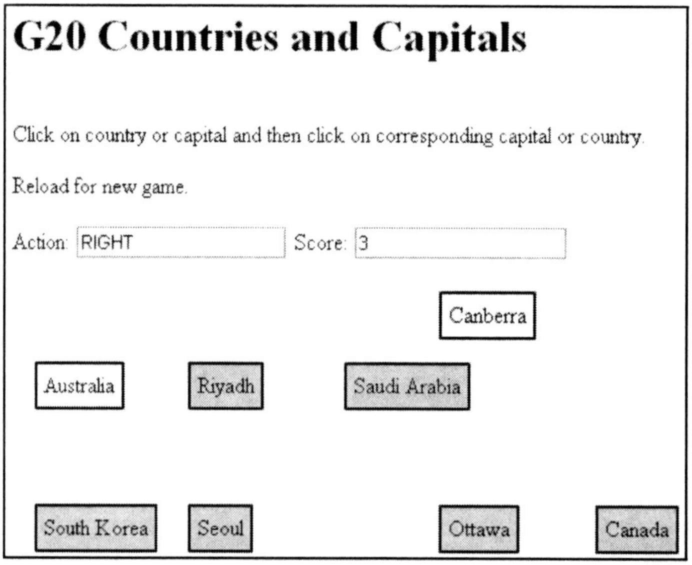

Figure 6-5. Choosing the correct match for Riyadh

The second version of the quiz provides more feedback to the player. Clicking on a country or capital turns its color to tan, as in Figure 6-6. If the attempted match is correct, the blocks become gold as in the first game. If not, the color changes back to white.

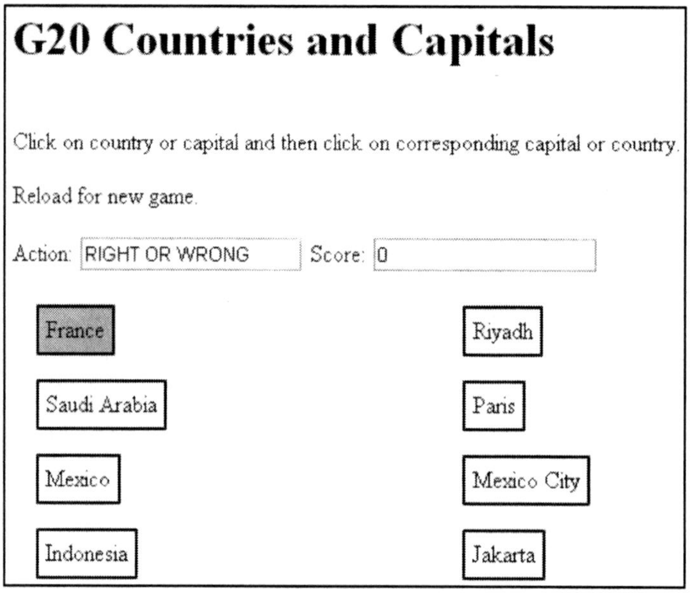

Figure 6-6. A first selection changes color.

Matching all four correctly results in a short video clip. Figure 6-7 shows the start of the video.

Figure 6-7. After success, a video clip

A game or, indeed, any application, must communicate effectively with the user. Sometimes, you may want to be subtle, but a good rule is to provide feedback for every user action, or at least think carefully and make a conscious decision to not provide direct feedback. The color changes are feedback. The video is feedback: the player who completes the game gets a visual reward.

This program should be considered a starting point. As designer, you will need to make decisions on retries, game completion, hints, and so forth. I decided to make this game a random selection of 4 questions from a set of 20. You could consider these sets of 4 questions rounds in a longer game. You could present one country along with several alternatives for its capital. And you could use images (img elements with the src values set by code) in place of names. See the "Building the Application and Making It Your Own" section for more ideas.

Our quiz program creates HTML elements that change and move around the screen as a result of player action. It also uses arrays of arrays to hold information, and it includes video that plays at a specific point in the game. It's hard to imagine a sophisticated game nowadays that wouldn't include such elements. Moreover, this program suggests the potential of games for education, certainly an area worth exploring.

Critical requirements

A quiz requires a way to store information or, to use a fancier term, a knowledge base. We need a way to choose specific questions to ask, hopefully randomly, so the player sees a different set of challenges each time. Since what we're storing is simply pairs of names, we can use a simple technique.

Next we need to present questions to the player and provide feedback, something different each time. In this example, the player sees the country and capital names in blocks on the screen, and then clicks on the appropriate blocks to indicate a possible match. This means we need a way to generate JavaScript to detect mouse clicks on specific blocks and then reposition the first block clicked on to be next to the second block. We want a correct pairing to be indicated by a change in color as well as text, and an increase in the score.

Notice that we are not using the <canvas> element. We could have, and you can read the Comment below for a comparison of dynamically created HTML markup and the canvas. The Hangman application in Chapter 9 includes dynamically generated HTML elements *and* drawing on a canvas element.

Since video is such an important advance for HTML5, I wanted to demonstrate it in an example. A critical aspect of using video as a "reward" for a successful game is the need to hide the video until that point in the game and then start playing it. What makes this more challenging is that currently not all browsers accept the same video encodings. Still, as mentioned earlier, the new capability in HTML5 means that developers can make very precise use of video without relying on third-party plug-ins.

HTML5, CSS, and JavaScript features

Now let's delve into the specific features of HTML5, CSS, and JavaScript that provide what we need to implement the quiz. I again build on what has been explained before, with some redundancy just in case you skipped around in your reading.

Storing and retrieving information in arrays

You may remember that an array is a sequence of values and that a variable can be set up as an array. The individual components of an array can be any data type—including other arrays! Recall that in the memory games in Chapter 5, we used an array variable named pairs in which each element was itself an array of two elements, the matching photo image files.

```
var pairs = [
            ["allison1.jpg","allison2.jpg"],
            [ "grant1.jpg","grant2.jpg"],
            ["liam1.jpg","liam2.jpg"],
            ["aviva1.jpg","aviva2.jpg"],
            ["daniel1.jpg","daniel2.jpg"]
```

The pairs array had 5 elements, each of which was an array. The inner arrays consisted of two elements and each of these elements was a string of characters, the name of an image file.

In the quiz application, we will again use an array of arrays. For the quiz show, we set up a variable named facts as an array to hold the information about the G20 members. Each element of the facts array is itself an array. My first thought on creating the application was that these inner arrays would each hold two elements, the country name and the capital city name. Later, I added a third element to hold whether or not this country/capital pair had been chosen in this round of the quiz. This meant that the inner arrays had three different elements: two character strings and a Boolean (true/false) value.

The individual components of an array are accessed or set using square brackets. Arrays in JavaScript are indexed starting from zero and ending at one less than the total number of elements in the array. One trick to remember that the indexing starts from zero is to imagine the array all lined up. The first element will be at the start; the second 1 unit away; the third 2 units away, and so on.

The length of the array is kept in an attribute of the array named `length`. To access the first component of the `facts` array, you use `fact[0]`; for the second element, `fact[1]`, and so on. You will see this in the coding.

A common way to do something with each element in an array is to use a `for` loop. (See also the explanation for setting up the gradient in the walls of the bounding box in Chapter 3.) Suppose you have an array named `prices` and your task is to write code to increase each of the prices by 15%. Further, each price has to increase by a minimum of 1, even if 1 is more than the 15%. You could use the construct in Table 6-1 to perform this task. As you can see in the Explanation column, the `for` loop does the same thing for each component of the array, using the indexing variable `i` in this example. This example also shows the use of the `Math.max` method.

Table 6-1. Increasing Prices in an Array Using a For Loop

Code	Explanation
`for(var i=0;i<prices.length;i++) {`	Do the statements inside the brackets, changing the value of `i`, starting at 0 and increasing by 1 (that's what i++ does) until the value is not less than `prices.length`, the number of elements in the array.
`prices[i] += Math.max`↪ `(prices[i]*.15,1);`	Remember to interpret this from the inside out. Compute .15 times the ith element of the array `prices`. See what's greater, this value or 1. If it is this value, that's what `Math.max` returns. If it is 1 (if 1 is more than `prices[i]*.15`), use 1. Add this value to the current value of `prices[i]`. That's what += does.
`}`	Close the `for` loop

Notice that the code does not state the size of the `prices` array explicitly. Instead it is represented in the expression `prices.length`. This is good because it means that the value of `length` changes automatically if and when you add elements to the array. Of course, in our example we know the number to be 20, but in other situations it's better to keep things flexible. This application can be a model for a quiz involving any number of facts when a fact is two pieces of information.

Our `facts` array is an array of arrays, which means you'll see the following in the code:

`facts[i][0]` the country name

`facts[i][1]` the capital city name

`facts[i][2]` the true/false value indicating this country/capital has been used

These expressions are interpreted as the 0th element of the ith element of the `facts` array and so on. I do refer to the inner arrays as rows, but keep in mind that there are not really any columns. Some programming languages support multi-dimensional arrays as a primitive data type, but JavaScript only supports one-dimensional arrays. The facts array is one-dimensional. The facts[0] element is itself an array, and so on.

> *Note: If the knowledge base was much more complex or if I were sharing the information or accessing it from somewhere else, I might need to use something other than an array of arrays. I could also store the knowledge base separate from the HTML document, perhaps using an eXtended Markup Language (XML) file. JavaScript has functions for reading in and accessing XML.*

The design for the quiz is to present a randomly chosen set of four facts for each game, so we define a variable nq (standing for number in a quiz) to be 4. This never changes, but making it a variable means that if we wanted to change it, it would be easy to do.

The HTML that's created dynamically (see next section) will take up two columns on the screen, with the countries in the left column and the capitals in the right. I don't want the pairs to line up, so I use the Math.random facility to position the capitals in the nq different positions. I think of these as slots. The logic, presented here in pseudo-code, is the following

Make a random choice, from 0 to facts.length. If this fact has been used, try again
Mark this choice as used.
Create new HTML to be a block for the country and place in the next ↪
position on the left.
Make a random choice, 0 to 3, to determine the slot for the capital. ↪
If this slot has been taken, try again.
Mark this slot as used.

So how do we code this? As indicated earlier, the fact array contains arrays and the third element of the inner arrays is a Boolean variable. Initially, these values will each be false, meaning the elements haven't yet been used in the game. After a time, of course, some facts will have been used, so I use another type of loop, a do-while construct that will keep trying until it comes to a fact that hasn't been used:

```
do {c = Math.floor(Math.random()*facts.length);}
while (facts[c][2]==true)
```

The do-while exits as soon as facts[c][2] is false, that is, when the element at index c is available for use.

We use similar coding to determine the slot for the capital. We define an array called slots. Now, we could have made the values in the slots array Booleans, but instead we're going to store the value c that holds the index in the facts array once the code determines what that value is. For an initial value for each element of slots, we'll use an arbitrary value of -100. The used values are in the range 0 to 19 (facts.length). The coding is:

```
do {s = Math.floor(Math.random()*nq);}
while (slots[s]>=0)
slots[s]=c;
```

Creating HTML during program execution

An HTML document typically consists of the text and markup you include when you initially write the document. However, you can also add to the document while the file is being interpreted by the browser, specifically, when the JavaScript in the `script` element is being executed (called *execution time* or *runtime*). This is what I mean by creating HTML dynamically. For the quiz application, I created two types of elements that we'll add, with the names "country" and "cap". For each of these, we insert an element of type `div`, a general element type that suits our purposes here. (Be aware that HTML5 has added several other types—for example, `header`, `footer`, `article`, and `section`—that convey more specific meaning and should be considered for your applications. Chapter 1 shows one use of `section`, and in Chapter 10, I'll show `footer`.)

The div is a block type, meaning it can contain other elements as well as text, and it is displayed with line breaks before and after. Table 6-2 shows methods we'll use.

Table 6-2. Methods for Creating HTML

Code	Explanation
`createElement`	Creates the HTML element
`appendChild`	Adds the element to the document by appending it to something in the document
`getElementbyID`	Gets a reference to the element

One trick needed for applications such as this is to come up with unique `id` values for the elements that are created. We'll do this using a variable that's incremented for each set of country and capital. The id value consists of that number, converted to a string and then preceded by a "c" or a "p". Why a "p"? Because I'm using "c" for country and "p" came to mind when thinking of capital. By the way, the id values don't have to be numbers or take any particular form. As you see, in our application, they are single letters followed by numbers.

The matching country and capital city will have the same number so we can use the `id` values to check for a match. We use a `String` method, `substring`, that extracts a portion of any string of characters. Let's look at a couple of examples. To use `substring`, you specify the starting position and, optionally, one more than the ending position. That is, the extracted string starts at the first parameter and goes up until the second. If our code doesn't include the second parameter, the extract goes to the end of the string. Suppose you had a variable

`var class ;`

for course or class names. Most colleges use specific patterns for such names, such as three letters for department and then perhaps four numbers to indicate the specific course. Now let's suppose the variable `class` has been assigned the value "MAT1420". In that case,

`class.substring(0,3)` would produce "MAT"

`class.substring(3)` would produce "1420"

`class.substring(3,7)` would produce "1420"

`class.substring(3,6)` would produce "142"

`class.substring(3,4)` would produce "1"

> Tip: JavaScript and many other languages also provide a string method called *substr* that works a little differently. The second argument of *substr* is the length of the piece of string. For the class name example,
>
> *class.substr(0,3)*, coincidentally, also produces "MAT"
>
> *class.substr(3,4)* produces "1420"
>
> *class.substr(3,1)* produces "1"

In our implementation of the quiz, we use the portion of the string starting from the position numbered 1, that is, the second position, to the end of the string.

Once we create these new HTML elements, we use addEventListener to set up events and event handlers. The addEventListener method is used for a variety of events. Remember, we used it on the canvas element in Chapter 4.

For the quiz application, the following statement sets up the JavaScript engine to "listen" for clicks for each element and to invoke the pickelement function that we'll create.

```
thingelem.addEventListener('click',pickelement,false);
```

(The false in this statement refers to a technicality involving other possible listeners for this event.)

In the pickelement function, you'll see code containing the term this, such as

```
thisx= this.style.left;
```

In the code, this refers to the current instance, namely the element that the player clicked. We set up listening for the event for each element so when pickelement is executed, the code can refer to the specific element that *heard* the click using the this. When the player clicks on the Brazil block, the code *knows* it, where by "knows" I am anthropomorphizing the program more than I would like. Putting it another way, the same pickelement function will be invoked for all the blocks we have placed on the screen, but, by using this, the code can refer to the specific one that the player clicks on each time.

> Note: If we didn't have these elements and the capability to do the addEventListener and refer to the attributes using the this (forgive the awkward English) and instead drew stuff on a canvas, we would need to perform calculations and comparisons to determine where the mouse cursor was and then look up the corresponding information in some way to check for matches. (Recall the coding for the Slingshot in Chapter 4.) Instead, the JavaScript engine is doing much of the work, and doing it more efficiently—faster—than we could by writing the code ourselves.

After the new HTML is created, its contents are set using the innerHTML attribute. Next, the new element is added to the document by being appended as a child of the body element. This may seem odd, but it is how things are done.

```
d.innerHTML = (
    "<div class='thing' id='"+uniqueid+"'>placeholder</div>");
    document.body.appendChild(d);
```

The `placeholder` text will be replaced and the whole thing will be repositioned. We set the text by assigning a value to the attribute `textContent`. Next, we'll look at how to use CSS with our code to position the elements and change their color.

You'll see the code in complete context in the Building the Application section.

Changing elements by modifying CSS using JavaScript code

Cascading Style Sheets (CSS) lets you specify the formatting of parts of an HTML document. Chapter 1 showed a very basic example of CSS, which is powerful and useful even for static HTML. Essentially, the idea is to use CSS for the formatting, that is, the look of the application, and to reserve HTML for structuring the content. See David Powers' *Getting StartED with CSS* (friends of ED, 2009) for more information on CSS.

Let's take a brief look here at what we'll use to generate the dynamically created blocks holding the country and capital names.

A style element in an HTML document holds one or more styles. Each style refers to

- an element type using the element type name; or
- a specific element, using the `id` value; or
- a class of elements.

In Chapter 1, we used a style for the body element and for the section elements. For the video, we'll use a reference to a specific element. Here is a fragment of the coding, starting with what goes in the style element:

```
#vid {position:absolute; visibility:hidden; z-index: 0; }
```

where `vid` is the id used in the video element in the body element.

```
<video id="vid" controls="controls"  preload="auto">
```

We'll get into the details of this soon when I discuss the video element and its visibility.

Now let's set the formatting for a class of elements. The class is an attribute that can be specified in any element starting tag. For this application, I came up with a class `thing`. Yes, I know it's lame. It refers to a thing our code will place on the screen. The style is

```
.thing {position:absolute;left: 0px; top: 0px; border: 2px; border-style: double;↩
 background-color: white; margin: 5px; padding: 5px; }
```

The period before `thing` indicates that this is a class specification. The `position` is set to `absolute` and `top` and `left` include values that can be changed by code.

The `absolute` setting refers to the way the `position` is specified in the document window—as specific coordinates. The alternative is `relative`, which you'd use if the part of the document was within a containing block that could be anywhere on the screen. The unit of measurement is the pixel and so the positions from the left and from the top are given as 0px for 0 pixels, and the border, margin, and padding measurements are 2 pixels, 5 pixels, and 5 pixels, respectively.

Now let's see how to use the style attributes to position and format the blocks. For example, after creating a dynamic element to hold a country, we can use the following lines of code to get a reference to the `thing` just created, put the text holding the country name into the element, and then position it at a specified point on the screen.

```
thingelem = document.getElementBy(uniqueid);
thingelem.textContent=facts[c][0];
thingelem.style.top = String(my)+"px";
thingelem.style.left = String(mx)+"px";
```

Here, my and mx are numbers. Setting style.top and style.left requires a string, so our code converts the numbers to strings and adds the "px" at the ends of the strings.

We want to change the color of both boxes when there is a correct match. We can do this pretty much as when changing the top and left to reposition the block. However, the name of the attribute for JavaScript is slightly different than the one in the CSS: no dash.

```
elementinmotion.style.backgroundColor = "gold";
this.style.backgroundColor = "gold";
```

The gold is one of the set of established colors, including red, white, blue, etc. that can be referred to by name. Alternatively, you can use the hexadecimal RGB values available from a program such as Corel Paint Shop Pro, Adobe Photoshop, or Adobe Flash. For the second version of the game, I used tan and white.

> Tip: You can specify a font in the style section. You can put 'safe web fonts' in any search engine and get a list of fonts purported to be available on all browsers and all computers. However, an alternative approach is to specify an ordered list of fonts so if the first one is not available, the browser will attempt to find the next. See Chapter 8 for more information.

Text feedback using form and input elements

The player gets feedback in two ways in the two applications: in both versions, a selected block always gets moved. In the second version of the game, the first block clicked gets changed to tan. If the match is correct, the color of both blocks is set to gold. Otherwise, both blocks revert to white. Text feedback is given using input fields of a form element. This form is not used for input and so there's no button, either as a separate button element or as an input element of type submit.

The following two lines set one input field to RIGHT and the other to one more than the previous value. Note that the value must be converted from text to number before incrementing, then converted back.

```
document.f.out.value = "RIGHT";
document.f.score.value =String(1+Number(document.f.score.value));
```

What if our pesky player clicks twice on the same block? We have code to check for this.

```
if (makingmove) {
  if (this==elementinmotion) {
        elementinmotion.style.backgroundColor = "white";
        makingmove = false;
        return;
  }
}
```

This makes the player start over with a new move if she clicks twice on the same block. Since the block will change back to white, this should be clear to the player.

Presenting video

HTML5 provides the new video element for presenting video, either as part of a static HTML document or under the control of JavaScript. This may well become the new standard. For more information, see Silvia Pfeiffer's *The Definitive Guide to HTML5 Video* (Apress, 2010).

In brief, video comes in different file types, just like images do. The file types vary based on the containers for the video and the associated audio, as well as on how the video and the audio are encoded. The browser needs to know how to handle the container and how to decode the video to display the frames—the still images making up the video—in succession on the screen, and how to decode the audio to send the sound to the computer speakers.

Videos involve a considerable amount of data, so people still are working on the best ways to compress the information, taking advantage, for example, of what is similar between frames without losing too much quality. Web sites are now displayed on small screens on cell phones as well as large high-definition TV screens, so it's important to take advantage of any knowledge of what the display device will be. With this in mind, though we can hope that browser makers standardize on one format in the future, the HTML5 video element provides a way to work around the lack of standardization by referencing multiple files. Developers, therefore, and that includes those of us creating this quiz application, need to produce different versions of the same video.

I downloaded a Fourth of July fireworks video clip and then used a free tool (Miro video converter) to create three different versions with different formatting of the same short video clip. I then used the new HTML5 video element as well as the source element to code references to all three video files. The codecs attribute in the source element provides information on what the encoding is for the file specified in the `src` attribute.

```
<video controls="controls">
<source src="sfire3.mp4" type='video/mp4; codecs="avc1.42E01E, mp4a.40.2"'>
<source src="sfire3.theora.ogv" type='video/ogg; codecs="theora, vorbis"'>
<source src="sfire3.webmvp8.webm" type="video/webm; codec="vp8, vorbis"'">
</video>
```

Including `controls="controls"` puts the familiar controls on the screen to allow the player/user to start or pause the video clip. This code, as part of a standard HTML document, produces what is shown in Figure 6-8.

Figure 6-8. Video clip with controls

Note that the display will vary slightly across the different browsers.

The tag for the video element provides other attributes, including a standard width and height and autoplay and preload. Three different source files are indicated in the HTML. The type attribute supplies information on both the video and audio encoding, and you must use the single and double quotation marks. That is, the double quotation marks indicate something within the longer single quote. The browser interprets the HTML starting from the first source element. As soon as the determination is made that this is a file type the browser can display, that file is downloaded to the client computer.

This is the basic way to present video. However, as mentioned earlier, for our quiz application we are going to hide the video until it is time to play it. To do this, we define a style for the video element specifying the visibility as hidden. We also need the video clip to be on top of any other elements, including the elements created dynamically in the code. Placing elements on top of other elements is controlled by the z-index, what you might consider the third dimension after x and y. To do this we need the following style:

```
#vid {position:absolute; visibility:hidden; z-index: 0; }
```

This style specifies the original settings. The code will change it when it is time to play the video. #vid refers to the id of the video element.

```
<video id="vid" controls="controls"  preload="auto">
<source src="sfire3.mp4" type='video/mp4; codecs="avc1.42E01E, mp4a.40.2"'>
<source src="sfire3.theora.ogv" type='video/ogg; codecs="theora, vorbis"'>
<source src="sfire3.webmvp8.webm" type="video/webm; codec="vp8, vorbis"'">
Your browser does not accept the video tag.
 </video>
```

We not only want the video to appear, we also want it to be on top of everything else. To do this, we will modify the z-index. Think of z as the dimension coming out of the screen toward the user.

Note that the position is never changed, but the z-index only works if `position` has been specified in a style.

When the code calculates that it is time for the video clip, it changes the visibility and the z-index and then invokes the `play` method.

```
v = document.getElementById("vid");
v.style.visibility = "visible";
v.style.zIndex = "10000";
v.play();
```

> Tip: CSS has its own language, sometimes involving hyphens in terms. The CSS term for expressing how elements are layered on the screen is z-index; the JavaScript term is zIndex.

With this considerable JavaScript, HTML, and CSS knowledge, we are now ready to describe the details of the quiz application.

Building the application and making it your own

The knowledge base for the quiz is represented in the `facts` variable, which is an array of arrays. If you want to change the quiz to another topic, one that consists of pairs of names or other text, you just need to change `facts`. Of course, you also need to change the text that appears as an h1 element in the `body` element to let the player know the category of questions. I defined a variable named `nq`, for number in each quiz (the number of pairs to appear onscreen) to be 4. You can, of course, change this value if you want to present a different number of pairs to the player. The other variables are used for the original positions of the blocks and to hold status information, such as whether it's a first click or a second click.

I created three functions for this application: `init`, `setupgame` and `pickelement`. I could have combined `init` and `setupgame`, but made them separate to facilitate a replay button. Table 6-3 describes these functions and what they call or are called by.

Table 6-3. Functions in the Quiz Application

Function	Invoked By / Called By	Calls
init	Invoked by the action of the onLoad in the <body> tag	setupgame
setupgame	called by init	
pickelement	Called as a result of the addEventListener calls in setupgame	

The `setupgame` function is where the HTML is created for the blocks. Briefly, an expression using `Math.random` is evaluated to pick one of the rows in the `facts` array. If that row has been used, the code tries again. When an unused row is found, it is marked as used (the third element, index value 2) and the blocks are created.

An alternative approach would be to remove a used fact from the array and to keep going until all rows have been chosen. Look back to the use of `splice` in Chapter 4 for an idea of how you could achieve this.

The block for the capital is placed randomly in one of the four available slots. This produces the countries and capital cities in two columns, but mixed up. The `pickelement` function does one thing if it is a first click and another if it is a second click, determined by the value of `makingmove`, which starts off being false and then is set to true at a first click.

Table 6-4 supplies a line-by-line explanation of the code.

Table 6-4. The Complete Code for the First Quiz Application

Code	Explanation
`<html>`	Starting `html` tag
`<head>`	Starting head tag
`<title>Quiz</title>`	Complete `title` element
`<style>`	Start of `style` section

`.thing {position:absolute;left: 0px;`↪
`top: 0px; border: 2px;`↪
`border-style: double;`↪
`background-color: white; margin:`
`5px;`↪
`padding: 5px; }`
	A style for all elements of the class `thing`. The original position is at the top, left corner of the window. There's a thick border and a white background color.

`</style>`	End of `style` element
`<script>`	Start `script` element
`var facts = [`	Start of declaration of the `facts` variable, array of arrays
`["China","Beijing",false],`	Each row is a complete array, 3 elements, country, capital, false The `false` field will be changed if this row is chosen to be presented
`["India","New Delhi",false],`	
`["European Union","Brussels",false],`	
`["United States","Washington,` `DC",false],`	

Code	Explanation
`["Indonesia","Jakarta",false],`	
`["Brazil","Brasilia",false],`	
`["Russia","Moscow",false],`	
`["Japan","Tokyo",false],`	
`["Mexico","Mexico City",false],`	
`["Germany","Berlin",false],`	
`["Turkey","Ankara",false],`	
`["France","Paris",false],`	
`["United Kingdom","London",false],`	
`["Italy","Rome",false],`	
`["South Africa","Pretoria",false],`	
`["South Korea","Seoul",false],`	
`["Argentina","Buenos Aires",false],`	
`["Canada","Ottawa",false],`	
`["Saudi Arabia","Riyadh",false],`	
`["Australia","Canberra",false]`	
`    ];`	Closing the array
`    var thingelem;`	Variable declaration for created elements
`    var nq = 4;`	Number of pairs presented to the player
`    var elementinmotion;`	Variable to hold the first element clicked on
`    var makingmove = false;`	Variable to distinguish first click situation and second click situation

Code	Explanation
`var inbetween = 300;`	Variable holding the distance between the original two columns
`var col1 = 20;`	Variable holding the horizontal position of the first column
`var row1 = 200;`	Variable holding the vertical position of the first row
`var rowsize = 50;`	Variable holding the height of a row (the block itself and the spacing) for creation of all the rows
`var slots = new Array(nq);`	An array variable to hold which slots in the right column have been filled
`function init(){`	Start of `init` function
`  setupgame();`	Invoked `setupgame();`
`}`	Close of `init` function
`function setupgame() {`	Start of `setupgame` function
`  var i;`	Variable used for the for loops
`  var c;`	Variable used for the choice of row (inner array) of facts
`  var s;`	Variable used for choice of slots
`  var mx = col1;`	Variable holding the horizontal position
`  var my = row1;`	Variable holding the initial vertical position
`  var d;`	Variable holding the created `html` element
`  var uniqueid;`	Variable holding the created id
`  for (i=0;i<facts.length;i++) {`	Start of a `for` loop to mark all facts as not being used
`    facts[i][2] = false;`	Set (reset) the third value, index 2, to be false
`  }`	Close the `for` loop
`  for (i=0;i<nq;i++) {`	Start of a `for` loop to set all the slots to unused

Code	Explanation
`slots[i] = -100;`	Used values will be 0 to 19
`}`	Close of `for` loop
`for(i=0;i<nq;i++) {`	Start of `for` loop to choose `nq` country/capital pairs Recall our `nq` is set to 4, 4 country-capital pairs
`do {c = Math.floor(Math.`↪ `random()*facts.length);}`	Start of do/while loop. What is in the brackets is done at least once. The variable `c` is set to a random value 0 to 1 less than the length of the array.
`while (facts[c][2]==true)`	Do this again if this inner array (country/capital pair) has been chosen
`facts[c][2]=true;`	Outside of loop, now set this country/capital pair array as being used
`uniqueid = "c"+String(c);`	Construct the id for the country block

`d =`
`document.createElement`↪
`('country');`
	Create an `html` element of type `country`

`d.innerHTML = (`	Set its `innerHTML` to be
`"<div class='thing'` `id='"+uniqueid+"'>placeholder</div>");`	… a div of class `thing` with the id. The contents of the element will be changed
`document.body.appendChild(d);`	Add this element to the document as a child of the `body` element
`thingelem =` `document.getElementById(uniqueid);`	Get a pointer to the element just created
`thingelem.textContent=`↪ `facts[c][0];`	Set its `textContent` to the country name
`thingelem.style.top =`↪ `String(my)+"px";`	Position it vertically by changing the `top` style
`thingelem.style.left =`↪ `String(mx)+"px";`	… and horizontally by changing the `left` style

Code	Explanation
`thingelem.addEventListener('click',↩ pickelement,false);`	Set up to listen for the `click` event
`uniqueid = "p"+String(c);`	Now construct the id for the capital block
`d = document.createElement('cap');`	Create a new element
`d.innerHTML = (`	Set its `innerHTML` to be
`"<div class='thing' id='"+uniqueid+"'>placeholder</div>");`	a div, class `thing`, with the id. `placeholder` will be changed
`document.body.appendChild(d);`	Add this to the document as a child to the `body` element
`thingelem = document.getElementById(uniqueid);`	Get a pointer to the `thing` element
`thingelem.textContent=facts[c][1];`	Set its `textContent` to the capital city name
`do {s = Math.floor↩ (Math.random()*nq);}`	Start a do `while` loop, the code in brackets is executed at least once. Determine a random choice from empty slots.
`while (slots[s]>=0)`	But repeat if this slot IS already taken
`slots[s]=c;`	Store away the country/capital number
`thingelem.style.top = String↩ (row1+s*rowsize)+"px";`	Position this block according to formula based on which slot and `rowsize` vertically
`thingelem.style.left = String↩ (col1+inbetween)+"px";`	Position this block horizontally in the second column (`inbetween` over from `col1`)
`thingelem.addEventListener('click',↩ pickelement,false);`	Set up to listen for the `click` event
`my +=rowsize;`	Increase the `my` value to prepare for the next block
`}`	Close loop

Code	Explanation
`document.f.score.value = "0";`	Set score to 0
`return false;`	This is done to prevent an HTML reloading of the page
`}`	Close `setupgame` function
`function pickelement(ev) {`	Start of `pickelement` function
`var thisx;`	Variable to hold the horizontal position of `this` element (the element that received the `click` event)
`var thisxn;`	Variable to hold the number represented by `thisx`, which is text
`if (makingmove) {`	Is this a second click?
`thisx= this.style.left;`	Set `thisx`
`thisx = thisx.substring↪` `(0,thisx.length-2);`	Remove the `px` from the string.
`thisxn =↪` `Number(thisx) + 110;`	Turn `this` into a number and then add fudge factor to position the element first clicked to the right of this element
`elementinmotion.style.left =↪` `String(thisxn)+"px";`	`elementinmotion` holds the first click element. position it horizontally to the calculated `thisxn` value.
`elementinmotion.style.top =↪` `this.style.top;`	Position it vertically the same as the `this` element
`makingmove = false;`	Set `makingmove` back to false
`if (this.id.substring(1)==↪` `elementinmotion.id.substring(1)) {`	Check if this is a match by comparing the ids, after using `substring` to leave off the first character
`elementinmotion.style.↪` `backgroundColor = "gold";`	If it was a match, change the color of `elementinmotion` and
`this.style.backgroundColor = "gold";`	this element
`document.f.out.value = "RIGHT";`	Output the value `RIGHT`

Code	Explanation
`document.f.score.value = String` ↪ `(1+Number(document.f.score.value));`	Increment the score (need to change value to number, add 1, and then change back to text)
`}`	Close if match true clause
`else {`	Else
`document.f.out.value = "WRONG";}`	Output the value WRONG
`}`	Close `else` clause
`else {`	If it wasn't a second click
`makingmove = true;`	Check `makingmove`
`elementinmotion = this;`	Save `this` element in the `elementinmotion` variable
`}`	End `else` clause
`}`	End `pickelement`
`</script>`	End `script`
`</head>`	End `head`
`<body onLoad="init();">`	Start body tag. Set up call to `init` on loading.
`<h1>G20 Countries and` ↪ `capitals </h1> `	Heading on the screen
`Click on country or capital` ↪ `and then click on corresponding` ↪ `capital or country.`	Directions
`<p>`	Paragraph
`Reload for new game.`	Directions
`<form name="f" >`	Start of form
`Action: <input name="out" type=` ↪ `"text" value="RIGHT OR WRONG"/>`	Text label and then input field

Code	Explanation
Score: `<input name="score" type=`↪ `"text" value="0"/>`	Text label and then input field
`</form>`	Close form
`</p>`	Close paragraph
`</body>`	Close body
`</html>`	Close html

The first step to making this application your own is to choose the content of your quiz. It needs to be pairs of values. The values here are names, held in text, but they could be numbers, or numbers and text. You also could create `img` tags and use the information kept in the array to set the `src` values of `img` elements. More complicated, but still doable is to incorporate audio. Start simple, with something resembling the G20 facts, and then be more daring.

You can change the look of the application by modifying the original HTML and/or the created HTML. You can modify or add to the CSS section.

You can easily change the number of questions, or change the four-question game to a four-question round and make a new round happen automatically after a certain number of guesses or when clicking on a button. You would need to decide if country/capital pairs are to be repeated from round to round.

You can also incorporate a time feature. There are two general approaches: keep track of time and simply display it when the player completes a game/round successfully (see the memory games in Chapter 5) or impose a time limit. The first approach allows someone to compete with themselves but imposes no significant pressure. The second does put pressure on the player and you can decrease the allowed time for successive rounds. It could be implemented using the `setTimeout` command.

Table 6-5 shows the code for the second version of the game, which includes changing a first selection to tan, and the video. As was the case in other chapters with multiple versions, think about what is the same in this game, and what we've changed or added.

Table 6-5. The Complete Code for the Second Version of the Quiz Application

Code	Explanation
`<html>`	
`<head>`	
`    <title>Quiz (multiple videos)</title>`	
`<style>`	

Code	Explanation
`.thing {position:absolute;left: 0px;`↪ `top: 0px; border: 2px; border-style:`↪ `double; background-color: white;`↪ `margin: 5px; padding: 5px; }`	
`#vid {position:absolute; visibility:`↪ `hidden; z-index: 0; }`	Style for the video element.
`</style>`	
`    <script type="text/javascript">`	
`    var facts = [`	
`        ["China","Beijing",false],`	
`        ["India","New Delhi",false],`	
`        ["European Union","Brussels",false],`	
`        ["United States","Washington,` `DC",false],`	
`        ["Indonesia","Jakarta",false],`	
`        ["Brazil","Brasilia",false],`	
`        ["Russia","Moscow",false],`	
`        ["Japan","Tokyo",false],`	
`        ["Mexico","Mexico City",false],`	
`        ["Germany","Berlin",false],`	
`        ["Turkey","Ankara",false],`	
`        ["France","Paris",false],`	
`        ["United Kingdom","London",false],`	
`        ["Italy","Rome",false],`	

Code	Explanation
["South Africa","Pretoria",false],	
["South Korea","Seoul",false],	
["Argentina","Buenos Aires",false],	
["Canada","Ottawa",false],	
["Saudi Arabia","Riyadh",false],	
["Australia","Canberra",false]	
];	
var thingelem;	
var nq = 4;	
var elementinmotion;	
var makingmove = false;	
var inbetween = 300;	
var col1 = 20;	
var row1 = 200;	
var rowsize = 50;	
var slots = new Array(nq);	
function init(){	
setupgame();	
}	
function setupgame() {	
var i;	

Code	Explanation
`var c;`	
`var s;`	
`var mx = col1;`	
`var my = row1;`	
`var d;`	
`var uniqueid;`	
`for (i=0;i<facts.length;i++) {`	
`    facts[i][2] = false;`	
`}`	
`for (i=0;i<nq;i++) {`	
`    slots[i] = -100;`	
`}`	
`for(i=0;i<nq;i++) {`	
`    do {c = Math.floor⮕` `(Math.random()*facts.length);}`	
`    while (facts[c][2]==true)`	
`    facts[c][2]=true;`	
`    uniqueid = "c"+String(c);`	
`    d = document.createElement⮕` `('country');`	
`    d.innerHTML = (`	
`        "<div class='thing'⮕` `id='"+uniqueid+"'>placeholder</div>");`	

Code	Explanation
`document.body.appendChild(d);`	
`thingelem = document.`↵ `getElementById(uniqueid);`	
`thingelem.textContent=facts[c][0];`	
`thingelem.style.top =`↵ `String(my)+"px";`	
`thingelem.style.left =`↵ `String(mx)+"px";`	
`thingelem.addEventListener`↵ `('click',pickelement,false);`	
`uniqueid = "p"+String(c);`	
`d = document.createElement`↵ `('cap');`	
`d.innerHTML = (`	
`"<div class='thing'`↵ `id='"+uniqueid+"'>placeholder</div>");`	
`document.body.appendChild(d);`	
`thingelem = document.`↵ `getElementById(uniqueid);`	
`thingelem.textContent=facts[c][1];`	
`do {s = Math.floor`↵ `(Math.random()*nq);}`	
`while (slots[s]>=0)`	
`slots[s]=c;`	
`thingelem.style.top =`↵ `String(row1+s*rowsize)+"px";`	

Code	Explanation
```thingelem.style.left =↪``` ```String(col1+inbetween)+"px";```	
```thingelem.addEventListener↪``` ```('click',pickelement,false);```	
```my +=rowsize;```	
```}```	
```document.f.score.value = "0";```	
```return false;```	
```}```	
```function pickelement(ev) {```	
```var thisx;```	
```var thisxn;```	
```var sc;```	Variable for the number of correct matches
```if (makingmove) {```	
```if (this==elementinmotion) {```	Check that the player hasn't clicked twice on the same block
```elementinmotion.style.backgroundColor =↪``` ```"white";```	If so, reset color to white
```makingmove = false;```	Reset ```makingmove```
```return;```	Return
```}```	Close ```if``` clause
```thisx= this.style.left;```	
```thisx = thisx.substring↪``` ```(0,thisx.length-2);```	

Code	Explanation
`thisxn = Number(thisx) + 115;`	
`elementinmotion.style.left =`↪ `String(thisxn)+"px";`	
`elementinmotion.style.top =`↪ `this.style.top;`	
`makingmove = false;`	
`if (this.id.substring(1)==`↪ `elementinmotion.id.substring(1)) {`	
`elementinmotion.`↪ `style.backgroundColor = "gold";`	
`this.style.`↪ `backgroundColor = "gold";`	
`document.f.out.value =` `"RIGHT";`	
`sc = 1+Number`↪ `(document.f.score.value);`	Pick up the score, convert to number, and increment by 1
`document.f.score`↪ `.value = String(sc);`	
`if (sc==nq) {`	If game over
`v = document`↪ `.getElementById("vid");`	...find video element
`v.style`↪ `.visibility = "visible";`	...set visibility to visible
`v.style.zIndex="10000";`	...set zIndex to a very big number
`v.play();`	...play the video
`}`	...close if clause

Code	Explanation
``` } ```	
``` else { ```	
``` document.f.out↪ .value = "WRONG"; ```	
``` elementinmotion.↪ style.backgroundColor = "white"; ```	
``` } ```	
``` } ```	
``` else { ```	
``` makingmove = true; ```	
``` elementinmotion = this; ```	
``` elementinmotion.style.↪ backgroundColor = "tan"; ```	Set first block color to tan
``` } ```	
```} ```	
```</script> ```	
```</head> ```	
```<body onLoad="init();"> ```	
```<h1>G20 Countries and capitals </h1> ```	
```Click on country or capital and then↪ click on corresponding capital or country. ```	
```<p> ```	
```Reload for new game. ```	
```<form name="f" > ```	

Code	Explanation
`Action: <input name="out" type=↪` `"text" value="RIGHT OR WRONG"/>`	
`Score: <input name="score" type=↪` `"text" value="0"/>`	
`</form>`	
`</p>`	
`<video id="vid" controls=↪` `"controls"  preload="auto">`	Video with controls
`<source src="sfire3.mp4" type='video/↪` `mp4; codecs="avc1.42E01E, mp4a.40.2"'>`	Source for the mp4 file
`<source src="sfire3.theora.ogv" type=↪` `'video/ogg; codecs="theora, vorbis"'>`	Source for the ogv file
`<source src="sfire3.webmvp8.webm" type=↪` `"video/webm; codec="vp8, vorbis"'">`	Source for the webm file
`Your browser does not accept the video tag.`	Message to noncompliant browsers
`</video>`	Closing tag
`</body>`	
`</html>`	

To make this game your own, consider other questions from geography or even other entirely different categories. As suggested earlier, you can make one or both of the pairs of information images. The video treat can vary depending on the content or even the player's performance.

You can identify links to web sites that discuss the facts or to Google map locations as mini-awards for correct answers—or as clues.

You may not like the way the quiz blocks remain on the screen while the video is showing. You can remove them using a loop that makes each element invisible. Look ahead to the Hangman application in Chapter 9 for ideas.

Testing and uploading the application

The random feature of the game does not impact the testing. If you wish, you can substitute fixed choices after the `Math.random` coding, do the bulk of the testing, and then remove these lines of code and test again. The important thing to do for this and similar games is to make sure your testing involves both correct guesses and incorrect guesses. You also need to click on the country name first and then the capital, and then do it the other way. Check the color changes and the scores. If you add a *new round* feature, make sure that the score remains or is reset as you want.

> *Warning: The player can cheat! There is no check to prevent the player from repeating a correct move. See if you can make this improvement in the coding. You can add a new element to the inner arrays in* facts *to mark a correctly answered question.*

The basic G20 game is complete in the HTML file (which you can download from www.friendsofed.com/downloads.html). The game with the video reward requires you to download the video from the Friends of Ed site or use your own. To play your own choice of video, you must:

- create or acquire the video
- produce the different versions, assuming you want to support the different browsers
- upload all the files to the server

You may need to work with your server staff to make sure the different video types are properly specified. This involves something called the **htaccess** file. HTML5 still is new and this way of featuring video on web pages may be new to the server support crews.

Alternatively, you can identify video already online and use absolute URLs as the `src` attributes in the source elements in the video elements.

Summary

In this chapter, we implemented a simple quiz that asked a player to match the names of countries and capitals. The application used the following programming techniques and HTML5 features:

- creating HTML during runtime using `document.createElement`, `document.getElementById`, and `document.body.appendChild`
- setting up event handling for the mouse `click` event using `addEventListener`
- changing color of objects on the screen using code to change CSS settings
- an array of arrays to hold the quiz content
- `for` loops for iterating over the array
- do-while loops to make a random choice of an unused question set
- `substring` for determining a correct match
- `video` and `source` elements for displaying video encoded in formats acceptable by different browsers

You can make use of dynamically created and repositioned HTML along with the drawing on canvas that you learned in the previous chapters. The implementation of Hangman, described in Chapter 9, does just that. You can use video as a small part of an application, as was done here, or as the major part of a web site. In the next chapter we return to drawing on canvas as we build a maze and then travel through it.

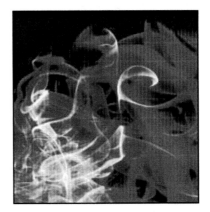

Chapter 7

Mazes

In this chapter, we will cover

- responding to mouse events
- calculation of collision between circles and lines
- responding to the arrow keys
- form input
- encoding, saving, decoding, and restoring information from local storage using `try` and `catch` for testing if coding is recognized
- using `join` and `split` to encode and decode information
- using `javascript:` in a button to invoke functions
- radio buttons

Introduction

In this chapter, we'll continue our exploration of programming techniques and HTML5 and JavaScript features, this time using programs that build and traverse mazes. Players will have the ability to draw a set of walls to make up a maze. They will be able to save and load their mazes, and to traverse them using collision detection to make sure they don't cross any walls.

The general programming techniques include using arrays for everything that needs to be drawn on the canvas as well as a separate array for the set of walls in the maze. The number of walls is not known before play starts, so a flexible approach is required. Once the maze is constructed, we'll see how to respond to presses of the arrow keys and how to detect collisions between the playing piece—a pentagon-shaped token—and the walls. With HTML5, we can handle mouse events so the player can press the mouse button down and then drag and release the button to define each wall of a maze; respond to the arrow keys to move the token; and save and retrieve the layout of walls on the local computer. As usual, we'll build more than one version of the application. In the first, everything is contained in one HTML file. That is, the player builds a maze, can travel through it, and can optionally save it to the local computer or restore a set of walls saved earlier. In the second version, there's one program to create the mazes and a second file that offers the player a choice of specific mazes to traverse, using radio buttons. Perhaps one person might build the mazes on a given computer and then ask a friend to try traversing them.

HTML5's local storage facility accepts only strings of characters, and so we'll look at how we can use JavaScript to encode the maze information into a character string and then decode it back to rebuild the walls of the maze. The saved information will remain on the computer even after it is turned off.

The individual capabilities we'll discuss in this chapter: building structures, using the arrow keys to move a game piece, checking for collisions, and encoding, saving, and restoring data on the user's computer, can all be reused in a variety of games and design applications.

Note: HTML files are generally called scripts, while the term program is typically reserved for languages such as Java or C. This is because JavaScript is an interpreted language: the statements are translated one at a time at execution time. In contrast, Java and C programs are compiled, that is, completely translated all at once, with the result stored for later use. Some of us are not so strict and use the terms script, program, application, or, simply, file for HTML documents with JavaScript.

Figure 7-1 shows the opening screen for both the all-in-one program and the first script of the second program.

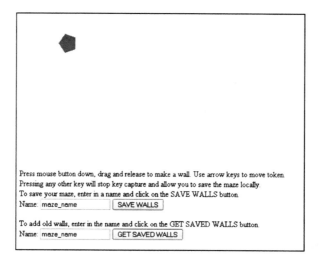

Figure 7-1. Opening screen for the maze game

Figure 7-2 shows the screen after some fairly sloppy walls have been placed on the canvas.

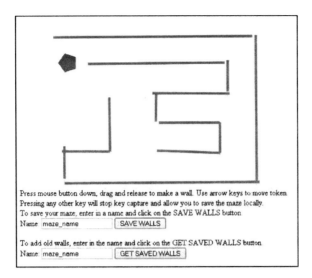

Figure 7-2. Walls for a maze

Figure 7-3 shows the screen after the player has used the arrow keys to move the token into the maze.

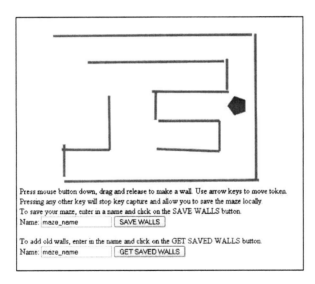

Figure 7-3. Moving the token inside the maze

If the player wants to save a set of walls, he or she types in a name and clicks on the button. To retrieve the walls, which are added to whatever is currently on the canvas, the player types in a name and presses the GET SAVED WALLS button. If there's nothing saved under that name, nothing happens.

The two-script application has the second script present the player with a choice. Figure 7-4 shows the opening screen.

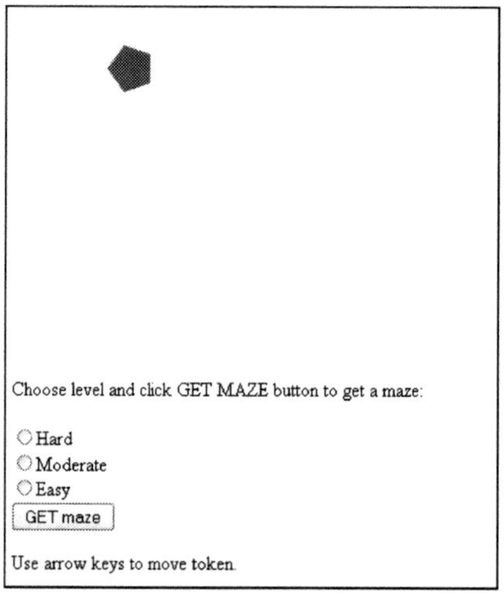

Figure 7-4. Opening screen of the travelmaze script

The two-script application assumes that someone has used the first script to create and save three mazes with the specific names used in the second script. Furthermore, the same browser must be used for creating a maze and for the travel maze activities. I do this to demonstrate the local storage facility of HTML5, which is similar to cookies—a way for Web application developers to store information about users.

Note: Cookies, and now HTML5 localStorage, are the basis of what is termed behavioral marketing. They bring convenience to us—we don't have to remember certain items of information such as passwords—but they are also a way to be tracked and the target of sales. I am not taking a position here, just noting the facility.

Figure 7-5 shows an easy maze.

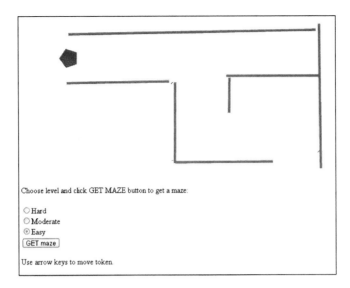

Figure 7-5. An easy maze

Figure 7-6 shows a slightly more difficult maze.

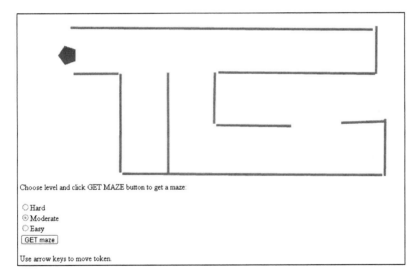

Figure 7-6. A moderate maze

Figure 7-7 shows a more difficult maze, more difficult mainly because the player needs to move away from the first entry point toward the bottom of the maze to make it through. Of course, it is up to the player/creator to design the mazes.

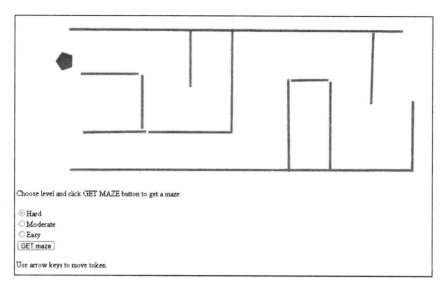

Figure 7-7. A harder maze

One important feature is that in the two-script application, clicking the GET maze button forces the current maze to be erased and the newly selected maze to be drawn. This is different from what happens in either the all-in-one program or the creation part of the second version, when old walls are added to what is present. As has been the case for the other examples, these are just stubs of programs, created to demonstrate HTML5 features and programming techniques. There is much opportunity for improvement to make the projects your own.

Critical requirements

The maze application requires the display of a constantly updated game board, as new walls are erected and the token is moved.

The maze-building task requires responding to mouse events to collect the information needed to build a wall. The application displays the wall being built.

The maze-traveling task requires responding to the arrow keys to move the token. The game must not allow the token to cross any wall.

The save and retrieve operations require the program to encode the wall information, save it on the local computer, and then retrieve it and use it to create and display the saved walls. Mazes are moderately complex structures: a set of some number of walls, with each wall defined by starting and ending coordinates, that is, pairs of numbers representing x,y positions on the canvas. For the local storage facility to be used, this information has to be turned into a single string of characters.

The two-document version makes use of radio buttons to select a maze.

HTML5, CSS, and JavaScript features

Now let's take a look at the specific features of HTML5 and JavaScript that provide what we need to implement the maze application. This builds on material covered in previous chapters: the general structure of an HTML document; using programmer-defined functions, including programmer-defined objects; drawing paths made up of line segments on a `canvas` element; programmer objects; and arrays. Previous chapters have addressed mouse events on the canvas (the cannonball and slingshot games in Chapter 4 and the memory game in Chapter 5) and mouse events on HTML elements (the quiz games in Chapter 6). New features we'll be covering include a different type of event: getting input from a player pressing on the arrow keys, called *keystroke capture*; and using local storage to save information on the local computer, even after the browser has been closed and the computer turned off. Remember, you can skip ahead to the "Building the Application" section to see all the code with comments and return to this section to read explanations of individual features and techniques.

Representation of walls and the token

To start, we'll define a function, `Wall`, to define a wall object, and another function, `Token`, to define a token object. We'll define these functions in a more general manner than required by this application, but I believe this is okay: the generality does not affect much, if anything, in terms of performance, while giving us the freedom to use the code for other applications, such as a game with different playing pieces. I chose the pentagon shape because I liked it, and use `mypent` as the variable name for the playing piece.

The properties defined for a wall consist of the start and finish points specified by the mouse actions. I name these `sx`, `sy`, `fx`, and `fy`. The wall also has a `width` and a `strokestyle` string, and a `draw` method is specified as `drawAline`. The reason this is more general than necessary is because all walls will have the same width and style string, and all will use the `drawAline` function. When it comes time to save the walls to local storage, I save only the `sx`, `sy`, `fx`, and `fy` values. You can use the same techniques to encode more information if and when you write other programs and need to store values.

The token that moves around the maze is defined by a call to the `Token` function. This function is similar to the `Polygon` function defined for the polygon memory game. The `Token` function stores the center of the token, `sx` and `sy`, along with a radius (`rad`), number of sides (`n`), a `fillstyle`, and it links to the `drawtoken` function for the `draw` method and the `movetoken` function for the `moveit` method. In addition, a property named `angle` is computed immediately as `(2*Math.PI)/n`. Recall that in the radian system for measuring angles, 2*Math.PI represents a full circle, so this number divided by the number of sides will be the angle from the center to the ends of each side.

As was the case with previous applications (see Chapter 4), after an object is created, the code adds it to the `everything` array. I also add all walls to the `walls` array. It is this array that is used to save the wall information to local storage.

Mouse events to build and position a wall

Recall that in previous chapters we used HTML5 and JavaScript to define an event and specify an event handler. The `init` function contains code that sets up event handling for the player pressing the main mouse button, moving the mouse, and releasing the button.

```
canvas1 = document.getElementById('canvas');
canvas1.addEventListener('mousedown',startwall,false);
```

```
canvas1.addEventListener('mousemove',stretchwall,false);
canvas1.addEventListener('mouseup',finish,false);
```

We'll also use a variable called inmotion to keep track of whether or not the mouse button is down. The startwall function determines the mouse coordinates (see Chapters 4 and 5 for accessing the mouse coordinates after an event), creates a new Wall object with a reference stored in the global variable curwall, adds the wall to the everything array, draws all the items in everything, and sets inmotion to be true. If inmotion is not true, then the stretchwall function returns immediately without doing anything. If inmotion is true, the code gets the mouse coordinates and uses them to set the fx and fy values of curwall. This happens over and over as the player moves the mouse with the button pressed down. When the button is released, the function finish is called. This function sets inmotion back to false and adds the curwall to an array called walls.

Detecting the arrow keys

Detecting that a key on the keyboard has been pressed and determining which one is called *capturing* a key stroke. This is another type of event that HTML5 and JavaScript can handle. We need to set up a response to a key event, which is analogous to setting up a response to a mouse event. The coding starts with invoking the addEventListener method, this time for the window:

```
window.addEventListener('keydown',getkeyAndMove,false);
```

The window is the object that holds the document defined by the HTML file. The third parameter, which could be omitted because false is the default, relates to the order of responding to the event by other objects. It isn't an issue for this application.

This means the getkeyAndMove function will be invoked if and when a key is pressed.

> Tip: Event handling is a big part of programming. Event-based programming is often more complex than demonstrated in this book. For example, you may need to consider if a contained object or a containing object also should respond to the event, or what to do if the user has multiple windows open. Devices such as cell phones can detect events such as tilting or shaking or using your fingers to stroke the screen. Incorporating video may involve invoking certain actions when the video is complete. HTML5 JavaScript is not totally consistent in handling events (setting up a time out or a time interval does not use addEventListener), but at this point, you know enough to do research to identify the event you want, try multiple possibilities to figure out what the event needs to be associated with (e.g., the window or a canvas element or some other object), and then write the function to be the event handler.

Now, as you may expect at this point, the coding to get the information for which key was pressed involves different code for different browsers. The following code, with two ways to get the number corresponding to the key, works in all current browsers recognizing other new features in HTML5:

```
if(event == null)
  {
    keyCode = window.event.keyCode;
        window.event.preventDefault();
  }
  else
```

```
{
  keyCode = event.keyCode;
      event.preventDefault();
}
```

The `preventDefault` method does what it sounds like: prevents any default action, such as a special shortcut action that is associated with the particular key in the particular browser. The only keys of interest in this application are the arrow keys. The following `switch` statement moves the `Token` referenced by the variable `mypent`; that is, the location information is changed so that the next time everything is drawn, the token will move. (This isn't quite true. The `moveit` function contains a collision check to make sure we don't hit any walls first, but that will be described later.)

```
switch(keyCode)
  {
  case 37:   //left arrow
    mypent.moveit(-unit,0);
    break;
  case 38:   //up arrow
    mypent.moveit(0,-unit);
     break;
   case 39: //right arrow
 mypent.moveit(unit,0);
     break;
  case 40:   //down arrow
    mypent.moveit(0,unit);
    break;
  default:
    window.removeEventListener('keydown',getkeyAndMove,false);
}
```

> Tip: Do put comments in your code as demonstrated by the comments indicating the keyCode for the different arrow keys. The examples in this book don't have comments because I've supplied an explanation for every line of code in the relevant tables, so this is a case of do as I say, not as I (mostly) do. Comments are critical for team projects and for reminding you of what's going on when you return to old work. In JavaScript, you can use the // to indicate that the rest of the line is a comment or surround multiple lines with /* and */. Comments are ignored by the JavaScript interpreter.

How did I know that the keycode for the left arrow was 37? You can look up keycodes on the Web (for example, `www.w3.org/2002/09/tests/keys.html`) or you can write code that issues an alert statement:

```
alert(" You just pressed keycode "+keyCode);
```

The default action for our maze application, which occurs when the key is not one of the four arrow keys, stops event handling on key strokes. The assumption here is that the player wants to type in a name to save or retrieve wall information to or from local storage. In many applications, the appropriate action to take would be a message, possibly using `alert`, to let the user know what the expected keys are.

Collision detection: token and any wall

To traverse a maze, the player must not move the token across any wall. We will enforce this restriction by writing a function, `intersect`, that returns true if a circle with given center and radius intersects a line segment. For this task, we need to be exacting in our language: a line segment is part of a line, going from `sx`, `sy` to `fx`, `fy`. Each wall corresponds to a finite line segment. The line itself is infinite. The `intersect` function is called for each wall in the array `walls`.

Tip: My explanation of the mathematics in the intersection calculation is fairly brief, but may be daunting if you haven't done any math in a while. Feel free to skip over it and accept the coding as is if you don't want to work through it.

The `intersect` function is based on the idea of a parameterized line. Specifically, the parameterized form of a line is (writing mathematical formula, as opposed to code)

Equation a: x = sx + t*(fx-sx);

Equation b: y = sy + t*(fy-sy);

As parameter t goes from 0 to 1, the x and y take on the corresponding values of x, y on the line segment. The goal is to determine if a circle with center cx,cy and radius rad overlaps the line segment. One way to do this is to determine the closest point on the line to cx,cy and see if the distance from that point is less than rad. In Figure 7-8, you see a sketch of part of a line with the line segment depicted with a solid line and the rest of what is shown of the line indicated by dots. The value of t at one end is 0 and the other end is 1.There are two points c1x,c1y and c2x, c2y. The c1x,c1y point is closest to the line outside the critical line segment. The point c2x,c2y is closest somewhere in the middle of the line segment. The value of t would be between 0 and 1.

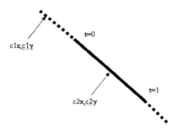

Figure 7-8. A line segment and two points

The formula for the distance between the two points (x,y) and (cx,cy) is

$$\text{distance} = ((cx-x)*(cx-x)+(cy-y)*(cy-y)).5$$

Substituting for x and for y using equations a and b, we get a formula for distance.

Equation c: distance = ((cx-sx+t*(fx-sx))*(cx- sx + t*(fx-sx))+(cy- sy + t*(fy-sy))*(cy- sy + t*(fy-sy)))$^{.5}$

For our purposes, we want to determine the value of t when distance is at a minimum. Lessons from calculus and reasoning about minimum versus maximum in this situation tell us first that we can use the distance squared in place of the distance and so avoid taking square roots. Moreover, the value is at a minimum when the derivative (with respect to t) is zero. Taking the derivative and setting that expression to zero, produces the value of t at which the cx,cy is closest to the line. In the code, we define two extra variables, dx and dy, to make the expressions simpler.

dx = fx-sx

dy = fy-sy;

t= 0.0 −((sx-cx)*dx+(xy-cy)*dy)/((dx*dx)+(dy*dy))

This will produce a value for t. The 0.0 is used to force the calculations to be done as floating point numbers (numbers with fractional parts, not restricted to whole numbers).

We use equations a and b to get the x,y point corresponding to the value of t. This is the x,y closest to cx,cy. If the value of t is less than 0, we check the value for t = 0, and if it is more than 1, we check the value for t = 1. This means that the closest point was not a point on the line segment, so we will check the appropriate end of the line segment closest to that point.

Is the distance from cx,cy to the closest point close enough to be called a collision? We again use distance squared and not distance. We evaluate the distance squared from cx, cy to the computed x,y. If it is less than the radius squared, there is an intersection of the circle with the line segment. If not, there is no intersection. Using the distance squared does not make a difference: if there is a minimum for the value squared, then there is a minimum for the value.

Now the very good news here is that most of the equations are not part of the coding. I did the work beforehand of determining the expression for the derivative. The intersect function follows, with comments:

```
function intersect(sx,sy,fx,fy,cx,cy,rad) {
   var dx;
   var dy;
   var t;
   var rt;
   dx = fx-sx;
   dy = fy-sy;
   t =0.0-((sx-cx)*dx+(sy-cy)*dy)/((dx*dx)+(dy*dy));   //closest t
   if (t<0.0) { //closest beyond the line segment at the start
     t=0.0; }
   else if (t>1.0) {   //closest beyond the line segment at the end
     t = 1.0;
   }

   dx = (sx+t*(fx-sx))-cx; // use t to define an x coordinate
   dy = (sy +t*(fy-sy))-cy; // use t to define a y coordinate
   rt = (dx*dx) +(dy*dy);   //distance squared
   if (rt<(rad*rad)) {   // closer than radius squared?
       return true; }    // intersect
else {
```

```
        return false;}    // does not intersect
}
```

In our application, the player presses an arrow key and, based on that key, the next position of the token is calculated. We call the `intersect` function to see if there would be an intersection of the token (approximated as a circle) and a wall. If `intersect` returns `true`, the token is not moved. The checking stops as soon as there is an intersection. This is a common technique for collision checking.

Using local storage

The Web was originally designed for files being downloaded from the server to the local, so-called client computer for viewing, but with no permanent storage on the local computer. Over time, people and organizations building web sites decided that some sort of local storage would be advantageous. So, someone came up with the idea of using small files called *cookies* to keep track of things, such as user IDs stored for the convenience of the user as well as the web site owner. The use of cookies, Flash's shared objects, and now HTML5 local storage has grown considerably with the commercial Web. Unlike the situation for the applications shown here, the user often does not know that information is being stored and by whom, and for what purpose the information is accessed.

The `localStorage` facility of HTML5 is browser-specific. That is, a maze saved using Chrome is not available to someone using FireFox.

Let's take a closer look at using local storage by examining a small application that saves date and time information. Local storage and the `Date` function, introduced in Chapter 1, provide a way to store date/time information. Think of local storage as a database in which strings of characters are stored, each under a specific name. The name is called the *key*, the string itself is the *value,* and the system is called *key/value pairs*. The fact that local storage just stores strings is a restriction, but the next section shows how to work around it.

Figure 7-9 shows a screen shot from the opening screen of a simple date saving application.

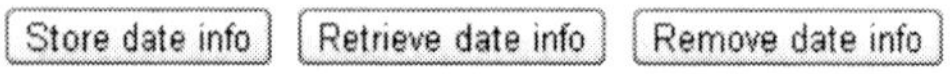

Figure 7-9. A simple save date application

The user has three options: store information on the current date and time, retrieve the last information saved, and remove the date information. Figure 7-10 shows what happens when clicking "Retrieve date info" the very first time using this application (or after the date has been removed).

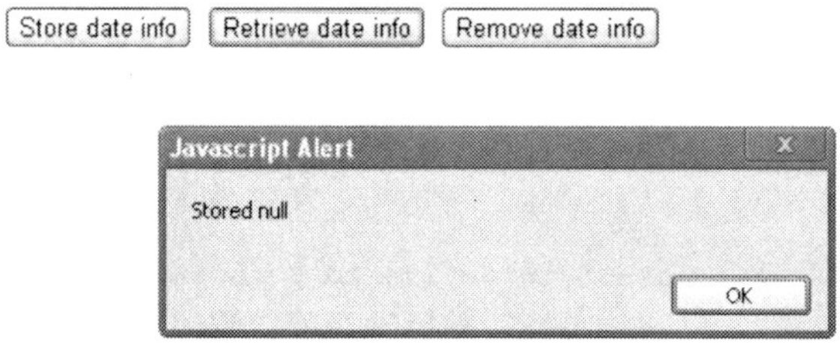

Figure 7-10. Data not yet saved or after removal

Our application uses a JavaScript alert box to show a message. The user needs to click the OK button to remove the alert box from the screen.

Figure 7-11 shows the message after a user clicks the Store date info button.

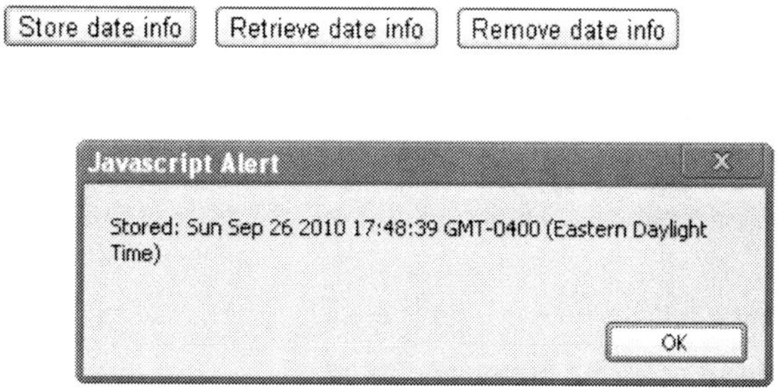

Figure 7-11. After storing date information

If the user later clicks on the Retrieve date info button, he'll see a message similar to Figure 7-12.

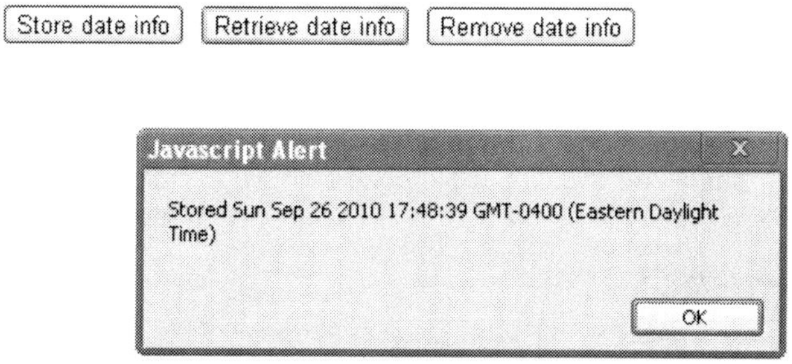

Figure 7-12. Retrieving the stored date information

You can give your players a way to remove the stored information using a Remove date info button. Figure 7-13 shows the result.

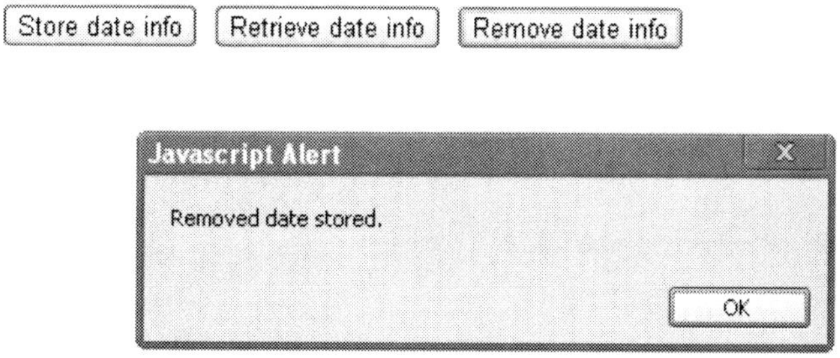

Figure 7-13. After removing stored information

HTML5 lets you save, fetch, and remove a key/value pair, using methods for the built-in object `localStorage`.

The command `localStorage.setItem("lastdate",olddate)` sets up a new key/value pair or replaces any previous one with the key equal to `lastdate`. The statement

```
last = localStorage.getItem("lastdate");
```

assigns the fetched value to the variable `last`. In the code for our simple example, we just display the results. You can also check for something being null and provide a friendlier message.

The command `localStorage.removeItem("lastdate")` removes the key/value pair with `lastdate` as the key.

For our simple date application, we set the `onClick` attribute of each button object to be some JavaScript code. For example:

```
<button onClick="javascript:store();">Store date info. </button>
```

causes `store()` to be invoked when the button is clicked.

You may be wondering if anyone can read any of the saved information in local storage. The answer is that access to each key/value pair in `localStorage` (and in other types of cookies) is restricted to the Web site that stored the information. This is a security feature.

The Chrome browser allows testing of local storage with HTML5 scripts stored on the local computer. Firefox does not. This means that to test these applications in Firefox, you'll need to upload the file to a server.

Because browsers may not support local storage or there may be other problems such as exceeding limits set by the user for local storage and cookies, it is a good practice to include some error checking. You can use the JavaScript function `typeof` to check if `localStorage` is accepted by the browser:

```
if (typeof(localStorage)=="undefined")
```

Figure 7-14 shows the result of loading the date application and clicking on the Store date info button in an old version of Internet Explorer. (By the time you read this book, the latest version of IE may be out and this will not be a problem.)

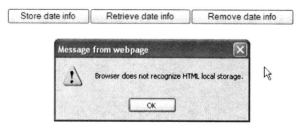

Figure 7-14. The browser didn't recognize `localStorage`.

JavaScript also provides a general mechanism for avoiding the display of errors. The compound statement `try` and `catch` will `try` to execute some code and if it doesn't work, go to the `catch` clause.

```
try {
        olddate = new Date();
        localStorage.setItem("lastdate",olddate);
```

```
        alert("Stored: "+olddate);
 }
 catch(e) {
         alert("Error with use of local storage: "+e);}
 }
```

If you removed the if (typeof(localStorage) test and tried the code in the old IE, you'd see the message shown in Figure 7-15.

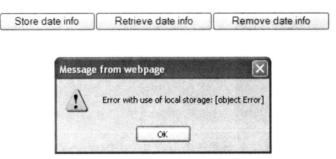

Figure 7-15. Browser error, caught in a try/catch

The Table 7-1 shows the complete date application. Remember: you may need to upload this to a server to test it.

Table 7-1. Complete Code for the Date Application

Code	Explanation
`<html>`	Opening html tag
`<head>`	Opening head tag
`<title>Local Storage test</title>`	Complete title
`<script>`	Opening script
`function store() {`	Store function header
`        if (typeof(localStorage) == "undefined") {`	Check if localStorage recognized
`        alert("Browser does not recognize HTML local storage.");`	Display alert message
`}`	Close if clause
`else {`	Else

Code	Explanation
`try {`	Set up try clause
`olddate = new Date();`	Define new Date
`localStorage.setItem("lastdate",olddate);`	Store in local storage using the key "lastdate"
`alert("Stored: "+olddate);`	Display message to show what was stored
`}`	Close try clause
`Catch(e) {`	Start catch clause: if there was a problem
`alert("Error with use of local storage: "+e);}`	Display message
`}`	Close try clause
`Return false;`	Return false to prevent any page refresh
`}`	Close function
`function remove() {`	Remove function header
`if (typeof(localStorage) == "undefined") {`	Check if localStorage recognized
`alert("Browser does not recognize HTML local storage.");`	Display alert message
`}`	Close if clause
`else {`	Else
`localStorage.removeItem('lastdate');`	Remove the item stored using the key 'lastdate'.
`alert("Removed date stored.");`	Display message indicating what was done

Code	Explanation
`}`	Close clause
`    return false;`	Return `false` to prevent page refresh.
`}`	Close function
`function fetch() {`	Fetch function header
`        if (typeof(localStorage) == "undefined")` `{`	Check if `localStorage` recognized.
`        alert("Browser does not recognize HTML` `local storage.");`	Display `alert` message
`}`	Close `if` clause
`else {`	Else
`                alert("Stored` `"+localStorage.getItem('lastdate'));`	Fetch the item stored under the key `'lastdate'` and display it.
`    }`	Close clause
`    return false;`	Return `false` to prevent page refresh.
`}`	Close function
`</script>`	Close `script` element
`</head>`	Close `head` element
`<body>`	Opening `body` tag
`<button onClick="javascript:store();">Store date info` `</button>`	Button for storing
`<button onClick="javascript:fetch();">Retrieve date` `info </button>`	Button for retrieving, that is, fetching the stored data.
`<button onClick="javascript:remove();">Remove date` `info </button>`	Button for removing

Code	Explanation
`</body>`	Closing `body` tag
`</html>`	Closing `html` tag

Combining the `Date` function with `localStorage` lets you do many things. For example, you can calculate the elapsed time between a player's current and last use of the application or, perhaps, the player winning two games. In Chapter 5, we used `Date` to compute the elapsed time using the `getTime` method. Recall that `getTime` stores the number of milliseconds from January 1, 1970. You can convert that value to a string, store it, and then when you fetch it back, do arithmetic to calculate elapsed time.

The localStorage key/value pairs last until they are removed, unlike JavaScript cookies, for which you can set a duration.

Encoding data for local storage

For simplicity's sake, the first application consists of just one HTML document. You can use this version to create mazes, store and retrieve them, and move the token through the maze. The second version of the application involves two HTML documents. One script is the same as the first application and can be used for building, traversing, and saving mazes as well as traveling each maze. The second script is just for traveling one of a fixed list of saved mazes. A set of radio buttons allows the player to pick from easy, moderate, and hard options, assuming someone has created and saved mazes with the names *easymaze, moderatemaze,* and *hardmaze*. These names can be anything you want and as many as you want. You just need to be consistent between what you create in one program and what you reference in the second program.

Now let's address the issue that `localStorage` just stores character strings. The applications described here must store enough information about the walls so that these walls can be added to the canvas. In the one-document version, the old walls are actually added to whatever is on the canvas. The two-document version erases any old maze and loads the requested one. I use two forms, each with an input field for the name and a submit button. The player chooses the name for saving a maze and must remember it for retrieving.

The data to be stored is a character string, that is, a piece of text. We will create the text holding the information for a set of walls by doing the following for each wall:

- Combine the `sx`, `sy`, `fx`, `fy` into an array called `w` for a single wall.
- Using the `join` method, use the `w` array to generate a string separated by + signs.
- Add each of these strings to an array called `allw`, for all the walls.
- Using the `join` method again, use the `allw` array to produce a string called `sw`.

The `sw` string variable will hold all the coordinates (four numbers for each wall) for all the walls. The next step is to use the `localStorage.setItem` method to store `sw` under the name given by the player. We do this using the `try` and `catch` construction explained in the last section.

```
try {
    localStorage.setItem(lsname,sw);
}
```

```
catch (e) {
    alert("data not saved, error given: "+e);
}
```

This is a general technique that will try something, suppress any error message, and if there is an error, it will invoke the code in the catch block.

> Note: This may not always work as you intend. For example, when executing this application on Firefox directly on a computer, as opposed to a file downloaded from a server, the `localStorage` statement does not cause an error, but nothing is stored. This code does work when the HTML file is downloaded from a server using Firefox and the creation script works both as a local file and when downloaded using Chrome. The two-script version must be tested using a server for each of the browsers.

Retrieving the information works in a corresponding way. The code extracts the name given by the player to set the variable `lsname` and then uses

```
swalls = localStorage.getItem(lsname);
```

to set the variable `swalls`. If this is not null, we use the string method `split` to do the opposite of join: split the string on the symbol given (we split at every semicolon) and assign the values to the successive elements of an array. The relevant lines are

```
wallstgs = swalls.split(";");
```

and

```
sw = wallstgs.split("+");
```

Next, the code uses the information just retrieved and the fixed information for wall width and wall style to create a new `Wall` object:

```
curwall = new Wall(sx,sy,fx,fy,wallwidth,wallstyle);
```

Finally, there is code to add `curwall` to both the `everything` array and the `walls` array.

Radio buttons

Radio buttons are sets of buttons in which only one member of the set can be selected. If the player makes a new choice, the old choice is deselected. They are an appropriate choice for the hard/moderate/easy selection for this application. Here's the HTML markup in the `<body>` section:

```
<form name="gf" onSubmit="return getwalls()" >
<br/>
<input type="radio" value="hard" name="level" />Hard <br/>
<input type="radio" value="moderate" name="level" />Moderate <br/>
<input type="radio" value="easy" name="level" />Easy<br/>
<input type="submit" value="GET maze"/><br/>
</form>
```

Notice that all three input elements have the same name. This is what defines the group of buttons of which only one may be selected. In this case, the markup creates an array called `level`. The `getwalls` function will be shown in full in the next section. It is similar to the function in the all-in-one script. However, in this case, the name of the `localStorage` item is determined from the radio buttons. The code is

```
for (i=0;i<document.gf.level.length;i++) {
 if (document.gf.level[i].checked) {
     lsname= document.gf.level[i].value+"maze";
        break;
    }
}
```

The `for` loop iterates over all the input items. The `if` test is based on the `checked` attribute. When it detects a true condition, the variable `lsname` is constructed from the value attribute of that item, and the `break;` statement causes execution to leave the `for` loop. If you want your radio buttons to start with one of the items checked, use code like this:

```
<input type="radio" value="easy" name="level" checked />
```

or

```
<input type="radio" value="easy" name="level" checked="true" />
```

Building the application and making it your own

Now let's take a look at the coding for the maze applications, first the all-in-one script and then the second script of the two-script version.

Table 7-2 shows the functions in the script for creating, saving, and retrieving, and traveling the maze. Notice that much of the invoking of functions is done through event handling: `onLoad`, `onSubmit`, `addEventListener` calls. These do not invoke the functions directly or immediately, but set up the call to be made when the indicated event occurs.

Table 7-2. Functions in the Maze Application

Function	Invoked By / Called By	Calls
init	Invoked by action of onLoad in body tag	drawall
drawall	init startwall stretchwall getkeyAndMove getwalls	draw method for Walls and for token: drawtoken and drawAline
Token	var statement declaring mypent	
Wall	startwall	

Function	Invoked By / Called By	Calls
drawtoken	drawwall using draw method for the token object in the everything array	
movetoken	getkeyAndMove using the moveit method for mypent	intersect
drawAline	drawwall using draw method for Wall objects in the everything array	
startwall	Invoked by action of an addEventListener call in init	drawwall
stretchwall	Invoked by action of an addEventListener call in init	drawwall
finish	Invoked by action of an addEventListener call in init	
getkeyAndMove	Invoked by action of an addEventListener call in init	movetoken using the moveit method for mypent
savewalls	Invoked by action of onSubmit for the sf form	
getwalls	Invoked by action of onSubmit for the gf form	drawwall

Table 7-3 shows the complete code for the maze application, with comments.

Table 7-3. Complete Code for the All-in-one Maze Application

Code	Explanation
`<html>`	Opening html tag
`<head>`	Opening head tag
`<title>Build maze & travel maze</title>`	Complete title element
`<script type="text/javascript">`	Opening script tag
`var cwidth = 900;`	To clear canvas
`var cheight = 350;`	To clear canvas
`var ctx;`	To hold canvas context

Code	Explanation
`var everything = [];`	To hold everything
`var curwall;`	For wall in progress
`var wallwidth = 5;`	Fixed wall width
`var wallstyle = "rgb(200,0,200)";`	Fixed wall color
`var walls = [];`	Hold all walls
`var inmotion = false;`	Flag while wall being built by dragging
`var unit = 10;`	Unit of movement for token
`function Token(sx,sy,rad,stylestring,n) {`	Function header to build token
`this.sx = sx;`	Set `sx` property
`this.sy = sy;`	... `sy`
`this.rad = rad;`	... `rad` (radius)
`this.draw = drawtoken;`	Set the `draw` method
`this.n = n;`	... `n` number of sides
`this.angle = (2*Math.PI)/n`	Compute and set angle
`this.moveit = movetoken;`	Set `moveit` method
`this.fillstyle = stylestring;`	Set color
`}`	Close function
`function drawtoken() {`	Function header drawtoken
`ctx.fillStyle=this.fillstyle;`	Set color
`var i;`	Index
`var rad = this.rad;`	Set `rad`

Code	Explanation
`ctx.beginPath();`	Begin path
`ctx.moveTo(this.sx+rad*Math.cos➥` `(-.5*this.angle),this.sy+rad*Math.sin➥` `(-.5*this.angle));`	Move to first vertex of the token polygon (which is a pentagon)
`for (i=1;i<this.n;i++) {`	For loop to draw the n sides of the token: 5 sides in this case
`ctx.lineTo(this.sx+rad*Math.cos➥` `((i-.5)*this.angle),this.sy+rad*Math.sin➥` `((i-.5)*this.angle));`	Specify line to next vertex, setting up the drawing of a side of the pentagon
`}`	Close `for`
`ctx.fill();`	Draw token
`}`	Close function
`function movetoken(dx,dy) {`	Function header
`this.sx +=dx;`	Increment x value
`this.sy +=dy;`	Increment y value
`var i;`	Index
`var wall;`	Used for each wall
`for(i=0;i<walls.length;i++) {`	Loop over all walls
`wall = walls[i];`	Extract i[th] wall
`if (intersect(wall.sx,➥` `wall.sy,wall.fx,wall.fy,this.sx,this.sy,➥` `this.rad)) {`	Check for intersect. If there is an intersection between the new position of the token and this specific wall
`this.sx -=dx;`	… change x back—don't make this move
`this.sy -=dy;`	… change y back—don't make this move
`break;`	Leave `for` loop because it isn't necessary to do any more checking if there is a collision with one wall.

Code	Explanation
`        }`	Close if true clause
`    }`	Close for loop
`}`	Close function
`function Wall(sx,sy,fx,fy,width,stylestring) {`	Function header to make Wall
`    this.sx = sx;`	Set up sx property
`    this.sy = sy;`	... sy
`    this.fx = fx;`	... fx
`    this.fy = fy;`	... fy
`    this.width = width;`	... width
`    this.draw = drawAline;`	Set draw method
`    this.strokestyle = stylestring;`	... strokestyle
`}`	Close function
`function drawAline() {`	Function header drawAline
`    ctx.lineWidth = this.width;`	Set the line width
`    ctx.strokeStyle = this.strokestyle;`	Set the strokestyle
`    ctx.beginPath();`	Begin path
`    ctx.moveTo(this.sx,this.sy);`	Move to start of line
`    ctx.lineTo(this.fx,this.fy);`	Set line to finish
`    ctx.stroke();`	Draw the line
`}`	Close function
`var mypent = new Token(100,100,20,"rgb(0,0,250)",5);`	Set up mypent as a pentagonal shape to be the playing piece
`everything.push(mypent);`	Add to everything

Code	Explanation
`function init(){`	Function header init
`    ctx = document.getElementById↪('canvas').getContext('2d');`	Define the `ctx` (context) for all drawing
`    canvas1 = document.getElementById('canvas');`	Define `canvas1`, used for events
`    canvas1.addEventListener('mousedown',↪startwall,false);`	Set up handling for `mousedown`
`    canvas1.addEventListener('mousemove',↪stretchwall,false);`	Set up handling for `mousemove`
`    canvas1.addEventListener('mouseup',finish,↪false);`	Set up handling for `mouseup`
`    window.addEventListener('keydown',↪getkeyAndMove,false);`	Set up handling for use of the arrow keys
`    drawall();`	Draw everything
`}`	Close function
`function startwall(ev) {`	Function header `startwall`
`    var mx;`	Hold mouse x
`    var my;`	Hold mouse y
`    if ( ev.layerX ||  ev.layerX == 0) {`	Can we use `layerX` to determine the position of the mouse? Necessary because browsers are different.
`        mx= ev.layerX;`	Set mx
`        my = ev.layerY;`	Set my
`    } else if (ev.offsetX↪|| ev.offsetX == 0) {`	Else can we use `offsetX`?
`        mx = ev.offsetX;`	Set mx
`        my = ev.offsetY;`	Set my

Code	Explanation
`        }`	Close clause
`    curwall = new` `Wall(mx,my,mx+1,my+1,wallwidth,wallstyle);`	Create new wall. It is small at this point.
`    inmotion = true;`	Set inmotion to true
`    everything.push(curwall);`	Add curwall to everything
`    drawall();`	Draw everything
`}`	Close function
`function stretchwall(ev) {`	Function header stretchwall to that uses the dragging of the mouse to stretch out a wall while the mouse is dragged.
`    if (inmotion) {`	Check if inmotion
`      var mx;`	Hold mouse x
`      var my;`	Hold mouse y
`      if ( ev.layerX ||  ev.layerX == 0) {`	Can we use layerX?
`          mx= ev.layerX;`	Set mx
`        my = ev.layerY;`	Set my
`        } else if (ev.offsetX` ⮡ `|| ev.offsetX == 0) {`	Else can we use offsetX? This is necessary for different browsers.
`        mx = ev.offsetX;`	Set mx
`        my = ev.offsetY;`	Set my
`      }`	Close clause
`    curwall.fx = mx;`	Change curwall.fx to mx
`    curwall.fy = my;`	Change curwall.fy to my

Code	Explanation
`    drawall();`	Draw everything (will show growing wall)
`  }`	Close if `inmotion`
`}`	Close function
`function finish(ev) {`	Function header `finish`
`    inmotion = false;`	Set `inmotion` to false
`    walls.push(curwall);`	Add `curwall` to `walls`
`}`	Close function
`function drawall() {`	Function header `drawall`
`    ctx.clearRect(0,0,cwidth,cheight);`	Erase whole canvas
`    var i;`	Index
`    for (i=0;i<everything.length;i++) {`	Loop through `everything`
`        everything[i].draw();`	Draw `everything`
`    }`	Close loop
`}`	Close function
`function getkeyAndMove(event) {`	Function header `getkeyAndMove`
`  var keyCode;`	Hold `keyCode`
`  if(event == null) {`	If event `null`
`   keyCode = window.event.keyCode;`	Get `keyCode` using `window.event`
`    Window.event.preventDefault();`	Stop default action
`  }`	Close clause
`  else {`	Else

Code	Explanation
`keyCode = event.keyCode;`	Get `keyCode` from event
`event.preventDefault();`	Stop default action
`}`	Close clause
`switch(keyCode) {`	Switch on `keyCode`
`case 37:`	If left arrow
`mypent.moveit(-unit,0);`	Move back horizontally
`break;`	Leave switch
`case 38:`	If up arrow
`mypent.moveit(0,-unit);`	Move up screen
`break;`	Leave switch
`case 39:`	If right arrow
`mypent.moveit(unit,0);`	Move left
`break;`	Leave switch
`case 40:`	If down arrow
`mypent.moveit(0,unit);`	Move down screen
`break;`	Leave switch
`Default:`	Anything else
`window.removeEventListener('keydown',↪` `getkeyAndMove,false);`	Stop listening for keys. Assume player trying to save to local storage or retrieve from local storage.
`}`	Close switch
`Drawall();`	Draw everything

Code	Explanation
`}`	Close function
`Function intersect(sx,sy,fx,fy,cx,cy,rad) {`	Function header intersect
`var dx;`	For intermediate value
`var dy;`	For intermediate value
`var t;`	For expression in t
`var rt;`	For holding distance squared
`dx = fx-sx;`	Set x difference
`dy = fy-sy;`	Set y difference
`t =0.0-((sx-cx)*dx+(sy-cy)*dy)/↪` `((dx*dx)+(dy*dy));`	Taking the formula for the distance squared from each point to cx,cy. Take derivative and solve for 0.
`if (t<0.0) {`	If closest is at t <0
`t=0.0; }`	Check at 0 (this will be further)
`else if (t>1.0) {`	If closest is at t>1
`t = 1.0;`	Check at 1 (this will be further)
`}`	Close clause
`dx = (sx+t*(fx-sx))-cx;`	Compute difference at this value of t
`dy = (sy +t*(fy-sy))-cy;`	Compute difference at this value of t
`rt = (dx*dx) +(dy*dy);`	Compute distance squared
`if (rt<(rad*rad)) {`	Compare to rad squared
`Return true; }`	Return true
`else {`	Else

Code	Explanation
`    Return false;}`	Return false
`}`	Close function
`function savewalls() {`	Function `savewalls` header
`    var w = [];`	Temporary array
`    var allw=[];`	Temporary array
`    var sw;`	Hold final string
`    var onewall;`	Hold intermediate string
`    var i;`	Index
`    var lsname = document.sf.slname.value;`	Extract player's name for the local storage
`    for (i=0;i<walls.length;i++) {`	Loop over all walls
`        w.push(walls[i].sx);`	Add `sx` to `w` array
`        w.push(walls[i].sy);`	Add `sy` to `w` array
`        w.push(walls[i].fx);`	Add `fx` to `w` array
`        w.push(walls[i].fy);`	Add `fy` to `w` array
`        onewall = w.join("+");`	Make a string
`        allw.push(onewall);`	Add to `allw` array
`        w = [];`	Reset `w` to empty array
`    }`	Close loop
`    sw = allw.join(";");`	Now make `allw` into a string
`    try {`	Try
`        localStorage.setItem(lsname,sw);`	Save `localStorage`

Code	Explanation
`}`	End try
`catch (e) {`	If a catchable error
`alert("data not saved,↪` `error given: "+e);`	Display message
`}`	End catch clause
`return false;`	Return false to avoid refresh
`}`	Close function
`function getwalls() {`	Function header getwalls
`var swalls;`	Temporary storage
`var sw;`	Temporary storage
`var i;`	Index
`var sx;`	Hold the sw value
`var sy;`	Hold the sy value
`var fx;`	Hold the fx value
`var fy;`	Hold the fy value
`var curwall;`	Hold walls being created
`var lsname = document.gf.glname.value;`	Extract player's name for storage to be retrieved
`swalls=localStorage.getItem(lsname);`	Get the storage
`if (swalls!=null) {`	If something was fetched
`wallstgs = swalls.split(";");`	Split to make an array
`for (i=0;i<wallstgs.length;i++) {`	Loop through this array

Code	Explanation
`sw = wallstgs[i].split("+");`	Split individual item
`sx = Number(sw[0]);`	Extract 0th value and convert to number
`sy = Number(sw[1]);`	...1st
`fx = Number(sw[2]);`	...2nd
`fy = Number(sw[3]);`	...3rd
`curwall = new Wall(sx,sy,fx,fy,wallwidth,wallstyle);`	Create new `Wall` using extracted and fixed values
`walls.push(curwall);`	Add to `walls` array
`everything.push(curwall);`	Add to `everything` array
`}`	Close loop
`drawall();`	Draw everything
`}`	Close if not null
`Else {`	Was null
`alert("No data retrieved.");`	No data
`}`	Close clause
`window.addEventListener('keydown',↵ getkeyAndMove,false);`	Set up keydown action
`return false;`	Return false to prevent refresh
`}`	Close function
`</head>`	End head element
`<body onLoad="init();" >`	Start body, set up call to init
`<canvas id="canvas" width="900" height="350">`	Canvas tag
`Your browser doesn't support the HTML5 element canvas.`	Warning for certain browser.

Code	Explanation
`</canvas>`	Close canvas
` `	Line break
Press mouse button down, drag↦ and release to make a wall.	Instructions
Use arrow keys to move token. ` `	Instructions and line break
Pressing any other key will stop key↦ capture and allow you to save the↦ maze locally.	Instructions
`<form name="sf" onSubmit="return savewalls()" >`	Form tag, set up call to savewalls
To save your maze, enter in a name and↦ click on the SAVE WALLS button. ` `	Instructions
`Name: <input name="slname" value="maze_name" type="text">`	Label and input field
`<input type="submit" value="SAVE WALLS"/>`	Submit button
`</form>`	Close form
`<form name="gf" onSubmit="return↦ getwalls()" >`	Form tag, set up call to getwalls
To add old walls, enter in the name and↦ click on the GET SAVED WALLS button. ` `	Instructions
`Name: <input name="glname" value="maze_name" type="text">`	Label and input field
`<input type="submit" value="GET↦ SAVED WALLS"/>`	Submit button
`</form>`	Close form
`</body>`	Close body
`</html>`	Close html

Creating the second maze application

The localStorage data can be accessed by a different application from the one that created the data, as long as it is on the same server. This is a security feature, as mentioned previously, restricting readers of local storage to scripts on the same server.

The second script is based on this feature. Table 7-4 shows the functions calling or being called; it is a subset of the previous one.

Table 7-4. Functions in the Travel Maze Script

Function	Invoked By / Called By	Calls
init	Invoked by action of onLoad in body tag	drawall
drawall	Init startwall stretchwall getkeyAndMove getwalls	draw method for Walls and for token: drawtoken and drawAline
Token	var statement declaring mypent	
Wall	startwall	
drawtoken	drawall using draw method for the token object in the everything array	
movetoken	getkeyAndMove using the moveit method for mypent	intersect
drawAline	drawall using draw method for Wall objects in the everything array	
getkeyAndMove	Invoked by action of an addEventListener call in init	movetoken using the moveit method for mypent
getwalls	Invoked by action of onSubmit for the gf form	drawall

The functions are exactly the same as in the all-in-one script with one exception, the getwalls function, so I've only commented the new or changed code. This application also has radio buttons in place of the form input fields. Table 7-5 shows the complete code for the travelmaze application.

Table 7-5. Complete Code for the Travel Maze Script

Code	Explanation
`<html>`	
`<head>`	
`<title>Travel maze</title>`	Travel maze
`<script type="text/javascript">`	
`var cwidth = 900;`	
`var cheight = 350;`	
`var ctx;`	
`var everything = [];`	
`var curwall;`	
`var wallwidth = 5;`	
`var wallstyle = "rgb(200,0,200)";`	
`var walls = [];`	
`var inmotion = false;`	
`var unit = 10;`	
`function Token(sx,sy,rad,stylestring,n) {`	
`this.sx = sx;`	
`this.sy = sy;`	
`this.rad = rad;`	
`this.draw = drawtoken;`	
`this.n = n;`	

Code	Explanation
`this.angle = (2*Math.PI)/n`	
`this.moveit = movetoken;`	
`this.fillstyle = stylestring;`	
`}`	
`function drawtoken() {`	
`ctx.fillStyle=this.fillstyle;`	
`ctx.beginPath();`	
`var i;`	
`var rad = this.rad;`	
`ctx.beginPath();`	
`ctx.moveTo(this.sx+rad*Math.cos`↪`(-.5*this.angle),this.sy+rad*Math.sin`↪`(-.5*this.angle));`	
`for (i=1;i<this.n;i++) {`	
`ctx.lineTo(this.sx+rad*Math.cos`↪`((i-.5)*this.angle),this.sy+rad*Math.sin`↪`((i-.5)*this.angle));`	
`}`	
`ctx.fill();`	
`}`	
`function movetoken(dx,dy) {`	
`this.sx +=dx;`	
`this.sy +=dy;`	
`var i;`	

Code	Explanation
`    var wall;`	
`    for(i=0;i<walls.length;i++) {`	
`        wall = walls[i];`	

`            if (intersect(wall.sx,wall.sy,↪`
`wall.fx,wall.fy,this.sx,this.sy,`
`this.rad)) {`	

`            this.sx -=dx;`	
`            this.sy -=dy;`	
`            break;`	
`            }`	
`        }`	
`}`	
`function Wall(sx,sy,fx,fy,width,stylestring)` `{`	
`    this.sx = sx;`	
`    this.sy = sy;`	
`    this.fx = fx;`	
`    this.fy = fy;`	
`    this.width = width;`	
`    this.draw = drawAline;`	
`    this.strokestyle = stylestring;`	
`}`	
`function drawAline() {`	

Code	Explanation
`ctx.lineWidth = this.width;`	
`ctx.strokeStyle = this.strokestyle;`	
`ctx.beginPath();`	
`ctx.moveTo(this.sx,this.sy);`	
`ctx.lineTo(this.fx,this.fy);`	
`ctx.stroke();`	
`}`	
`var mypent = new Token(100,100,20,"rgb(0,0,250)",5);`	
`everything.push(mypent);`	
`function init(){`	
`ctx = document.getElementById('canvas')`↪ `.getContext('2d');`	
`window.addEventListener('keydown',`↪ `getkeyAndMove,false);`	
`drawall();`	
`}`	
`function drawall() {`	
`ctx.clearRect(0,0,cwidth,cheight);`	
`var i;`	
`for (i=0;i<everything.length;i++) {`	
`everything[i].draw();`	
`}`	

Code	Explanation
`}`	
`function getkeyAndMove(event) {`	
`  var keyCode;`	
`  if(event == null)`	
`  {`	
`    keyCode = window.event.keyCode;`	
`      window.event.preventDefault();`	
`  }`	
`  else`	
`  {`	
`    keyCode = event.keyCode;`	
`      event.preventDefault();`	
`  }`	
`  switch(keyCode)`	
`  {`	
`    case 37:  //left arrow`	
`    mypent.moveit(-unit,0);`	
`      break;`	
`    case 38:  //up arrow`	
`    mypent.moveit(0,-unit);`	
`      break;`	

Code	Explanation
case 39: //right arrow	
mypent.moveit(unit,0);	
break;	
case 40: //down arrow	
mypent.moveit(0,unit);	
break;	
default:	
window.removeEventListener↪('keydown',getkeyAndMove,false);	
}	
drawall();	
}	
function intersect(sx,sy,fx,fy,cx,cy,rad) {	
var dx;	
var dy;	
var t;	
var rt;	
dx = fx-sx;	
dy = fy-sy;	
t =0.0-((sx-cx)*dx+(sy-cy)*dy)/((dx*dx)+(dy*dy));	
if (t<0.0) {	

Code	Explanation
`    t=0.0; }`	
`else if (t>1.0) {`	
`    t = 1.0;`	
`  }`	
`dx = (sx+t*(fx-sx))-cx;`	
`dy = (sy +t*(fy-sy))-cy;`	
`rt = (dx*dx) +(dy*dy);`	
`if (rt<(rad*rad)) {`	
`    return true; }`	
`else {`	
`    return false;}`	
`}`	
`function getwalls() {`	
`    var swalls;`	
`    var sw;`	
`    var i;`	
`    var sx;`	
`    var sy;`	
`    var fx;`	
`    var fy;`	
`    var curwall;`	

Code	Explanation
`var lsname;`	
`for (i=0;i<document.gf.level.length;i++) {`	Iterate through the radio buttons in the gf form, level group
`if (document.gf.level[i].checked) {`	Is this radio button checked?
`lsname= document.gf.level[i].value+"maze";`	If so, construct the local storage name using the value attribute of the radio button element
`break;`	Leave the `for` loop
`}`	Close if
`}`	Close for
`swalls=localStorage.getItem(lsname);`	Fetch this item from local storage
`if (swalls!=null) {`	If it is not null, it is good data
`wallstgs = swalls.split(";");`	Extract the string for each wall
`walls = [];`	Removes any old walls from walls array
`everything = [];`	Removes any old walls from `everything` array
`everything.push(mypent);`	Do add the pentagon-shaped token called `mypent` to everything
`for (i=0;i<wallstgs.length;i++) {`	Proceed to decode each wall. The remaining code is the same as the all-in-one application.
`sw = wallstgs[i].split("+");`	
`sx = Number(sw[0]);`	
`sy = Number(sw[1]);`	
`fx = Number(sw[2]);`	
`fy = Number(sw[3]);`	

Code	Explanation
`        curwall = new` `Wall(sx,sy,fx,fy,wallwidth,wallstyle);`	
`        walls.push(curwall);`	
`        everything.push(curwall);`	
`      }`	
`      drawall();`	
`    }`	
`    else {`	
`        alert("No data retrieved.");`	
`    }`	
`    window.addEventListener('keydown',↪` `getkeyAndMove,false);`	
`    return false;`	
`}`	
`</script>`	
`</head>`	
`<body onLoad="init();" >`	
`<canvas id="canvas" width="900"` `height="350">`	
`Your browser doesn't support the HTML5` `element canvas.`	
`</canvas>`	
` `	
`Choose level and click GET MAZE button to↪` ` get a maze:`	

Code	Explanation
`<form name="gf" onSubmit="return getwalls()">`	
` `	
`<input type="radio" value="hard" name="level"↵` `/>Hard  `	Set up radio button, common level, value hard
`<input type="radio" value="moderate" name="level"↵` `/>Moderate  `	Set up radio button, common level, value moderate
`<input type="radio" value="easy" name="level"↵` `/>Easy `	Set up radio button, common level, value easy
`<input type="submit" value="GET maze"/> `	
`</form>`	
`<p>`	
`Use arrow keys to move token.`	
`</p>`	
`</body>`	
`</html>`	

There are a number of ways you can make this application your own.

Some applications in which the user places objects on the screen by dragging limit the possibilities by doing what is termed snapping the end points to grid points, perhaps even limiting the walls for a maze to be strictly horizontal or vertical.

The second application has two levels of user: the creator of the mazes and the player who attempts to traverse the mazes. You may want to design very intricate mazes, and for that you would want an editing facility. Another great addition would be a timing feature. Look back at the timing for the memory game in Chapter 5 for ways to calculate elapsed time.

Just as we added a video treat for the quiz show in Chapter 6, you could play a video when someone completes a maze.

The ability to save to local storage is a powerful feature. For this, and any game or activity that takes a fair amount of time, you may want to add the ability to save the current state. Another common use for local storage is to save the best scores.

Do understand that I wanted to demonstrate the use of local storage for intricate data, and these applications did do that. However, you may want to develop maze programs using something other than local storage. To build on this application, you need to define the sequence of starting and stopping points, four numbers in all, for each wall, and define walls accordingly. Look ahead to the word list implemented as an external script file in the Hangman game in Chapter 9.

This chapter and the previous one demonstrated events and event handling for mouse, keys, and timing. New devices provide new events, such as shaking a phone or using multiple touches on a screen. With the knowledge and experience you've acquired here, you'll be able to put together many different interactive applications.

Testing and uploading application

The first application is complete in one HTML document, `buildmazesavelocally.html`. The second application uses two files, `buildmazes.html` and `travelmaze.html`. The `buildmazesavelocally.html` and `buildmaze.html` are identical, except for the titles. All three files are available on the friends of ED site. Please note that `travelmaze.html` will not work until you create mazes and save them using local storage on your own computer.

To test the save and restore feature, you need to load the file to a server for it to work using Firefox and, perhaps, other browsers. It works locally using Chrome. The two HTML documents for the two-script version must both be uploaded to a server to be tested.

Some people may limit the use of local storage and cookies. There are differences between these constructs. To use any of this in a production application requires considerable work. The ultimate fall-back is to store information on the server using a language such as php.

Summary

In this chapter, you learned how to implement a program to support the building of a maze of walls and to store it on the local computer. You also learned how to create a maze travel game. We used the following programming techniques and HTML5 features:

- programmer-defined objects
- capturing key strokes; that is, setting up event handling for key presses, and deciphering which key was pressed
- `localStorage` for saving the layout of the walls of the maze on the player's computer
- `try` and `catch` to check if certain coding is acceptable
- the `join` method for arrays and the `split` method for strings
- mouse events
- mathematical calculations for determining collisions between the token and the walls of the maze
- radio buttons to present a choice to the player.

The use of local storage was fairly intricate for this application, requiring the encoding and decoding of the maze information. A simpler use might be for storing the highest score or the current score on any game. You can go back to previous chapters and see if you can incorporate this feature. Remember that localStorage is tied to the browser. In the next chapter, you will learn how to implement the rock-paper-scissors game, and how to incorporate audio in your application.

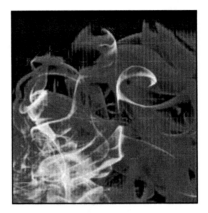

Chapter 8

Rock, Paper, Scissors

In this chapter, we will cover

- playing against a computer
- creating graphics to serve as buttons
- arrays of arrays for game rules
- the font-family property
- inherited style settings
- audio

Introduction

This chapter combines programming techniques with HTML5 JavaScript features to implement the familiar rock-paper-scissors game. In the school yard version of this game, each player uses hand symbols to indicate one of the three possibilities: rock, paper, or scissors. The terminology is that a player *throws* one of the three options. The game rules are stated this way:

- Rock crushes scissors.
- Paper covers rock.
- Scissors cuts paper.

So each symbol beats one other symbol: rock beats scissors; paper beats rock; and scissors beats paper. If both players throw the same thing, it's a tie.

Since this is a two-player game that our player will play against the computer, we have to create the computer's moves. We will generate random moves, and the player needs to trust that the program is doing this and not basing its move on what the player threw. The presentation must reinforce this trust.

The first version of our game just uses the visuals you'll see here. The second version adds audio, four different clips governed by the three winning events plus the tie option. You can either use the sound files provided in the download pack from www.friendsofed.com, or your own sounds. Note that you'll need to change the file names in the code to match the sound files you use.

This is a situation in which we want to use special graphics for the player moves. Figure 8-1 shows the opening screen of the application, consisting of three graphics that serve as buttons, as well as a field labeled with the string "Score:" that holds an initial value of zero.

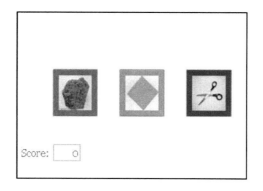

Figure 8-1. The Rock, Paper, Scissors opening screen

The player makes a move by clicking one of the symbols. Let's look at an example with the player clicking on the rock icon. We'll assume the computer chose scissors. After a short animated sequence in which a scissors symbol starts small and grows on the screen, a text message appears as shown in Figure 8-2. In the version with added audio, the audio clip would play a sound corresponding to a rock crushing a scissors. Notice that the score is now 1.

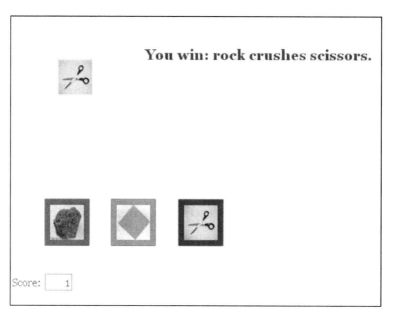

Figure 8-2. The player threw rock and computer threw scissors

Next in the game, the player and the computer tie, as shown in Figure 8-3. There's no change in the score when a tie occurs, so the score is still 1.

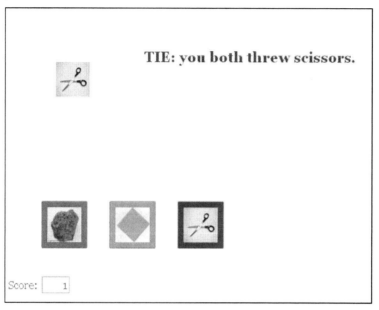

Figure 8-3. A tie

Later, the game has been even but the player loses and the score falls to negative 1, meaning the player is behind, as Figure 8-4 shows.

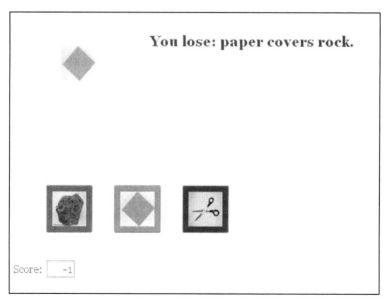

Figure 8-4. Later in the game, a losing move

This application, like all the examples in this book, is only a start. Both the plain and audio versions keep a running score for the player in which a loss results in a decrease. An alternative approach is to keep individual scores for player and computer, with only wins counted for either side. You could display a separate count of the games played. This is preferable if you don't want to show negative numbers. You could also save the player's score using `localStorage`, as described in the maze game in Chapter 7.

A more elaborate enhancement might feature video clips (look back at Chapter 6) or animated GIFs that show rock crushing scissors, paper covering rock, and scissors cutting paper. You can also look at this as a model for many different games. In all cases, you need to determine how to capture the player's moves and how to generate the computer's moves; you need to represent and implement the rules of the game; and you need to maintain the state of the game and display it for the player. The rock-paper-scissors game has no state information except for the running score. Putting it another way, a game consists of just one turn. This is in contrast to the dice game described in Chapter 2 in which a game can involve one to any number of throws of the dice, or the concentration game described in Chapter 5 in which a turn consists of two selections of cards and a completed game can take any number of turns with the minimum equal to half the number of cards.

> Note: There are competitions for rock-paper-scissors and also computer systems in which the computer makes moves based on the player's history of moves. You may find it interesting to check out the World RPS Society (`www.worldrps.com`) and the USA RPS League (`www.usarps.com`).

Critical requirements

The implementation of rock-paper-scissors makes use of many HTML5 and JavaScript constructs demonstrated in earlier chapters, put together here in different ways. Programming is similar to writing. It is putting the representation of ideas together in some logical order, just like combining words into sentences and the sentences into paragraphs, and so on. While reading this chapter, think back to what you have learned about drawing rectangles, images, and text on the canvas, detecting where the player has clicked the mouse, setting up a timing event using `setInterval` to produce animation, and using arrays to hold information. These are the building blocks for the rock-paper-scissors application.

In planning this application, I knew I wanted our player to click on buttons, one button for each of the types of throws in the game. Once the player makes a throw, I wanted the program to make its own move, namely a random choice, and have a picture corresponding to that move appear on the screen. The program would then apply the rules of the game to display the outcome. A sound would play, corresponding to the three possible situations in which one throw beats another, plus a groan when there was a tie.

This application starts off with what appear as buttons or icons on the screen. These are pictures that the player can click on to make his or her move. There is also a box for the score.

The application must generate the computer move randomly and then display it in a way that appears as if the computer and the player are throwing their moves at the same time. My idea for this is to have the appropriate symbol start small on the screen and then get larger, seemingly emerging from the screen as if the computer were making its throw towards the player. This action starts right after the player clicks on one of the three possible throws, but it is soon enough to give the impression that the two happened at the same time.

The rules of the game must be obeyed! This includes both what beats what and the folksy message displayed to explain it—"rock crushes scissors"; "paper covers rock", and "scissors cuts paper". The score displayed goes up by one, down by one, or stays the same depending on whether the turn is a win, loss, or tie.

The audio-enhanced version of the game must play one of four audio clips depending on the situation.

HTML5, CSS, and JavaScript features

Now let's take a look at the specific features of HTML5, CSS, and JavaScript that provide what we need to implement the game. Except for basic HTML tags and functions and variables, the explanations here are complete. If you've read the other chapters, you'll notice that much of this chapter repeats explanations given previously.

We certainly could have used the types of buttons demonstrated in the other chapters, but I wanted these buttons to look like the throws they represent. As you'll see, the way we implement the buttons is built on the concepts demonstrated in prior chapters. And we again use JavaScript pseudo-random processing for defining the computer move, and setInterval for animating the display of the computer move.

Our rock-paper-scissors game will demonstrate HTML5's native audio facility. We will integrate coding for audio with applying the rules of the game.

Providing graphical buttons for the player

There are two aspects to producing clickable buttons or icons on the screen: drawing the graphics on the canvas and detecting when the player has moved the mouse over a button and clicked the primary mouse button.

The buttons or icons we'll produce consist of the outline (stroke) of a rectangle, a solid rectangle, and then an image on top of the rectangle with a vertical and horizontal margin. Since the similar operations will occur for all three buttons, we can use the approach first introduced in the cannonball and slingshot games in Chapter 4. We will set up a programmer-defined class of objects by writing a function named Throw. Recall that objects consist of data and coding grouped together. The function, described as a *constructor* function, will be used with the operator new to create a new object of type Throw. The term this is used within the function to set the values associated with each object.

```
function Throw(sx,sy, smargin,swidth,sheight,rectcolor,picture) {
  this.sx = sx;
  this.sy = sy;
  this.swidth = swidth;
  this.bwidth = swidth + 2*smargin;
  this.bheight = sheight + 2*smargin;
  this.sheight = sheight;
  this.fillstyle = rectcolor;
  this.draw = drawThrow;
  this.img = new Image();
  this.img.src = picture;
  this.smargin = smargin;
}
```

The parameters of the function hold all the information. The selection of names sx, sy, and so on, avoids built-in terms by making a simple modification: putting s, for stored, in front. The location of the button is at sx, sy. The color of the rectangle is represented by rectcolor. The file name for the image is held by picture. What we can think of as the inner and outer widths and the inner and outer heights are calculated based on the inputs smargin, sheight, and swidth. The b in bheight and bwidth stands for big. The s stands for small and stored. Don't get too hung up on the proper name—there is no such thing. The names are up to you and if a name works, meaning you remember it, it works.

The img attribute of a Throw object is an Image object. The src of that Image object is what points to the file name that was passed to the function in the picture parameter.

Notice that the attribute this.draw is set to be drawThrow. This sets up the drawThrow function to be used as the draw method for all objects of type Throw. The coding is more general than it needs to be: each of the three graphics has the same margin and width and height. However, there's no harm in making the coding general, and if you want to build on this application to make one in which objects representing the player's choices are more complex, much of this code would work.

> Tip: Don't worry when writing programs if you have code such as this.draw = drawThrow; and you haven't written the drawThrow function yet. You will. Sometimes it is impossible to avoid referencing a function or variable before it has been created. The critical factor is that all this coding is done before you try to execute the program.

Here's the drawThrow method:

```
function drawThrow() {
  ctx.strokeStyle = "rgb(0,0,0)";
  ctx.strokeRect(this.sx,this.sy,this.bwidth,this.bheight);
  ctx.fillStyle = this.fillstyle;
  ctx.fillRect(this.sx,this.sy,this.bwidth,this.bheight);
  ctx.drawImage(this.img,this.sx+this.smargin,this.sy+this.smargin, ➥
      this.swidth,this.sheight);
}
```

As promised, this draws an outline of a rectangle using black for the color rgb(0,0,0). Recall that ctx is the variable set with the property of the canvas element that is used for drawing. Black is actually the default color, making this line unnecessary. However, we'll put it in just in case you reuse this code in an application where the color has been changed previously. Next, the function draws a filled-in rectangle using the rectcolor passed in for this particular object. Lastly, the code draws an image on top of the rectangle, offset by the margin amount horizontally and vertically. The bwidth and bheight are calculated to be bigger than the swidth and sheight, respectively, by twice the smargin value. This in effect centers the image inside the rectangle.

The three buttons are created as Throw objects through the use of var statements, in which the variable is initialized using the new operator, and a call to the Throw constructor function. To make this work, we need pictures of rock, paper, and scissors, which I've acquired by a variety of means. The three image files are located in the same folder as the HTML file.

```
var rockb = new Throw(rockbx,rockby,8,50,50,"rgb(250,0,0)","rock.jpg");
var paperb = new Throw(paperbx,paperby,8,50,50,"rgb(0,200,200)","paper.gif");
```

```
var scib = new Throw(scissorsbx,scissorsby,8,50,50,"rgb(0,0,200)","scissors.jpg");
```

As in our previous applications, an array named everything is declared and initialized to the empty array. We push all three variables onto the everything array so we can treat them systematically.

```
everything.push(rockb);
everything.push(paperb);
everything.push(scib);
```

For example, to draw all the buttons, we use a function called drawall that iterates over the elements in the everything array.

```
function drawall() {
  ctx.clearRect(0,0,cwidth,cheight);
  var i;
  for (i=0;i<everything.length;i++) {
    everything[i].draw();
  }
}
```

Again, this is more general than required, but it's useful, especially when it comes to object-oriented programming, to keep things as general as possible.

But how to make these graphics act as clickable buttons? Because these are drawn on the canvas, the code needs to set up the click event handling for the whole canvas and then use coding to check which, if any, button was clicked.

In the slingshot game described in Chapter 4, you saw code in which the function handling the mousedown event for the whole canvas made a calculation to see if the mouse cursor was on the ball. In the quiz show described in Chapter 6, we set up event handling for each country and capital block. The built-in JavaScript mechanism indicated which object had received, so to speak, the click event. This application is like the slingshot.

We set up the event handling in the init function, explained in full in the next section. The task is to get JavaScript to listen for the mouse click event and then do what we specify when the click happens. What we want is for the function choose to be invoked. The following two lines accomplish this task.

```
canvas1 = document.getElementById('canvas');
canvas1.addEventListener('click',choose,false);
```

> Tip: Our code needs to distinguish between the element with the id canvas and the property of this element returned by getContext('2d'). That's just the way the HTML5 folks decided to do it. It is not something you could have deduced on your own.

The choose function has the tasks of determining which type of throw was selected, generating the computer move and setting up the display of that move, and applying the rules of the game. Right now, we're just going to take a look at the code that determines what button has been clicked.

The code starts by handling differences among the browsers. Functions that are invoked as a result of a call to addEventListener are called with a parameter holding information about the event. This parameter, ev as we are calling it in the choose function, is examined to see what attributes exist to be used. This complexity is forced on us because the browsers implement event handling using different terms.

```
function choose(ev) {
var mx;
var my;
if ( ev.layerX ||  ev.layerX == 0) {
  mx= ev.layerX;
  my = ev.layerY;
} else if (ev.offsetX || ev.offsetX == 0) {
  mx = ev.offsetX;
  my = ev.offsetY;
}
```

The goal of this portion of the code is to make the variables mx and my respectively hold the horizontal and vertical coordinates for the mouse cursor when the mouse button is clicked. Certain browsers keep the cursor information in properties of the ev parameter named layerX and layerY and others use offsetX and offsetY. We will use local variables to make sure we track the cursor position across all browsers. The condition ev.layerX will evaluate as false if ev.layerX does not exist for this browser or if it does exist and has the value 0. Therefore, to check if the property exists, we need to use the compound condition (ev.layerX || ev.layerX == 0) to make sure the code works in all situations. By the way, if the second if test fails, nothing happens. This code works for Chrome, FireFox, and Safari, but presumably will work eventually with all browsers.

The next section of code iterates through the elements of everything (there are three elements, but that's not mentioned explicitly) to see if the cursor is on any of the rectangles. The variable ch holds a reference to a Throw and so all the Throw attributes, namely, sx, sy, bwidth, and bheight, can be used in the compare statements. This is shorthand for all the choices of throws held in the everything array.

```
var i;
for (i=0;i<everything.length;i++){
  var ch = everything[i];
  if ((mx>ch.sx)&&(mx<ch.sx+ch.bwidth)&&(my>ch.sy)&&(my<ch.sy+ch.bheight)) {
    ...
    break;
  }
}
```

The ... indicates coding to be explained later. The compound condition compares the point mx,my with the left side, right side, top, and bottom of the outer rectangle of each of the three objects representing possible throws by the player. Each of these four conditions must be true for the point to be within the rectangle. This is indicated by the && operator. Though long, this is a standard way to check for points inside rectangles and you will become accustomed to using it.

So that's how the graphics are drawn on the canvas and how they serve as buttons. Notice that if the player clicks outside of any button, nothing happens. Some people might recommend providing feedback to the player at this point, such as an alert box saying:

```
Please make your move by clicking on the rock, paper, or scissors!
```

Others would tell you to avoid cluttering on the screen and assume that the player will figure out what to do.

Generating the computer move

Generating the computer move is similar to generating a throw of the dice, as we did in the dice game in Chapter 2. In the rock-paper-scissors game, we want a random selection from three possible throws instead of six possible die faces. We get that number with the line:

```
var compch = Math.floor(Math.random()*3);
```

The call to the built-in method `Math.random()` produces a number from zero up to, but not including, 1. Multiplying this by 3 produces a number from 0 up to, but not including, 3. Applying `Math.floor` produces a whole number not larger than its argument. It rounds the number down, knocking off any values over the highest integer floor. Therefore, the expression on the right produces 0, 1, or 2, which is exactly what we want. This value is assigned to `compch` which is declared (set up) as a variable.

The code takes the computer move, one of the numbers 0, 1, or 2 chosen by the calculation involving the random function, and uses it as an index for the `choices` array:

```
var choices = ["rock.jpg","paper.gif","scissors.jpg"];
```

These three elements refer to the same three pictures used in the buttons.

At this point, just in case you were concerned, the ordering rock, paper, scissors is arbitrary. We need to be consistent, but the ordering does not matter. If, at every instance, we made the ordering paper, scissors, rock, everything would still work. The player never sees the encoding of 0 for rock, 1 for paper, and 2 for scissors.

The next lines in the `choose` function extract one of the file names and assign it to the `src` attribute of an Image variable `compimg`.

```
var compchn = choices[compch];
compimg.src = compchn;
```

The name of the local variable, `compchn`, stands for computer choice name. The `compimg` variable is a global variable holding an Image object. The code sets its `src` property to the name of the appropriate image file, which will be used to display the computer move.

To implement the rules of the game, I set up two arrays:

```
var beats = [
  ["TIE: you both threw rock.","You win: paper covers rock.", ➡
      "You lose: rock crushes scissors."],
  ["You lose: paper covers rock.","TIE: you both threw paper.", ➡
      "You win: scissors cuts paper."],
  ["You win: rock crushes scissors.","You lose: scissors cuts paper.", ➡
      "TIE: you both threw scissors"]];
```

And:

```
var points = [
  [0,1,-1],
  [-1,0,1],
  [1,-1,0]];
```

Each of these is an array of arrays. The first holds all the messages and the second holds the amount to add to the score of the player. Adding 1 increases the player's score. Adding a -1 decreases the player's score by 1, which is the effect we want when the player loses a round. Adding 0 leaves the score as is. Now, you may think that it would be easier to do nothing in the case of ties rather than add zero, but handling this in a uniform way is the easier approach in terms of coding, and adding zero may actually take less time than doing an `if` test to see if it was a tie.

The first index into each array will come from the computer move, `compch`, and the second index, `i`, indicating the element in the inner array, will come from the player move. The `beats` and `points` arrays are called parallel structures. The `beats` array is for the text message and the `points` array is for the scoring. Let's check that the information is correct by picking a computer move, say scissors, which corresponds to 2, and picking a player move, say rock, which corresponds to 0. In the `beats` array, the value for the computer move tells us to go to the array with index value 2. (I am avoiding saying the second array, since arrays start with index 0, not with 1. The value indicated by 2 is the third element of the array). The element is:

```
["You win: rock crushes scissors.","You lose: scissors cuts paper.", ➡
     "TIE: you both threw scissors"]];
```

Now use the player value, namely 0, to index this array. The result is `"You win: rock crushes scissors."` and this is exactly what we want. Doing the same thing with the `points` array, the element with index 2 is

```
[1,-1,0]
```

and the value with index 0 into this array is 1, also exactly what we want: the player's score will be adjusted by 1.

```
result = beats[compch][i];
…
newscore +=points[compch][i];
```

Recall that the operator += in a statement

```
a += b;
```

is interpreted as follows:

Get the value of the variable a

Apply the + operator to this value and the value of the expression b

Assign the result back to the variable a

The second step is written in a general way since this could apply to + interpreted as addition of numbers as well as concatenation of strings. In this particular situation, the second step is:

Add a and b

This result gets assigned back to the variable a.

The two variables, `result` and `newscore`, are global variables. This means they are available to other functions and this is how we use them: set in one function and referenced for use in another.

The score is presented using a `form` element in the `body` element of the HTML document.

```
<form name="f">
Score: <input name="score" value="0" size="3"/>
</form>
```

Just to show you how these things are done, we'll use styles for the score field. We set up two styles, one for the form, and one for the input field.

```
form {
  color: blue;
  font-family: Georgia, "Times New Roman", Times, serif;
  font-size:16px;
}
input {
  text-align:right;
  font:inherit;
  color:inherit;
}
```

We set the color for the text in the form to blue, and specified the font using the font-family property. This is a way to specify a particular font and backups if that font doesn't exist on the client computer. This is a powerful feature because it means you can be as specific as you want in terms of fonts and, with work, still make sure that everyone can read the material.

> *Tip: You can research online for Web-safe fonts to see which fonts are widely available. Then you can pick your favorite font for the first choice, one of the Web-safe fonts for the second, and make the last choice either serif or sans-serif. You can even specify more than three choices if you wants. Check out http://en.wikipedia.org/wiki/Web_typography for ideas.*

In this style, we specify the font named Georgia, then "Times New Roman", then Times, and then whatever the standard font with serifs is on the computer. Serifs are the little extra flags on letters. The quotation marks around Times New Roman are necessary because the name involves multiple terms. Quotation marks wouldn't be wrong around the other font names, but they aren't necessary. We also specify the size as 16 pixels. The input field inherits the font, including size, and the color from the form element, its parent. However, because the score is a number, we use the text-align property to indicate right alignment in the field. The label Score is in the form element. The actual score is in the input element. Using the inherit setting for the input style properties makes the two display in the same font, size, and color.

The value in the input field will be extracted and set using its name, score. For example,

```
newscore = Number(document.f.score.value);
```

Number is required here to produce the number represented by the text in the field; that is 0 as opposed to "0" (the character). If we left the value as a string and the code used a plus sign to add 1 to a string, this would not be addition; it would instead be the concatenation of strings. (This is termed *operator overloading*, by the way: the plus sign indicates different operations depending on the data type of the operands.) Concatenating a "1" onto a "0" would yield "01". You might think this is okay, but the next time around, we would get "011" or "010" or "01-1". Ugh. We don't want that, so we write the code to make sure the value is converted to a number.

To place an adjusted new score back into the field, the code is

```
document.f.score.value = String(newscore);
```

Now, as I frequently tell my students, I am compelled to tell you the truth. In fact, String may not be necessary here. JavaScript sometimes does these conversions, also termed *casts*, automatically. However, sometimes it doesn't, so it is good practice to make it explicit.

The size of the field is the maximum required for three characters. The Georgia font is not a monospace font—all characters are not the same size—so this is the largest space that might be necessary. You might notice different amounts of space left over depending on the text in the field.

> *Note: JavaScript makes use of parentheses, curly brackets, and square brackets. They are not interchangeable. The parentheses are used in function headers and in function and method calls; in if, for, switch, and while statement headers; and for specifying the order of operations in complex expressions. The curly brackets are used to delimit the definition of functions and the clauses of if, for, switch and while statements. The square brackets are used to define arrays and to return specific members of arrays. The language of Cascading Style Sheets puts curly brackets around each style. HTML markup includes < and >, often called pointy brackets or angle brackets.*

Displaying results using animation

You've seen examples of animation in the bouncing ball application in Chapter 3 and the cannonball and slingshot in Chapter 4. To recap, animation is produced by displaying a sequence of still pictures in quick succession. The individual pictures are called frames. In what is called *computed animation,* new positions for objects on the screen are calculated for each successive frame. One way to produce animation is to use the setInterval command to set up an interval event, like so:

```
tid = setInterval(flyin,100);
```

This causes the flyin function to be invoked every 100 milliseconds (10 times per second). The variable tid, for timer identifier, is set so the code can turn the interval event off. The flyin function will create Throw objects of increasing size holding the appropriate image. When an object reaches a designated size, the code displays the result and adjusts the score. This is why the variables result and newscore must be global variables—they are set in choose and used in flyin.

The flyin function also makes use of a global variable named size that starts off at 15 and is incremented by 5 each time flyin is invoked. When size is over 50, the timing event is stopped, the result message displayed, and the score changed.

```
function flyin() {
  ctx.drawImage(compimg, 70,100,size,size);
  size +=5;
  if (size>50) {
    clearInterval(tid);
    ctx.fillText(result,200,100,250);
    document.f.score.value = String(newscore);
  }
}
```

By the way, I had to modify the code in order to grab these screenshots. Figure 8-5 is the screen after the very first invocation of flyin.

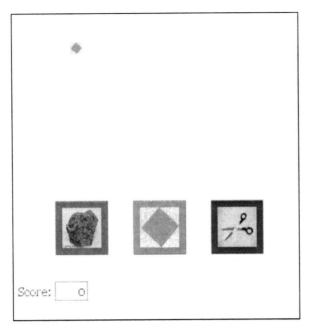

Figure 8-5. First call of `flyin`, with a tiny image representing the computer move

After a different modification of the code, Figure 8-6 shows the animation halted at a later step.

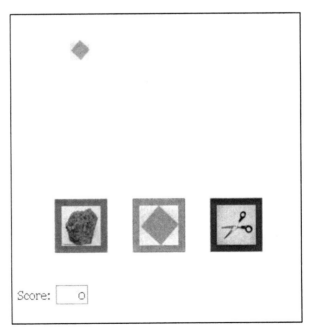

Figure 8-6. A step further in the animation

Figure 8-7 shows the animation completed, but just before the text messages with the results.

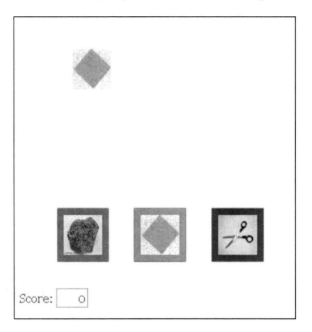

Figure 8-7. Just before text displayed on results

Now, here's a confession that should be informative. You may need to skip ahead or wait until you read through all the code to appreciate it. When I created this application the first time, I had the code for displaying the message and adjusting the score in the choose function. After all, that's where the code determined the values. However, this had a very bad effect. The player saw the results before seeing the computer move emerge out of the screen in the animation. It looked like the game was fixed! When I realized what the problem was, I changed the code in choose to store the message and the new score values in global variables and only display the message and set the updated score in the form input field *after* the animation was complete. Don't assume you can know everything about your application before you start. Do assume you will find problems and be able to resolve them. Companies have whole groups devoted solely to quality assurance.

Audio and DOM processing

The situation with audio is quite similar to the one with video (see Chapter 6). Again, the bad news is that browsers don't all recognize the same formats. And again, the good news is that HTML5 provides the <audio> element, and JavaScript supplies features for playing audio along with ways of referencing different formats for the audio accepted by the different browsers. Moreover, tools are available for converting from one format to another. The two formats I use for these examples are MP3 and OGG, which appear to be sufficient for Chrome, Firefox, and Safari. I used free sources for audio clips and found acceptable samples in WAV and MP3. I then used the Miro converter I had downloaded for working with the video to produce MP3 and OGG for the WAV file and OGG for the others. The Miro name for the OGG was theor.ogv and I changed it just to keep things simple. The main point here is that this approach requires two versions of each sound file.

The `<audio>` element has attributes I didn't use in the rock-paper-scissors game. The `autoplay` attribute starts play immediately on loading, though you do need to remember that with large files loading is not instantaneous. The `src` attribute specifies the source. However, good practice is to not use the `src` attribute in the `<audio>` tag, but to specify multiple sources using the `<source>` element as a child of the `<audio>` element. The `loop` attribute specifies looping, that is, repeating the clip. The `controls` attribute puts controls on the screen. This may be a good thing to do because the clips can be very loud. In order to make the audio a surprise, though, and to not add clutter to the visual presentation, I chose not to do this.

Here's a simple example for you to try. You will need to download `sword.mp3` from the book's download page at `www.friendsofed.com` or find your own audio file and reference it by name here. If you open the following HTML in Chrome

```
Audio example <br/>
<audio src="sword.mp3" autoplay controls>
Your browser doesn't recognize audio
</audio>
```

you'll see what's shown in Figure 8-8.

Figure 8-8. Audio tag with controls

Remember: for our game, we will play audio for the rock crushing the scissors, the paper covering the rock, the scissors cutting the paper, and a sigh for any tie. Here is the coding for the four audio clips in rock-paper-scissors:

```
<audio autobuffer>
<source src="hithard.ogg" />
<source src="hithard.mp3" />
</audio>
<audio autobuffer>
<source src="inhale.ogg" />
<source src="inhale.mp3" />
</audio>
<audio autobuffer>
<source src="sword.ogg" />
<source src="sword.mp3" />
</audio>
<audio autobuffer>
<source src="crowdohh.ogg" />
<source src="crowdohh.mp3" />
</audio>
```

This should appear reasonable for describing four sets of audio files, but you may be wondering how the code knows which one to play. We could insert id attributes in each <audio> tag. However, let's do something else instead in order to demonstrate more JavaScript that's useful in many situations. You have seen the method document.getElementById. There is a similar method: document.getElementsByTagname. The line:

```
musicelements = document.getElementsByTagName("audio");
```

extracts all elements of the tag name indicated by the parameter and creates an array, which, in this line of code, assigns the array to a variable named musicelements. We use this line in the init function so it's performed at the very start of the application. We construct another array of arrays, this one called music, and add two other global variables:

```
var music = [
  [3,1,0],
  [1,3,2],
  [0,2,3]];
var musicelements;
var musicch;
```

You can check that music and beats are *parallel structures* with 0 standing for rock crushing scissors, 1 for paper covering rock, 2 for scissors cutting paper, and 3 for a tie. The choose function will have the extra line:

```
musicch = music[compch][i];
```

The musicch variable—the name stands for choice for music—will hold 0, 1, 2, or 3. This sets up something to happen in the flyin function when the animation is complete. We don't play the clip immediately, as explained in my confession above.

```
musicelements[musicch].play();
```

The zeroth, first, second, or third element in musicelements is referenced by the indexing using musicch, then its play method is invoked and the clip is played.

Starting off

The application starts by setting up a call to a function in the onLoad attribute of the <body> tag. This has been the practice in the other games. The init function performs several tasks. It sets the initial score value to zero. This is necessary just in case the player reloads the document; it is a quirk of HTML that form data may not be reset by the browser. The function extracts values from the canvas element to be used for drawing (ctx) and for the event handling (canvas1). This needs to happen *after* the whole document is loaded because until then the canvas element does not exist. The function draws the three buttons and sets up the font for the text drawn on the canvas and the fill style. After that, nothing happens unless and until the player clicks the mouse button over one of the three symbols.

Now that we've examined the specific features of HTML5 and JavaScript used for this game, along with some programming techniques, such as the use of arrays of arrays, let's take a closer look at the code.

Building the application and making it your own

The basic rock-paper-scissors applications use styles, global variables, six functions, and HTML markup. The six functions are described in Table 8-1. I follow the convention that functions start with lower-case letters unless the function is a constructor for a programmer-defined object. I present the basic application first, and then show the modifications necessary to add audio.

Table 8-1. Functions in the Basic Rock-Paper-Scissors Application

Function	Invoked / Called By	Calls
init	Invoked by action of the onLoad in the <body> tag	drawall
drawall	init, choose	Invokes the draw method of each object, which in this application always in the function drawThrow
Throw	var statements for global variables	
drawThrow	drawall using the draw method of the Throw objects	
choose	Invoked by action of addEventListener call in init	drawall
flyin	Action of setInterval in choose	

As you can see from the table, most of the invocation of functions is done implicitly—by event handling, for example—as opposed to one function invoking another. After the init function does the set up, the main work is performed by the choose function. The critical information for the rules of the games is held in the two arrays of arrays.

Table 8-2 shows the code for the basic application, with comments for each line.

Table 8-2. Complete Code for the Basic Rock-Paper-Scissors Application

Code	Explanation
<html>	Starting html tag
<head>	Starting head tag
<title>Rock Paper Scissors</title>	Complete title element
<style>	Starting style section

Code	Explanation
`form {`	Style specified for all form elements. There is just one in this document.
`color: blue;`	Color of text set to blue, one of the 16 colors known by name
`font-family: Georgia, "Times New↪ Roman", Times, serif;`	Set up the fonts to try to use
`font-size:16px;`	Set size of characters
`}`	Close style
`input {`	Style specified for all input elements. There is just one.
`text-align:right;`	Make the text align to the right, appropriate for numbers
`font:inherit;`	Inherit any font information from parent, namely form
`color:inherit;`	Inherit color of text from parent, namely form
`}`	Close style
`</style>`	Close style element
`<script >`	Start script element
`var cwidth = 600;`	Canvas width, used for clearing
`var cheight = 400;`	Canvas height, used for clearing
`var ctx;`	Canvas ctx, used for all drawing
`var everything = [];`	Holds the 3 graphics
`var rockbx = 50;`	Horizontal position of rock symbol
`var rockby = 300;`	Vertical position of rock symbol
`var paperbx = 150;`	Horizontal position of paper symbol

Code	Explanation
`var paperby = 300;`	Vertical position of paper symbol
`var scissorsbx = 250;`	Horizontal position of scissors symbol
`var scissorsby = 300;`	Vertical position of scissors symbol
`var canvas1;`	Reference for setting up click event listening for canvas
`var newscore;`	Value to be set for new score
`var size = 15;`	Initial size for changing image for computer move
`var result;`	Value to be displayed as result message
`var choices = ["rock.jpg",↪ "paper.gif","scissors.jpg"];`	Names for symbol images
`var compimg = new Image();`	Image element used for each computer move
`var beats = [`	Start of declaration of array holding all the messages
`["TIE: you both threw↪ rock","You win: computer played rock",↪ "You lose: computer threw rock"],`	The set of messages when the computer throws rock
`["You lose: computer↪ threw paper","TIE: you both threw paper",↪ "You win: computer threw paper"],`	The set of messages when the computer throws paper
`["You win: computer↪ threw scissors","You lose: computer↪ threw scissors","TIE: you both threw↪ scissors"]];`	The set of messages when the computer throws scissors
`var points = [`	Start of declaration of array holding the increments for the score: 0 for a tie, 1 for the player winning, -1 for the player losing
`[0,1,-1],`	The set of increments when the computer throws rock

Code	Explanation
`[-1,0,1],`	The set of increments when the computer throws paper
`[1,-1,0]];`	The set of increments when the computer throws scissors
`function    Throw(sx,sy,    smargin,swidth,↪` `sheight,rectcolor,picture) {`	Header for constructor function to be used for the 3 game symbols. Parameters include x and y coordinates, margin, inner width and height, color for the rectangle, and the picture file
`this.sx = sx;`	Assign the `sx` attribute
`this.sy = sy;`	... `sy` attribute
`this.swidth = swidth;`	... `swidth` attribute
`this.bwidth = swidth + 2*smargin;`	Calculate and assign the outer width. This is the inner width plus 2 times the margin.
`this.bheight = sheight + 2*smargin;`	Calculate and assign the outer height. This is the inner height plus 2 times the margin.
`this.sheight = sheight;`	Assign `sheight` attribute
`this.fillstyle = rectcolor;`	Assign `fillstyle` attribute
`this.draw = drawThrow;`	Assign the draw method to be `drawThrow`
`this.img = new Image();`	Create a new `Image` object
`this.img.src = picture;`	Set its `src` to be the picture file
`this.smargin = smargin;`	Assign the `smargin` attribute. It is still needed for drawing.
`}`	Close function
`function drawThrow() {`	Header for function to draw the symbols
`ctx.strokeStyle = "rgb(0,0,0)";`	Set the style for the rectangle outline to black.

Code	Explanation
`        ctx.strokeRect(this.sx,this.sy,↪` `this.bwidth,this.bheight);`	Draw rectangle outline
`        ctx.fillStyle = this.fillstyle;`	Set the style for the filled rectangle
`        ctx.fillRect(this.sx,this.sy,↪` `this.bwidth,this.bheight);`	Draw rectangle

`ctx.drawImage(this.img,this.sx+this.↪`
`smargin,this.sy+this.smargin,this.swidth,↪`
`this.sheight);`
	Draw the image offset inside the rectangle.

`}`	Close function
`function choose(ev) {`	Header for function called upon a click event
`    var     compch     =     Math.floor↪` `(Math.random()*3);`	Generate computer move based on random processing
`    var compchn = choices[compch];`	Pick out the image file
`    compimg.src = compchn;`	Set the `src` of the already created `Image` object
`    var mx;`	Used for mouse x
`    var my;`	Used for mouse y
`    if  (  ev.layerX  ||     ev.layerX↪` `== 0) {`	Check which coding applies in this browser
`        mx= ev.layerX;`	Set mx
`        my = ev.layerY;`	Set my
`    } else  if  (ev.offsetX  ||↪` `ev.offsetX == 0) {`	Else check if this coding works
`        mx = ev.offsetX;`	Set mx
`        my = ev.offsetY;`	Set my

Code	Explanation
`}`	Close clause
`var i;`	Used for indexing over the different symbols
`for (i=0;i<everything.length;i++){`	For header for indexing over the elements in the `everything` array, namely the three symbols
`var ch = everything[i];`	Get the ith element

`if ((mx>ch.sx)&&(mx<ch.sx+ch↪`
`.bwidth)&&(my>ch.sy)&&(my<ch.sy+ch.bheight))`
`{`
	Check if the `mx`, `my` position is within the bounds (the outer rectangle bounds) for this symbol

`drawall();`	If so, invoke the drawall function, which will erase everything and then draw everything in the `everything` array
`size = 15;`	Initial size of computer-move image
`tid = setInterval↪` `(flyin,100);`	Set up timed event
`result = beats↪` `[compch][i];`	Set the result message. See the section below the table for the addition for audio.
`newscore =↪` `Number(document.f.score.value);`	Get the current score, converted to a number
`newscore +=↪` `points[compch][i];`	Add the adjustment and save to be displayed later
`break;`	Leave the `for` loop
`}`	End the `if` clause
`}`	End the `for` loop
`}`	End the function
`function flyin() {`	Header for the function handling the timed interval event

Code	Explanation
`        ctx.drawImage(compimg,        70,↪` `100,size,size);`	Draw the computer-move image on the screen at the indicated place and with dimensions indicated
`        size +=5;`	Change the value of the dimensions by incrementing `size`
`        if (size>50) {`	Use the `size` variable to see if the process has gone on long enough
`            clearInterval(tid);`	Stop the timing event
`            ctx.fillText(result,↪` `200,100,250);`	Display the message
`            document.f.score.value↪` `  = String(newscore);`	Display the new score. See the section below the table for the addition for audio
`        }`	Close of if true clause
`}`	Close of function
`var rockb = new Throw(rockbx,rockby,8,50,↪` `50,"rgb(250,0,0)","rock.jpg");`	Create the rock object

`var         paperb         =         new`
`Throw(paperbx,paperby,8,50,↪`
`50,"rgb(0,200,200)","paper.gif");`
	Create the paper object

`var scib = new Throw(scissorsbx,scissorsby,↪` `8,50,50,"rgb(0,0,200)","scissors.jpg");`	Create the scissors object
`everything.push(rockb);`	Add the rock object to the `everything` array
`everything.push(paperb);`	Add the paper object to the `everything` array
`everything.push(scib);`	Add the scissors object to the `everything` array
`function init(){`	Header for function called on load of the document
`    document.f.score.value = "0";`	Set score to zero. I also could use

Code	Explanation
	... = String(0); (and it actually isn't necessary since JavaScript will convert a number to a string in this situation)
`    ctx        =        document.getElementById↪('canvas').getContext('2d');`	Set the variable to be used for all drawing
`    canvas1      =        document.getElementById↪('canvas');`	Set the variable to be used for the mouse click event handling
`    canvas1.addEventListener↪('click',choose,false);`	Set up click event handling
`    drawall();`	Draw everything
`    ctx.font="bold 16pt Georgia";`	Set the font to be used for the result messages
`    ctx.fillStyle = "blue";`	Set the color
`}`	Close the function
`function drawall() {`	Header for the function
`        ctx.clearRect(0,0,cwidth,cheight);`	Clear the canvas
`        var i;`	Variable for indexing
`        for (i=0;i<everything.length;i++) {`	Iterate through the `everything` array
`            everything[i].draw();`	Draw the individual elements
`        }`	Close the `for` loop
`}`	Close the function
`</script>`	Close the `script` element
`</head>`	Close the `head` element
`<body onLoad="init();">`	Starting body tag. Set up call to the `init` function

Code	Explanation
`<canvas id="canvas" width="600" height=↪"400">`	Starting canvas tag
`Your browser doesn't support the HTML5↪ element canvas.`	Message for noncompliant browsers
`</canvas>`	Closing tag
` `	Line break
`<form name="f">`	Starting tag for form, giving form a name
`Score: <input name="score" value="0"↪ size="3"/>`	Label and then input field, with initial value and size
`</form>`	Closing tag for form
`</body>`	Closing tag for body
`</html>`	Closing tag for html document

The audio enhanced version required three more global variables along with additions in the `init`, `choose` and `flyin` functions. The new global variables are

```
var music = [
    [3,1,0],
    [1,3,2],
    [0,2,3]];
var musicelements;
var musicch;
```

Here is the clause in the `choose` function with the new line highlighted.

```
if ((mx>ch.sx)&&(mx<ch.sx+ch.bwidth)&&(my>ch.sy)&&(my<ch.sy+ch.bheight)) {
    drawall();
    size = 15;
    tid = setInterval(flyin,100);
    result = beats[compch][i];
    musicch = music[compch][i];
    newscore = Number(document.f.score.value);
    newscore +=points[compch][i];
    break;
}
```

Similarly, here's the complete `flyin` function with the new line in bold:

```
function flyin() {
  ctx.drawImage(compimg, 70,100,size,size);
  size +=5;
  if (size>50) {
    clearInterval(tid);
    ctx.fillText(result,200,100,250);
    document.f.score.value = String(newscore);
    musicelements[musicch].play();
  }
}
```

Adding the audio enhancement, like adding video, provides an exercise in examining just what needs to be changed and what remains the same. It certainly makes sense to develop a basic application first.

My idea was to make sounds for the four results. You could also have applause for any player win, booing for any player loss, and something in between for the ties.

Some people like to include additional possible moves, with funny remarks describing what beats what, or even replacing rock, paper, and scissors with three or more other possibilities. A few students of mine have produced this game using a different language, such as Spanish. The more challenging task is to make the application multilingual in a systematic way, by isolating the spoken language components. One approach would involve changing the beats array to an array of arrays of arrays, with the first index corresponding to the language. The label in the markup that holds the word Score also would need to change, which you could accomplish by making it an input field and using CSS to remove its border. Preparing applications for what is termed *localization* has emerged as an important area of development for the Web.

Testing and uploading the application

You need to create or acquire (a polite term for finding something and copying the file to your computer) the three images to represent rock, paper, and scissors. If you decide to enhance the application by adding sounds, you need to produce or find the audio clips, convert these to the two common formats, and upload all the sounds: this is 4 files times 2 formats for a total of 8 files.

Because this application involves a random element, make a concerted effort to do all the testing. You want to test a player throwing each of the three possibilities versus each of the three computer moves. You also want to test that the score goes up and down and stays the same as the situation dictates. Typically, my testing routine is to make the rock throw repeatedly until I see all three computer moves at least two times. Then I move on to paper, and then scissors, and then I keep changing my throw, say, paper, rock, paper, scissors.

Test the basic program and then decide on what enhancements you'd like to make to the presentation and to the scoring. The images and the HTML document need to be uploaded when you've tested the program on your local computer and decide to upload it to a server. If you decide to use different images for computer moves than for player moves, you'll have to find and upload even more. Some people like to put images and audio files in subfolders. If you do this, don't forget to use the correct names in the code.

Summary

In this chapter, you learned how to implement a familiar game using features of HTML5, JavaScript, and CSS, along with general programming techniques. These included

- styles, in particular the `font-family` property
- form and input fields for displaying the score
- event handling using `addEventListener` for the mouse click event
- animation using `setInterval` and `clearInterval`
- `audio` elements for sound and `source` elements for working with different browsers
- `getElementByTagname` and `play` for specific control of audio clips
- programmer-defined objects for drawing programmer-created buttons on the screen, with logic for determining if the mouse cursor was clicked on a specific button
- arrays of arrays for game rules

The next chapter describes another familiar, childhood game: Hangman. It combines techniques of drawing on canvas and creating HTML elements using code that you have learned in previous chapters along with some new CSS and JavaScript features.

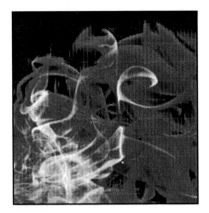

Chapter 9

Hangman

In this chapter, we will be covering

- CSS styles
- generating markup for alphabet buttons
- using an array for a sequence of drawings
- using a character string for the secret word
- an external script file for the word list
- setting up and removing event handling

Introduction

The goal for this chapter is to continue demonstrating programming techniques and the features of HTML5, Cascading Style Sheets (CSS), and JavaScript, combining dynamic creation of HTML markup along with drawing graphics and text on the canvas. The example for this chapter is another familiar game—the paper-and-pencil game of Hangman.

Just in case you need to brush up on the rules, the game is played as follows: One player thinks of a secret word and writes out dashes to let the other player know how many letters are in that word. The other person guesses individual letters. If the letter appears in the word, player one replaces the dash representing each occurrence of the guessed letter with the actual letter. If the letter does *not* appear in the secret word, the first player draws the next step in a progression of stick figure drawings of a hanging. In my example shown in Figure 9-1, the gallows are already on the screen. Next comes the head, then the body, left arm, right arm, left leg, right leg, and finally, the rope. Players can come to an agreement on how many steps are allowed. Player two loses the game if the hanging is complete before the word is guessed. Yes, this is a ghoulish game, but it is popular and even considered educational.

In our game, the computer takes the role of player one and picks the secret word from a word list (in this case an admittedly very short list). You may use my list. When you make your own game, use your own. It makes sense to start small and, once you are happy with your game, make a longer list. My technique of using an external file for the word list supports this approach.

For the user interface, I chose to place blocks with each letter of the alphabet on the screen. The player chooses a letter by clicking a block. After a letter is selected, its block disappears. This decision was influenced by the fact that most people playing the pencil-and-paper version write out the alphabet and cross out the letters as they are chosen.

Figure 9-1 shows the opening screen. The computer has selected a word with four letters. Notice that in our program, the gallows appears on the screen already. Alternatively, you can choose to make that the first one or two steps of the progression of drawings.

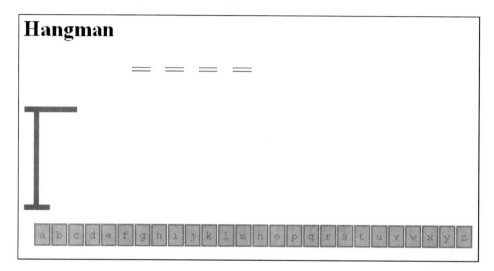

Figure 9-1. Opening screen

One advantage to using a small word bank is that I know what the word is now, even though my coding uses a random process to select the word. This means I can develop the game without any stress in playing it. I decided to select an *a* first. As Figure 9-2 shows, this letter does not appear in the secret word, so an oval for a head is drawn on the screen, and the block for the letter *a* disappears.

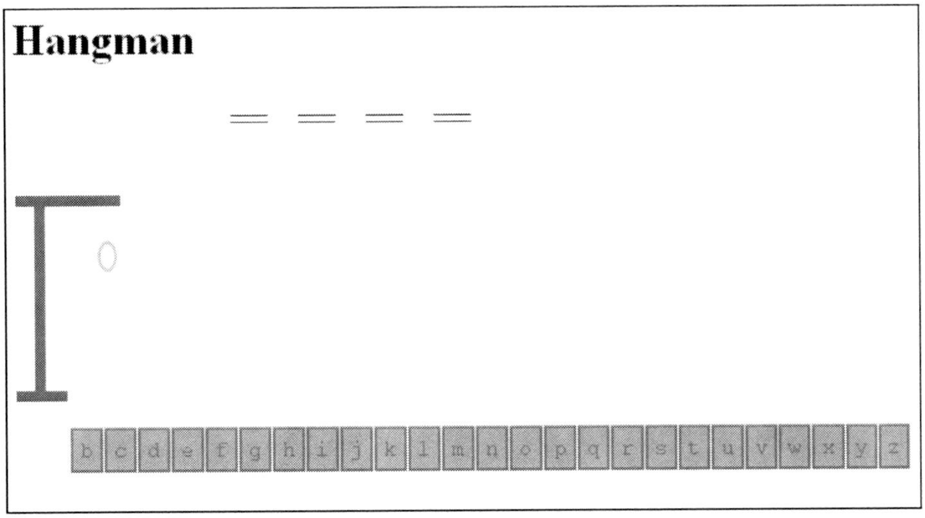

Figure 9-2. Screenshot after guessing an a

Working through the vowels, I guess an *e*, with results shown in Figure 9-3.

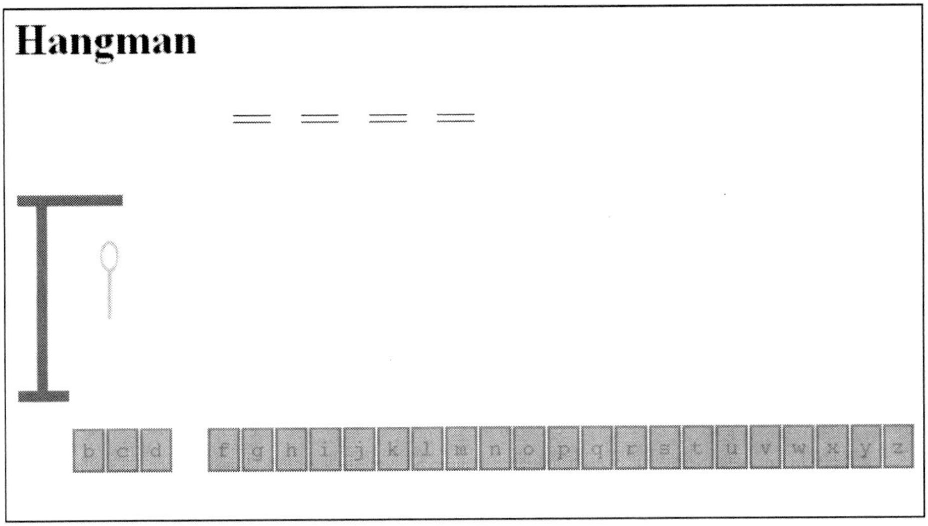

Figure 9-3. The game after guessing an e

Next, I guess an *i*, resulting in my third wrong move, as shown in Figure 9-4.

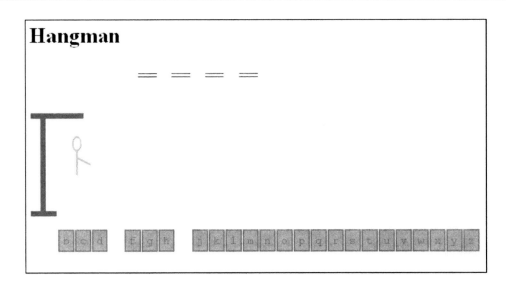

Figure 9-4. The game screen after three incorrect selections

Now, I guess an *o*, and this turns out to be correct (as I knew since I have insider information), and an o appears as the third letter in the word, as shown in Figure 9-5.

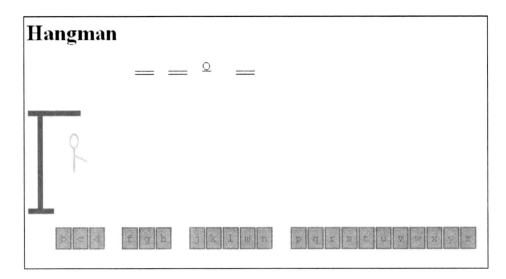

Figure 9-5. A correct guess of *o*

I try the next vowel, *u*, and that is correct also, as Figure 9-6 indicates.

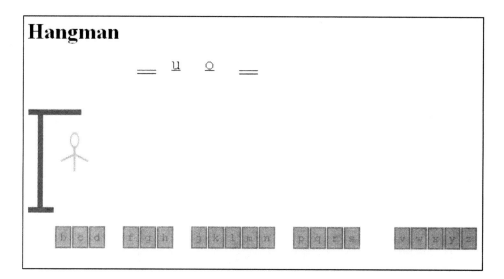

Figure 9-6. Two letters have been identified.

I now make some more guesses, first a *t*, as shown in Figure 9-7.

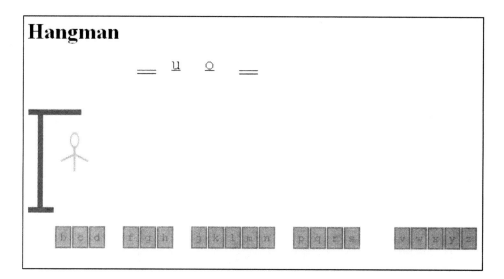

Figure 9-7. Another wrong guess of *t*

Then, I make another wrong guess, this time, an *s*, as shown in Figure 9-8.

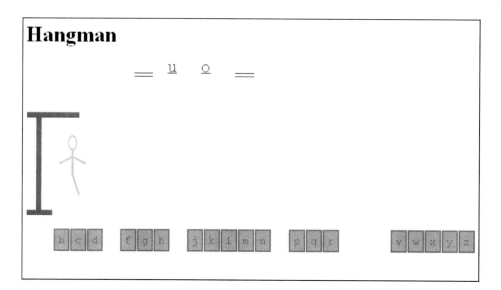

Figure 9-8. After a wrong guess of *s*

Figure 9-9 shows yet another wrong guess.

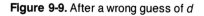

Figure 9-9. After a wrong guess of *d*

I decide to make a correct guess, namely *m*. Figure 9-10 shows three identified letters and most of the person drawn on the screen.

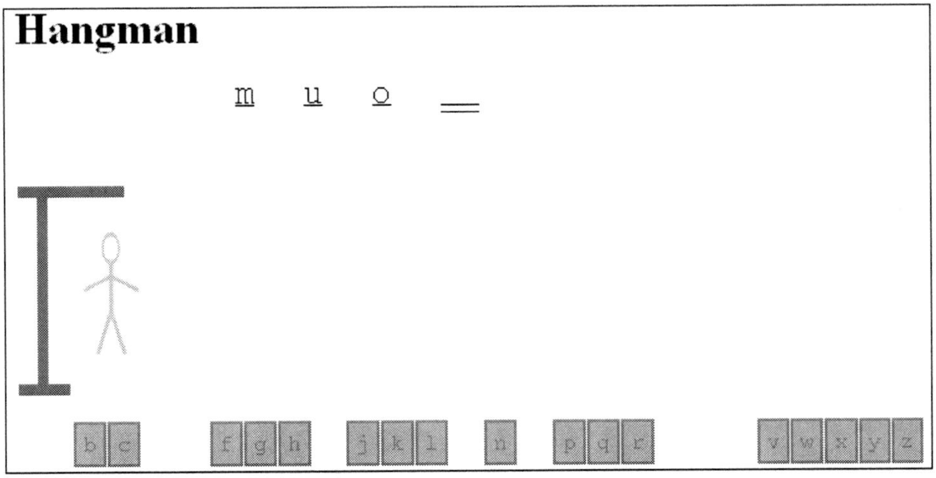

Figure 9-10. After a correct guess of *m*

At this point, I am trying to lose, so I guess *b*. This results in what is depicted in Figure 9-11.

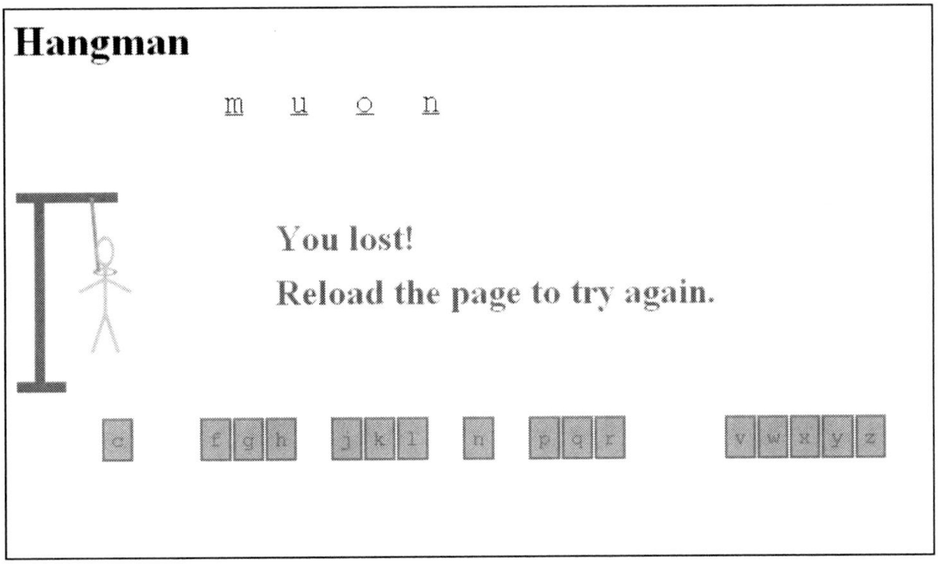

Figure 9-11. Game lost

Notice that the drawing shows a noose; the complete secret word is revealed; and a message appears telling the player that the game is lost and to reload to try again.

Figure 9-12 shows a screenshot from another game, and the computer has responded to a guess of the letter *e* by showing it in two positions. Handling letters appearing more than once is not difficult, but that certainly was not obvious to me before I started the programming.

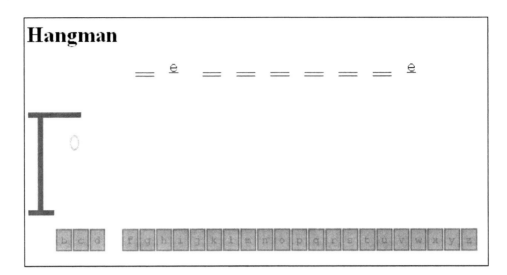

Figure 9-12. In this game, e appears in two spots.

I make some other guesses and finally get this word correct. Again, the list from which the choices are made is not very long, so I can guess the words from the number of letters. Figure 9-13 shows a screenshot from a winning game. Notice that there are two *e*'s and three *f*'s in the secret word.

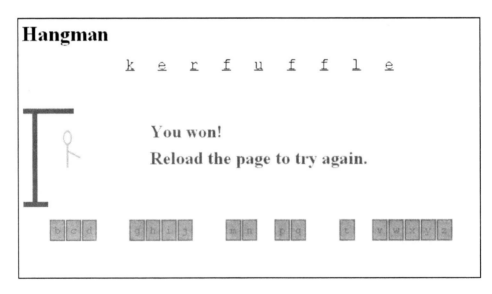

Figure 9-13. Winning the game

The programming techniques and language features include manipulating character strings; using an array holding the letters of the English alphabet; creating markup elements to hold the alphabet and the spaces that represent the secret word, which may or may not be replaced by letters; handling events for the created alphabet blocks; setting up a set of functions for drawing the steps of the hanging; and placing the names of the functions in an array. This implementation also demonstrates the use of external script files for holding the word list. This game has turns within a game, unlike, say, rock, paper, scissors, so the program must manage the game state internally as well as display it on the screen.

Critical requirements

As was true in the previous chapter, the implementation of this game makes use of many HTML5 and JavaScript constructs demonstrated in earlier chapters, but they are put together here in different ways. Programming is similar to writing. In programming, you put together various constructs, just like you write sentences composed of words that you know, and then put these into paragraphs, and so on. While reading this chapter, think back to what you have learned about drawing lines, arcs, and text on the canvas; creating new HTML markup; setting up a mouse click event for markup on the screen; and using if and for statements.

To implement Hangman, we need access to a list of words. Creating and testing the program does not require a long list, which could be substituted later. I decided to make it a requirement that the word list be separate from the program.

The user interface for player moves could have manifested in one of several ways, for example, an input field in a form. However, I decided a better approach was to make the interface include graphics representing the letters of the alphabet. It was necessary to make each of the graphics act as a clickable button *and* provide a way to make each letter disappear after it has been selected.

The pencil-and-paper version of the game involves a progression of drawings ultimately resulting in a stick figure with a noose around its neck. The computer game must show the same progression of drawings. The drawings can be simple lines and ovals.

The secret word must be represented on the screen, initially as all blanks and then filled in with any correctly identified letters. I chose to use double lines as blanks, because I wanted identified letters to be underlined. An alternative could be question marks.

Last, the program must monitor the progress of the game and correctly determine when the player has lost and when the player has won. The game state is visible to the player, but the program must set up and check internal variables to make the determination that the game is won or lost.

HTML5, CSS, JavaScript features

Let's now look at the specific features of HTML5, CSS, and JavaScript that provide what we need to implement Hangman. Except for basic HTML tags and the workings of functions and variables, the explanations here are complete. However, much of this chapter repeats explanations given in earlier chapters. As before, you may choose to look at all the code in the "Building the Application" section first and return to this section if you need explanations of specific features.

Storing a word list as an array defined in an external script file

The Hangman game requires access to a list of legal words, which can be called the word bank. It would be a pretty sure bet to say that one approach is to use an array. The short array we'll use for this initial example follows:

```
var words = [
    "muon", "blight","kerfuffle","qat"
    ];
```

Notice that the words are all different lengths. This means that we can use the random processing code that we will want for the final version and still know what word has been selected when we're testing. We'll make sure the code uses words.length so that when you substitute a bigger array, the coding still works.

Now, the question is how to use different arrays for this purpose if we want to bring in a different list of words. It certainly is possible to change the HTML document. However, in HTML5 (or previous versions of HTML), it is possible to include a reference to an external script file in place of or in addition to a script element in the HTML document. We can take the three lines that declare and define the variable words and place them in a file named words1.js. We can include this file with the rest of the document using the following line of code:

```
<script src="words1.js" defer></script>
```

The defer method will cause this file to be loaded while the browser is continuing with the rest of the base HTML document. We could not load these two files simultaneously if the external file contained part of the body, but it works in this situation.

A more elaborate program could include multiple files with code for the player to select from among different levels or languages.

Generating and positioning HTML markup, then making the markup be buttons, and then disabling the buttons

The creation of the alphabet buttons and the secret word dashes is done with a combination of JavaScript and CSS.

We'll write code to create HTML markup for two parts of the program: the alphabet icons and the blanks for the secret word. (You can go to the quiz game in Chapter 6 for more on creating HTML markup.) In each case, HTML markup is created using the following built-in methods:

- document.createElement(x): Creates HTML markup for the new element type x
- document.body.appendChild (d): Adds the d element as another child element of the body element
- document.getElementById(id): Extracts the element with id the value of id

The HTML is created to include a unique id for each element. The code involves setting certain properties:

- d.innerHTML is set to hold the HTML
- thingelem.style.top is set to hold the vertical position
- thingelem.style.left is set to hold the horizontal position

With this background, here is the coding for setting up the alphabet buttons. We first declare a global variable alphabet:

```
var alphabet = "abcdefghijklmnopqrstuvwxyz";
```

The setupgame function has this code for making the alphabet buttons:

```
var i;
   var x;
   var y;
   var uniqueid;
   var an = alphabet.length;
   for(i=0;i<an;i++) {

       uniqueid = "a"+String(i);
       d = document.createElement('alphabet');
        d.innerHTML = (
          "<div class='letters' id='"+uniqueid+"'>"+alphabet[i]+"</div>");
       document.body.appendChild(d);
       thingelem = document.getElementById(uniqueid);
       x = alphabetx + alphabetwidth*i;
       y = alphabety;
       thingelem.style.top = String(y)+"px";
       thingelem.style.left = String(x)+"px";
       thingelem.addEventListener('click',pickelement,false);
   }
```

The variable i is used for iterating over the alphabet string. The unique id is *a* concatenated with the index value, which will go from 0 to 25. The HTML inserted into the created element is a div with text containing the letter. The string is surrounded by double quotation marks, and the attributes inside this string are surrounded by single quotation marks. The elements are spaced across the screen, starting at the position alphabetx, alphabety (each global variable is declared earlier in the document), and incremented horizontally by alphabetwidth. The top and left attributes need to be set to strings and end with "px", for pixels. The last step is to set up event handling so these elements act as buttons.

The creation of the elements for the secret word is similar. A difference is that each of these elements has two underscores as its text content. On the screen, these two underscores look like one long underscore. The assignment to ch (for choice) is how our program selects the secret word.

```
var ch = Math.floor(Math.random()* words.length);
   secret = words[ch];
   for (i=0;i<secret.length;i++) {
       uniqueid = "s"+String(i);
       d = document.createElement('secret');
           d.innerHTML = (
               "<div class='blanks' id='"+uniqueid+"'> __ </div>");
       document.body.appendChild(d);
       thingelem = document.getElementById(uniqueid);
       x = secretx + secretwidth*i;
       y = secrety;
       thingelem.style.top = String(y)+"px";
       thingelem.style.left = String(x)+"px";
   }
```

At this point, you may be asking, how did the alphabet icons get to be letters inside blocks with borders? The answer is that I used CSS. The usefulness of CSS goes far beyond fonts and colors. The styles provide the look and feel of critical parts of the game. Notice that the alphabet div elements have a class setting of 'letters', and the secret word letter div elements have a setting of 'blanks'. The style section contains the following two styles:

```
<style>
.letters {position:absolute;left: 0px; top: 0px; border: 2px; border-style: double;↪
 margin: 5px; padding: 5px; color:#F00; background-color:#0FC; font-family:"Courier↪
New", Courier, monospace;
}
.blanks {position:absolute;left: 0px; top: 0px; border:none; margin: 5px; padding:↪
 5px; color:#006; background-color:white; font-family:"Courier New", Courier,↪
 monospace; text-decoration:underline; color: black; font-size:24px;
}
</style>
```

The designation of a dot followed by a name means this style applies to all elements of that class. This is in contrast to just a name, such as form in the last chapter, in which a style was applied to all form elements, or to a # followed by a name that refers to the one element in the document with an id of that name. Notice that the style for letters includes a border, a color, and a background color. Specifying a font family is a way to pick your favorite font for the task and then specify backups if that font is not available. This feature of CSS provides a wide latitude to designers. My choices here are "Courier New", with a second choice of Courier, and a third choice of any monospace font available (in a *monospace font*, all the letters are the same width). I decided to use a monospace font to facilitate making icons that are the same in size and space nicely across the screen. The margin attribute sets to the spacing outside the border, and padding refers to the spacing between the text and the border.

We want the buttons representing letters of the alphabet to disappear after they are clicked. The code in the pickelement function can use the term this to refer to the clicked object. These two statements (which could be squeezed into one) make this happen by setting the display attribute:

```
var id = this.id;
document.getElementById(id).style.display = "none";
```

When the game is over, either through a win or a loss, we remove the click event handling for all the letters by iterating over all the elements:

```
for (j=0;j<alphabet.length;j++) {
    uniqueid = "a"+String(j);
    thingelem = document.getElementById(uniqueid);
    thingelem.removeEventListener('click',pickelement,false);
}
```

The removeEventListener event does what it sounds like: it removes the event handling.

Creating progressive drawings on a canvas

In the chapters so far, you have read about drawing rectangles, text, images, and also paths. The paths consist of lines and arcs. For Hangman, the drawings are all paths. For this application, code has set the variable ctx to point to the 2D context of the canvas. Drawing a path involves setting a line width by setting ctx.lineWidth to a numerical value and setting ctx.strokeStyle to a color. We will use different line widths and colors for various parts of the drawing.

The next line in the code is `ctx.beginPath();`, and it's followed by a sequence of operations to draw lines or arcs or move a virtual pen. The method `ctx.moveTo` moves the pen without drawing and `ctx.lineTo` specifies the drawing of a line from the current pen position to the point indicated. Please keep in mind that nothing is drawn until the call of the `stroke` method. The `moveTo`, `lineTo`, and `arc` commands set up the path that is drawn whenever either the `stroke` or `fill` methods are invoked. In our draw functions, the next step is calling `ctx.stroke();`, and the last step is calling `ctx.closePath();` to end the path. For example, the gallows is drawn by the following function:

```
function drawgallows() {
    ctx.lineWidth = 8;
    ctx.strokeStyle = gallowscolor;
    ctx.beginPath();
    ctx.moveTo(2,180);
    ctx.lineTo(40,180);
    ctx.moveTo(20,180);
    ctx.lineTo(20,40);
    ctx.moveTo(2,40);
    ctx.lineTo(80,40);
    ctx.stroke();
    ctx.closePath();
}
```

The head and the noose require ovals. The ovals will be based on circles, so first I will review how to draw a circle. You also can go back to Chapter 2. Drawing a circular arc is done with the `ctx.arc` command with the following parameters: coordinates for the center of the circle, a length for the radius, the starting angle in radians, the ending angle, and `false` for counter-clockwise or `true` for clockwise. *Radians* are intrinsic measurements in which a full circle is `Math.PI*2`. The conversion from degrees to radians is to divide by `Math.PI` and multiply by `180`, but that is not needed for this example because we are drawing complete arcs.

However, we want to draw an oval in place of a circle for the head (and later for part of the noose). The solution is to use `ctx.scale` to change the coordinate system. In Chapter 4, we changed the coordinate system to rotate the rectangle representing a cannon. Here, we manipulate the coordinate system to squeeze one dimension to make a circle an oval. What our code does is first use `ctx.save()` to save the current coordinate system. Then for the head, it uses `ctx.scale(.6,1);` to shorten the x axis to 60 percent of its current value and keep the y axis the same. Use the code for drawing an arc and then use `ctx.restore();` to restore the original coordinate system. The function for drawing the head follows:

```
function drawhead() {
    ctx.lineWidth = 3;
    ctx.strokeStyle = facecolor;
    ctx.save();  //before scaling of circle to be oval
    ctx.scale(.6,1);
    ctx.beginPath();
    ctx.arc (bodycenterx/.6,80,10,0,Math.PI*2,false);
    ctx.stroke();
    ctx.closePath();
    ctx.restore();
}
```

The `drawnoose` function makes use of the same technique, except that, for the noose, the oval is wide as opposed to narrow; that is, the vertical is squeezed and not the horizontal.

Each step in the progression of drawings is represented by a function, such as `drawhead` and `drawbody`. We list all of these in an array called `steps`:

```
var steps = [
      drawgallows,
      drawhead,
      drawbody,
      drawrightarm,
      drawleftarm,
      drawrightleg,
      drawleftleg,
      drawnoose
      ];
```

A variable, `cur`, keeps track of the current step, and when the code confirms the condition that `cur` is equal to the length of `steps`, the game is over.

After experimenting with these, I decided that I needed to draw the head and draw a neck on top of the noose. This is done by putting in calls to `drawhead` and `drawneck` in the `drawnoose` function. The order is important.

Use the draw functions as models for you to make your own drawings. Do change each of these individual functions. You also can add or take away functions. This means you would be changing the number of steps in the progression, that is, the number of wrong guesses the player can make before losing the game.

> *Tip: If you haven't done so already (or even if you have), experiment with drawing. Create a separate file just for drawing the steps of the hanging. Experiment with lines and arcs. You also can include images.*

Maintaining the game state and determining a win or loss

The requirement to encode and maintain the state of an application is a common one in programming. In Chapter 2, our program kept track of whether the next move was a first throw or a follow-up throw of the dice. The state of the Hangman game includes the identity of the hidden word, what letters in the word have been correctly guessed, what letters of the alphabet have been tried, and the state of the progression of the hanging.

The `pickelement` function, invoked when the player clicks on an alphabet block, is where the critical action takes place, and it performs the following tasks:

- Check if the player's guess, kept in the variable `picked`, matches any of the letters in the secret word held in the variable `secret`. For each `match`, the corresponding letter in the blank elements is revealed by setting `textContent` to that letter.
- Keep track of how many letters have been guessed using the variable `lettersguessed`.

- Check if the game has been won by comparing `lettersguessed` to `secret.length`. If the game is won, remove event handling for the alphabet buttons and display the appropriate messages.
- If the selected letter did not match any letters in the secret word (if the variable `not` is still `true`), advance the hanging using the variable `cur` for an index into the array variable `steps`
- Check if the game has been lost by comparing `cur` to `steps.length`. If the two values are equal, reveal all the letters, remove event handling, and display the appropriate messages.
- Whether or not there is a match, make the clicked alphabet button disappear by setting the `display` attribute to `none`.

These tasks are performed using `if` and `for` statements. The check if the game has been won is done after determining that a letter has been guessed correctly. Similarly, the check if the game has been lost is done only when it is determined that a letter has *not* been correctly identified and the hanging has advanced. The state of the game is represented in the code by the `secret`, `lettersguessed`, and `cur` variables. The player sees the underscores and filled-in letters of the secret word and the remaining alphabet blocks.

The code for the whole HTML document with line-by-line comments is in the "Building the Application" section. The next section describes the critical first task of handling a player's guess. One general tactic to keep in mind is that several tasks are accomplished by doing something for every member of an array even if it may not be necessary for certain elements of the array. For example, when the task is to reveal all the letters in the secret word, all have the `textContent` changed even if some of them have already been revealed. Similarly, the variable `not` may be set to `false` multiple times.

Checking a guess and revealing letters in the secret word by setting textContent

The player makes a move by clicking a letter. The `pickelement` function is set up as the event handler for each letter icon. Therefore, within the function, we can use the term `this` to refer to the object that received (listened for and heard) the click event. Consequently, the expression `this.textContent` will hold the selected letter. Therefore, the statement

```
var picked = this.textContent;
```

assigns to the local variable `picked` the specific letter of the alphabet the player is guessing. The code then iterates over all the letters in the secret word held in the variable `secret` and compares each letter to the guess of the player. The created markup that starts out being the double underlines corresponds to the letters in the secret word, so when there is a correct guess, the corresponding element will be changed; that is, its `textContent` will be set to the letter guessed by the player, which is held in `picked`:

```
for (i=0;i<secret.length;i++) {
    if (picked==secret[i]) {
        id = "s"+String(i);
        document.getElementById(id).textContent = picked;
                not = false;
                lettersguessed++;
            ...
```

The iteration does not stop when a guess is correct; it keeps going. This means that all instances of any one letter will be discovered and revealed. The variable not is set to false each time there is a match. If there were two or more instances of the same letter, this variable is set more than once, which is not a problem. I included the word *kerfuffle* to make sure that repeated letters were handled correctly (besides the fact that I like the word). You can examine all the code in the next section.

Building the application and making it your own

The Hangman application makes use of CSS styles, HTML markup created by JavaScript, and JavaScript coding. There are two initializing and set up functions (init and setupgame) and the function that does most of the work (pickelement), plus eight functions that draw steps in the hanging. The functions are described in Table 9-1.

Table 9-1. Functions Invoked or Called by Calls

Function	Invoked / Called By	Calls
init	Invoked by the action of onLoad in the <body> tag	setupgame
setupgame	init	The first of the drawing functions, namely drawgallows
pickelement	Invoked by the action of the addEventListener calls in setupgame	One of the drawing functions through call of steps[cur]()
drawgallows	Call of steps[cur]() in pickelement	
drawhead	Call of steps[cur]() in pickelement, drawnoose	
drawbody	Call of steps[cur]() in pickelement	
drawrightarm	Call of steps[cur]() in pickelement	
drawleftarm	Call of steps[cur]() in pickelement	
drawrightleg	Call of steps[cur]() in pickelement	
drawleftleg	Call of steps[cur]() in pickelement	
drawnoose	Call of steps[cur]() in pickelement	drawhead, drawnoose
drawneck	drawnoose	

Note the indirect pattern of most of the function calls. This pattern provides considerable flexibility if you decide to change the hanging progression. Note also that you can remove the very first call in the setupgame function if you want the player to start with a blank page and not with the representation of the wooden beams of the gallows.

The complete implementation of Hangman is shown in Table 9-2.

Table 9-2. The Complete Implementation of Hangman

Code	Explanation
`<html>`	Opening tag
`<head>`	Opening tag
`    <title>Hangman</title>`	Completes the title element
`<style>`	Opens the style element

`.letters {position:absolute;left: 0px;↪`
`top: 0px; border: 2px; border-style: double;↪`
`margin: 5px; padding: 5px; color:#F00;↪`
`background-color:#0FC; font-family:↪`
`"Courier New", Courier, monospace;`
	Specifies styling for any element with designated class letters, including the border, colors, and font

`}`	Closing style directive

`.blanks {position:absolute;left: 0px;↪`
`top: 0px; border:none; margin: 5px;↪`
`padding: 5px; color:#006; background-color:↪`
`white; font-family:"Courier New", Courier,↪`
`monospace; text-decoration:underline; color:`
`black;`
	Specifies styling for any element with designated class blanks, including the border, spacing, color, and font, and puts in underlines

`}`	Closing style directive
`</style>`	Closes the style element
`<script src="words1.js" defer></script>`	Element calling for inclusion of external file, with directive to load the file at same time as the rest of this document
`    <script >`	Opening tag for the script element
`  var ctx;`	Variable used for all drawing
`    var thingelem;`	Variable used for created elements

Code	Explanation
`var alphabet = "abcdefghijklmnopqrstuvwxyz";`	Defines letters of the alphabet, used for alphabet buttons
`var alphabety = 300;`	Vertical position for all alphabet buttons
`var alphabetx = 20;`	Starting alphabet horizontal position
`var alphabetwidth = 25;`	Width allocated for the alphabet elements
`var secret;`	Will hold the secret word
`var lettersguessed = 0;`	Keeps count of letters guessed
`var secretx = 160;`	Horizontal starting position for secret word
`var secrety = 50;`	Vertical position for secret word
`var secretwidth = 50;`	Width allocated for each letter in display of secret word
`var gallowscolor = "brown";`	Color for the gallows
`var facecolor = "tan";`	Color for the face
`var bodycolor = "tan";`	Color for the body
`var noosecolor = "#F60";`	Color for the noose
`var bodycenterx = 70;`	Horizontal position for the body
`var steps = [`	Holds the functions constituting the sequence of drawings for the progression toward the hanging
`drawgallows,`	Draws the gallows
`drawhead,`	Draws the head
`drawbody,`	Draws the body
`drawrightarm,`	Draws the right arm
`drawleftarm,`	Draws the left arm

Code	Explanation
`drawrightleg,`	Draws the right leg
`drawleftleg,`	Draws the left leg
`drawnoose`	Draws the noose
`];`	Ends the array steps
`var cur = 0;`	Points to the next drawing in steps
`function drawgallows() {`	Header for the function drawing the gallows
`ctx.lineWidth = 8;`	Sets the line width
`ctx.strokeStyle = gallowscolor;`	Sets the color
`ctx.beginPath();`	Begins the drawing path
`ctx.moveTo(2,180);`	Moves to the first position
`ctx.lineTo(40,180);`	Draws a line
`ctx.moveTo(20,180);`	Moves to the next position
`ctx.lineTo(20,40);`	Draws a line
`ctx.moveTo(2,40);`	Moves to the next position
`ctx.lineTo(80,40);`	Draws the line
`ctx.stroke();`	Actually draws the whole path
`ctx.closePath();`	Closes the path
`}`	Closes the function
`function drawhead() {`	Header for the function drawing the head of the victim
`ctx.lineWidth = 3;`	Sets the line width
`ctx.strokeStyle = facecolor;`	Sets the color

Code	Explanation
`ctx.save();`	Saves the current stage of the coordinate system
`ctx.scale(.6,1);`	Applies scaling, namely squeezes the x axis
`ctx.beginPath();`	Start a path
`ctx.arc (bodycenterx/.6,80,10,0,↪` `Math.PI*2,false);`	Draws an arc. Note that the x coordinate is modified to work for the scaled coordinate system. The complete arc will be an oval.
`ctx.stroke();`	Actually does the drawing
`ctx.closePath();`	Closes the path
`ctx.restore();`	Restores (goes back to) the coordinates before the scaling
`}`	Closes function
`function drawbody() {`	Header for the function that draws the body, a single line
`ctx.strokeStyle = bodycolor;`	Sets the color
`ctx.beginPath();`	Starts the path
`ctx.moveTo(bodycenterx,90);`	Moves to the position (right below head)
`ctx.lineTo(bodycenterx,125);`	Draws the line
`ctx.stroke();`	Actually draws the path
`ctx.closePath();`	Closes the path
`}`	Closes the function
`function drawrightarm() {`	Header for the function that draws the right arm
`ctx.beginPath();`	Starts the path
`ctx.moveTo(bodycenterx,100);`	Moves to the position

Code	Explanation
`ctx.lineTo(bodycenterx+20,110);`	Draws the line
`ctx.stroke();`	Actually draws the path
`ctx.closePath();`	Closes the path
`}`	Closes the function
`function drawleftarm() {`	Header for the function that draws the left arm
`ctx.beginPath();`	Starts the path
`ctx.moveTo(bodycenterx,100);`	Moves to the position
`ctx.lineTo(bodycenterx-20,110);`	Draws the line
`ctx.stroke();`	Actually draws the path
`ctx.closePath();`	Closes the path
`}`	Closes the function
`function drawrightleg() {`	Header for the function that draws the right leg
`ctx.beginPath();`	Starts the path
`ctx.moveTo(bodycenterx,125);`	Moves to the position
`ctx.lineTo(bodycenterx+10,155);`	Draws the line
`ctx.stroke();`	Actually draws the path
`ctx.closePath();`	Closes the path
`}`	Closes the function
`function drawleftleg() {`	Header for the function that draws the left leg
`ctx.beginPath();`	Starts the path
`ctx.moveTo(bodycenterx,125);`	Moves to the position

Code	Explanation
`ctx.lineTo(bodycenterx-10,155);`	Draws the line
`ctx.stroke();`	Actually draws the path
`ctx.closePath();`	Closes the path
`}`	Closes the function
`function drawnoose() {`	Header for the function that draws noose
`ctx.strokeStyle = noosecolor;`	Sets the color
`ctx.beginPath();`	Starts the path
`ctx.moveTo(bodycenterx-10,40);`	Moves to the position
`ctx.lineTo(bodycenterx-5,95);`	Draws the line
`ctx.stroke();`	Actually draws the path
`ctx.closePath();`	Closes the path
`ctx.save();`	Saves the coordinate system
`ctx.scale(1,.3);`	Does the scaling, which, squeezes the image vertically (on the y axis)
`ctx.beginPath();`	Starts a path
`ctx.arc(bodycenterx,95/.3,8,0,Math.➥ PI*2,false);`	Draws a circle (which will become an oval)
`ctx.stroke();`	Actually draws the path
`ctx.closePath();`	Closes the path
`ctx.restore();`	Restores the saved coordinate system
`drawneck();`	Draws the neck on top of the noose
`drawhead();`	Draws the head on top of the noose

Code	Explanation
`}`	Closes the function
`function drawneck() {`	Header for the function for drawing the neck
`    ctx.strokeStyle=bodycolor;`	Sets the color
`    ctx.beginPath();`	Starts the path
`    ctx.moveTo(bodycenterx,90);`	Moves to the position
`    ctx.lineTo(bodycenterx,95);`	Draws the line
`    ctx.stroke();`	Actually draws the path
`    ctx.closePath();`	Closes the path
`}`	Closes the function
`function init(){`	Header for the function called on document load
`    ctx = document.getElementById➥` `('canvas').getContext('2d');`	Sets up the variable for all drawing on canvas
`    setupgame();`	Invokes the function that sets up the game
`    ctx.font="bold 20pt Ariel";`	Sets the font
`}`	Closes the function
`function setupgame() {`	Header for the function that sets up the alphabet buttons and the secret word
`    var i;`	Creates the variable for iterations
`    var x;`	Creates the variable for position
`    var y;`	Creates the variable for position
`    var uniqueid;`	Creates the variable for each of each set of created HTML elements
`    var an = alphabet.length;`	Will be 26

Code	Explanation
`for(i=0;i<an;i++) {`	Iterates to create alphabet buttons
`uniqueid = "a"+String(i);`	Creates a unique identifier.
`d = document.createElement('alphabet');`	Creates an element of type `alphabet`
`d.innerHTML = (`	Defines the contents as specified in the next line
`"<div class='letters'`↪ `id='"+uniqueid+"'>"+alphabet[i]+"</div>");`	Specifies a `div` of class `letters` with a unique identifier and text content, which is the `i`th letter of the alphabet
`document.body.appendChild(d);`	Adds to body
`thingelem = document.getElementById`↪ `(uniqueid);`	Gets the element with the id
`x = alphabetx + alphabetwidth*i;`	Computes its horizontal position
`y = alphabety;`	Sets the vertical position
`thingelem.style.top = String(y)+"px";`	Using the style `top`, sets the vertical position
`thingelem.style.left = String(x)+"px";`	Using the style `left`, sets the horizontal position
`thingelem.addEventListener('click',`↪ `pickelement,false);`	Sets up event handling for the mouse click event
`}`	Closes the `for` loop
`var ch = Math.floor(Math.random()*`↪ `words.length);`	Chooses, at random, an index for one of the words
`secret = words[ch];`	Set the global variable `secret` to be this word
`for (i=0;i<secret.length;i++) {`	Iterates for the length of the secret word
`uniqueid = "s"+String(i);`	Creates a unique identifier for the word
`d = document.createElement('secret');`	Creates an element for the word

Code	Explanation
`d.innerHTML = "<div class='blanks' id='"`↪ `+uniqueid+"'> __ </div>");`	Sets the contents to be a `div` of class `blanks`, with the id of the word the `uniqueid` just created. The text content will be an underscore.
`document.body.appendChild(d);`	Appends the created element as a child of the body
`thingelem = document.getElementById`↪ `(uniqueid);`	Gets the created element
`x = secretx + secretwidth*i;`	Calculates the element's horizontal position
`y = secrety;`	Sets its vertical position
`thingelem.style.top = String(y)+"px";`	Using the style `top`, sets the vertical position
`thingelem.style.left = String(x)+"px";`	Using the style `left`, sets the horizontal position
`}`	Closes the `for` loop
`steps[cur]();`	Draws the first function in the steps list, the gallows
`cur++;`	Increments `cur`
`return false;`	Returns `false` to prevent any refreshing of the HTML page
`}`	Closes the function
`function pickelement(ev) {`	Header for the function invoked as a result of a click
`var not = true;`	Sets `not` to `true`, which may or may not be changed
`var picked = this.textContent;`	Extracts the text content, namely the letter, from the object this references
`var i;`	Iterates

Code	Explanation
`var j;`	Iterates
`var uniqueid;`	Used to create unique identifiers for elements
`var thingelem;`	Holds the element
`var out;`	Displays a message
`for (i=0;i<secret.length;i++) {`	Iterates over the letters in the secret word
`if (picked==secret[i]) {`	Says, "If the player guessed letter is equal to this letter in secret…"
`id = "s"+String(i);`	Constructs the identifier for this letter
`document.getElementById(id).↪` `textContent = picked;`	Changes the text content to be the letter
`not = false;`	Sets not to false
`lettersguessed++;`	Increment the number of letters identified correctly
`if (lettersguessed==secret.length) {`	Says, "If the whole secret word has been guessed…"
`ctx.fillStyle=gallowscolor;`	Sets the color, which uses the brown of the gallows but could be anything
`out = "You won!";`	Sets the message
`ctx.fillText(out,200,80);`	Displays the message
`ctx.fillText("Re-load the page to↪` `try again.",200,120);`	Displays another message
`for (j=0;j<alphabet.length;j++) {`	Iterates over the whole alphabet
`uniqueid = "a"+String(j);`	Constructs the identifier
`thingelem = document.getElementById↪` `(uniqueid);`	Gets the element

Code	Explanation
`thingelem.removeEventListener('click',`↪ `pickelement,false);`	Removes the event handling
`        }`	Closes the `j` for loop iteration
`      }`	Closes `if (lettersguessed….)`, that is, the all-done test
`    }`	Closes the `if (picked==secret[i])` true clause
`  }`	Closes the `for` loop over letters in the secret word iteration
`  if (not) {`	Checks if no letters were identified
`    steps[cur]();`	Proceeds with the next step of the hanging iteration
`    cur++;`	Increments the counter
`    if (cur>=steps.length) {`	Checks to see if all steps are finished
`      for (i=0;i<secret.length;i++) {`	Starts a new iteration over the letters in the secret word to reveal all the letters
`        id = "s"+String(i);`	Constructs the identifier
`        document.getElementById(id).textContent`↪ `= secret[i];`	Obtains a reference to the element and sets it to that letter in the secret word
`      }`	Close the iteration
`      ctx.fillStyle=gallowscolor;`	Set the color
`      out = "You lost!";`	Sets the message
`      ctx.fillText(out,200,80);`	Displays the message
`          ctx.fillText("Re-load the`↪ `page to try again.",200,120);`	Displays the reload message

Code	Explanation
`for (j=0;j<alphabet.length;j++) {`	Iterates over all of the letters in the alphabet
`uniqueid = "a"+String(j);`	Constructs the unique identifier
`thingelem = document.getElementById↪` `(uniqueid);`	Gets the element
`thingelem.removeEventListener('click',↪` `pickelement,false);`	Removes the event handling for this element
`}`	Closes the j iteration
`}`	Closes the cur test to determine if the hanging is complete
`}`	Closes the if (not) test (bad guess by player)
`var id = this.id;`	Extracts the identifier for this element
`document.getElementById(id).style.display↪` `= "none";`	Makes this particular alphabet button disappear
`}`	Closes the function
`</script>`	Closes the script
`</head>`	Closes the head
`<body onLoad="init();">`	Opening tag that sets up call to init
`<h1>Hangman</h1>`	Puts the name of game in big letters
`<p>`	Opening tag for paragraph
`<canvas id="canvas" width="600" height="400">`	Opening tag for canvas element. Includes dimensions.
`Your browser doesn't support the HTML5↪` `  element canvas.`	Message for people using browsers that don't recognize canvas
`</canvas>`	Closing tag for canvas

Code	Explanation
`</body>`	Closes the body
`</html>`	Closes the document

A variation of Hangman uses common sayings in place of words. Building on this game to create that one is a challenge for you. The critical steps are handling of blanks between the words and the punctuation. You probably want to reveal each instance of blanks between words and periods, commas, and question marks immediately, making these things hints to the player. This means that you need to make sure that `lettersguessed` starts off with the correct count. Do not be concerned that the selected letters are compared to blanks or punctuation.

Another variation would be to change the alphabet. I carefully replaced all the instances of 26 with `alphabet.length`. You would also need to change the language for the messages for winning and losing.

A suitable enhancement of the game is to make a New Word button. To do so, you need to split up the workings of the `setupgame` button into two functions: One function creates new alphabet icons and the positions for the longest possible secret word. The other makes sure all the alphabet icons are visible and set up for event handling and then selects and sets up the blanks for secret word, making sure the appropriate number are visible. If you do this, you may want to include display of a score and a number of games.

Continuing with the educational idea and assuming you use unusual words, you may want to include definitions. The definition can be revealed at the end, by writing text on the canvas. Or you can make a button to click to reveal the definition as a hint to the player. Alternatively, you could create a link to a site such as Dictionary.com.

Testing and uploading the application

To test this application, you can download my word list or create your own. If you create your own, start off with a short word list prepared as plain text, giving it the name `words1.js`. When testing, do not always guess in the same pattern, such as choosing the vowels in order. Misbehave and try to keep guessing after the game is over. When you are satisfied with the coding, create a longer word list, and save it under the name `words1.js`. Both the HTML and `words1.js` files need to be uploaded to your server.

Summary

In this chapter, you learned how to implement a familiar game using features of HTML5, JavaScript, and CSS along with general programming techniques, which included the following:

- using the `scale` method to change the coordinate system to draw an oval, as opposed to a circle, by saving and restoring before and after
- creating HTML markup dynamically
- setting up and removing event handling using `addEventListener` and `removeEventListener` for individual elements

- using styles to remove elements from display
- using arrays of function names to set up a progression of drawings
- manipulating variables to maintain the state of the game, with calculations to determine if there is a win or a loss
- creating an external script file to hold the word list for increased flexibility
- using CSS, including `font-family` for the selection of fonts, `color`, and `display`

The next and final chapter of this book will describe the implementation of the card game, blackjack, also called 21. It will build on what you have learned already and describe some new techniques in programming, elements added to HTML5, and more CSS.

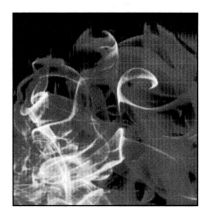

Chapter 10

Blackjack

In this chapter, we will be covering

- the footer and header tags, which are new to HTML5
- capturing key presses
- programmer-defined objects
- generating Image elements using a set of external image files
- shuffling a deck of cards

Introduction

The objective of this chapter is to combine programming techniques and HTML5 and JavaScript features to implement the card game blackjack, also called 21. The implementation will make use of new tags introduced in HTML5, namely footer and header. We will make use of the footer to give credit to the source for the card images and the web site we are using for the shuffling algorithm. The cards are created using programmer-defined objects and Image objects, with coding to generate the names of the image files. The player makes moves using key presses.

The rules of blackjack are as follows: The player plays against the dealer (also known as the house). The player and dealer are each dealt two cards. The first card of the dealer is hidden from the player, but the other is visible. The value of a card is its face value for the numbered cards, 10 for a jack, queen, or king, and either 1 or 11 for an ace. The value of a hand is the sum of the cards. The object of the game is to have a hand with a value as close to 21 as possible without going over *and* to have a value greater than the other person. Thus an ace and a face card count as 21, a winning hand. The actions are to request another card or to hold.

Since this is a two-person game, our player will play against the computer, and as was the case with rock, paper, scissors, we have the task of generating the computer moves. However, we are guided by the practice of casinos—the dealer (house) will use a fixed strategy. Our dealer will request another card if the value of the hand is under 17 (the game strategy in casinos may be slightly more complicated and may be dependent on the presence of aces). Similarly, our game does declare a tie if the player and house have the same total if the total is under 21; some casinos may have a different practice.

An opening screenshot is shown in Figure 10-1.

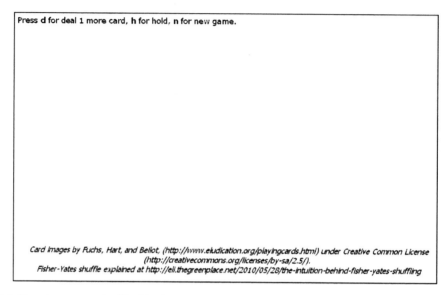

Figure 10-1. Opening screen for blackjack

After the user presses the n key, the next screen would look something like Figure 10-2. Remember that there are random processes involved, so this same set of cards is not guaranteed to appear each time.

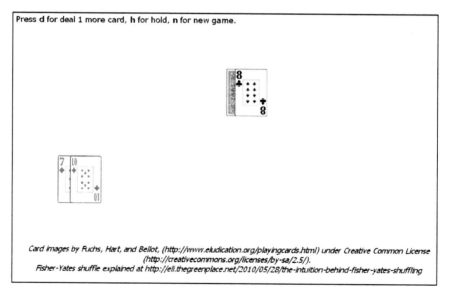

Figure 10-2. Cards dealt

Figure 10-2 shows what the player sees: all of his or her own hand and all but one card of the dealer's hard. The virtual dealer does not have knowledge of the player's hand. In this situation, the player's hand has a value of 7 plus 10 for a total of 17. The dealer is showing an 8. The player probably should hold, but let's be daring and press d for one more card. Figure 10-3 shows the result.

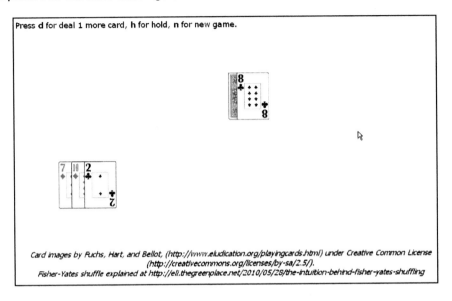

Figure 10-3. Player with 19

Now, the player clicks h to see what the dealer has. The result is shown in Figure 10-4.

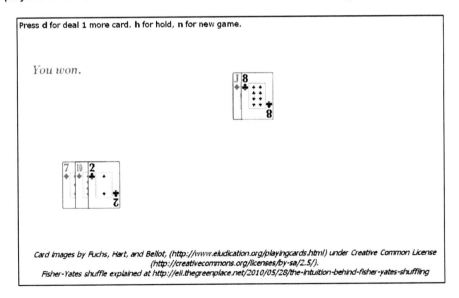

Figure 10-4. Player wins with 19 versus the dealer's 18

The player wins, since 19 is closer to 21 than 18.

The player can start a new game by pressing the n key or reloading the document. Reloading the document would mean starting with a complete, freshly shuffled deck. Pressing the n key continues with the current deck. Anyone who wants to practice **card counting**, a way of keeping track of what still is in the deck and varying your play accordingly, should opt to press the n key.

Figure 10-5 shows a new game.

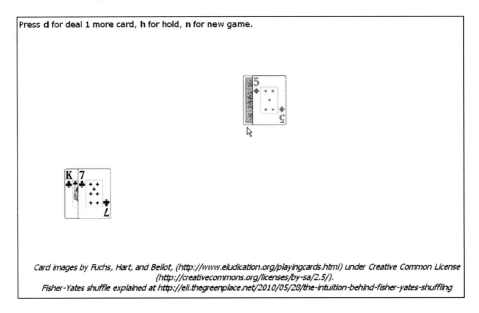

Figure 10-5. A new game

This time, the player presses h to hold, and Figure 10-6 shows the result.

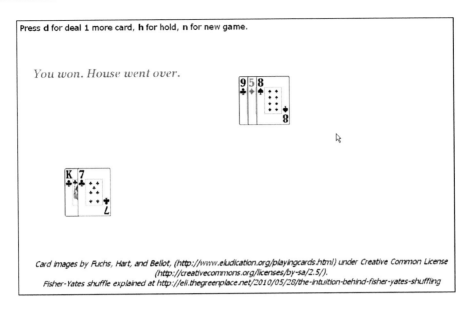

Figure 10-6. Player wins

The dealer was holding 9 plus 5 for a total of 14 and drew another card. The card drawn, an 8, took the hand over, so the player won.

Figure 10-7 shows the player being conservative by holding on 16. The dealer drew a card to add to the 10 (for the king) and 6 and then stopped with 19, beating the player.

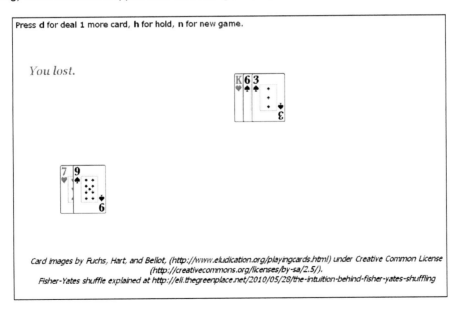

Figure 10-7. The house wins.

The actual practices of dealers at casinos may be different from this. This is an opportunity for research! The player also can bluff the house by going over and not revealing it. This may lead the house to request another card and go over also. The game is decided if and only if the player clicks the h key to hold, and thus stop drawing cards.

You may want to provide feedback to the player when a key that is not d, h, or n is pressed, as shown in Figure 10-8.

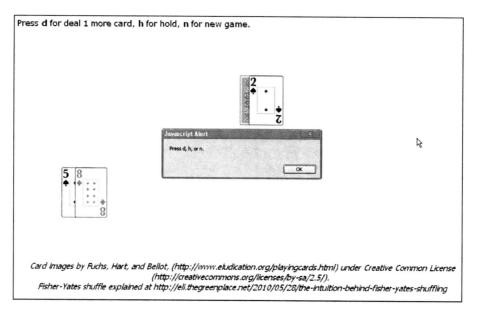

Figure 10-8. Feedback when a wrong key is pressed

Critical requirements

The blackjack game will make use of many of the HTML5, CSS, and JavaScript features described for the previous games.

The first issue I had when starting the implementation was to find a source of images for the card faces. I knew I could make my own drawings, but I preferred something more polished than I could produce.

The next challenge was how to design what a card was in programming terms so that I could implement dealing cards, showing the back or the face. I also wanted to investigate how to shuffle the deck.

Another challenge was implementing the way a player would play the game. I chose to use key presses: d to deal, h to hold, and n to begin a new game. There are, of course, alternatives, for example, displaying buttons with words or graphics or using other keys, such as the arrow keys. The absence of a clear, intuitive interface made it necessary to display the directions on the screen.

The last challenges are the general ones of maintaining the state of the game, the visible display, and internal information; generating the computer moves, and following the rules.

HTML5, CSS, and JavaScript features

Let's now look at the specific features of HTML5, CSS, and JavaScript that provide what we need to implement the blackjack card game. Except for basic HTML tags and functions and variables, the explanations here are complete. If you have read the other chapters, you will notice that much of this chapter repeats explanations given previously. Remember that you can skip ahead to the "Building the application" section to see the complete code for the game with comments and then return to this section for more explanation.

Source for images for card faces and setting up the Image objects

I did find an excellent source for the card faces: www.eludication.org/playingcards.html. This site uses something called the Creative Common License, and the rules of the Creative Common License are described at http://creativecommons.org/licenses/by-sa/2.5/. It requires any user to give credit, and I will demonstrate how I chose to do this.

After copying the files to your computer, we need a way to access 53 (52 cards plus one image for the back) image files without writing 53 different file names. This can be accomplished because the file names follow a pattern. The builddeck function is the following:

```
function builddeck() {
 var n;
 var si;
 var suitnames= ["clubs","hearts","spades","diamonds"];
 var i;
 i=0;
 var picname;
 var nums=["a","2","3","4","5","6","7","8","9","10","j","q","k"];
 for (si=0;si<4;si++) {
   for (n=0;n<13;n++) {
     picname=suitnames[si]+"-"+nums[n]+"-75.png";
     deck[i]=new MCard(n+1,suitnames[si],picname);
     i++;
   }
 }
}
```

Notice the nested for loops. A for statement is a way to program code to repeat, generally referred to as **looping,** for a specified amount of time. The three parts inside the parentheses specify an initial statement, a condition for continuing, and an increment action. These can be any expressions, but, typically, they refer to a single variable, called the **looping** or **index variable**. The first statement initializes the variable; the second indicates a comparison operation; and the third is an increment or decrement expression. for statements are common when dealing with arrays.

In this function, the outer loop manages the suits and the inner loop the cards within each suit. The picname variable will be set to the names of the files that we downloaded from the source. The MCard function is the constructor function to create a MCard object, that is, objects of the class we defined as a programmer-defined class of objects. n+1 will be used as the value of the card, and there will be some adjustment for the face cards.

> Note: The three statements in the nested for loops could be combined into
> `deck[i++]=new MCard(n+1,suitnames[si], suitnames[si]+"-"+nums[n]+"-75.png");`.
>
> This is because the ++ iteration operator takes place after the value has been generated for indexing the deck array. However, I recommend that in this learning example you don't do it! Using three statements is much easier to write and to understand.

Creating the programmer-defined object for the cards

JavaScript provides a way for programmers to create programmer-defined objects to group together data; the different pieces of data called **attributes** or **properties**, and we use dot notation to get at the different attributes. It is also possible to bundle together code into **methods**, but we don't need to do that in this example (recall that we did do this in other applications, such as cannonball and slingshot in Chapter 4). The function setting up the new object is called the **constructor** function. For cards, I defined MCard, which was shown in use in the previous section in the builddeck function. The definition of this function follows:

```
function MCard(n, s, picname){
    this.num = n;
    if (n>10) n = 10;
    this.value = n;
    this.suit = s;
    this.picture = new Image();
    this.picture.src = picname;
    this.dealt = 0;
}
```

The line of the function

```
    if (n>10) n = 10;
```

will be triggered by the face cards (jack, queen, king); remember, the value of each is 10. This line corrects the value to be 10 in these cases.

Notice that this if statement is structurally different from previous if statements. There are *not* any opening and closing curly brackets setting off the if-true clause. The single-statement clause is a legitimate form of the if statement. I generally avoid this form because if I later decide to add another statement, I will need to insert the curly brackets. However, it is OK in this situation. You will see both variations when examining code. Notice that nothing special is done when n equals 1. The rule for two possible values for an ace is handled elsewhere in the program.

The properties of MCard objects include a newly created Image object with its src attribute set to the picname passed in. The last attribute, dealt, initialized to 0, will be set to 1 or 2 depending on whether the card goes to the player or the dealer.

Dealing the cards

The builddeck function constructs the deck array of MCard objects. The player's hand is kept in an array called playerhand with pi holding the index of the next position. Similarly, the dealer's hand is kept in an array called househand with hi holding the index of the next position. An example showing the syntax (punctuation) for referencing an attribute of an MCard object when the object is an element of an array is playerhand[pi].picture.

The dealstart function has the task of dealing the first four cards: two to the player and two to the dealer. One of the dealer's cards is not shown; that is, the card's back is shown. The deal function is invoked when the player requests a new card (see later in this section). The deal function will deal a card to the player and see if the dealer is to get a new card. Both dealstart and deal accomplish the actual dealing by invoking the dealfromdeck function, adding the cards to the playerhand and househand arrays and drawing the cards on the canvas. Formally, the dealfromdeck is a function that returns a value of type MCard. Its call appears on the right side of assignment statements. If the face of the card is to show, the Image object drawn is the one referenced by the card. If the back of the card is to show, the Image object is the one held in the variable back.

Here is the dealstart function. Notice the four similar sets of statements: get the card, draw the image, increment the x position for the next time, and increase indexing variable, pi or hi.

```
function dealstart() {
    playerhand[pi] = dealfromdeck(1);
    ctx.drawImage(playerhand[pi].picture,playerxp,playeryp,cardw,cardh);
    playerxp = playerxp+30;
    pi++;
    househand[hi] = dealfromdeck(2);
    ctx.drawImage(back,housexp,houseyp,cardw,cardh);
    housexp = housexp+20;
    hi++;
    playerhand[pi] = dealfromdeck(1);
    ctx.drawImage(playerhand[pi].picture,playerxp,playeryp,cardw,cardh);
    playerxp = playerxp+30;
    pi++;
    househand[hi] = dealfromdeck(2);
    ctx.drawImage(househand[hi].picture,housexp,houseyp,cardw,cardh);
    housexp = housexp+20;
    hi++;
    }
```

The deal function is similar. A card is added to the player's hand and to the house if more_to_house returns true.

```
function deal() {
    playerhand[pi] = dealfromdeck(1);
    ctx.drawImage(playerhand[pi].picture,playerxp,playeryp,cardw,cardh);
    playerxp = playerxp+30;
    pi++;
    if (more_to_house()) {
    househand[hi] = dealfromdeck(2);
    ctx.drawImage(househand[hi].picture,housexp,houseyp,cardw,cardh);
    housexp = housexp+20;
    hi++;
    }
    }
```

Note that more_to_house is a function that generates a true or false value. This value will be based on a calculation of the dealer's total. If the total is 17 or greater, the value returned will be false; otherwise, it will be true. The function call is used as the condition of an if statement, so if more_to_house returns true, the statements within the if clause will be executed. The more_to_house code could be put inside the deal function, but dividing up large tasks into smaller ones is good practice. It means I can keep working on the deal function and postpone temporarily writing the more_to_house function. If you want to refine the more_to_house calculation, you know exactly where to do it.

Determining the specific card from the deck is the task of the dealfromdeck function. Again, I make this well-defined task its own function. The parameter is the recipient of the card. We don't need to keep track of which recipient in this application, but we'll keep that information in the code in to prepare for building other card games. What is critical is that the card has been dealt to someone. The dealt attribute changes from 0. Notice the line return card;, which does the work of making an MCard object be the result of invoking the function.

```
function dealfromdeck(who) {
  var card;
  var ch = 0;
  while ((deck[ch].dealt>0)&&(ch<51)) {
    ch++;
  }
  if (ch>=51) {
    ctx.fillText("NO MORE CARDS IN DECK. Reload. ",200,200);
    ch = 51;
  }
  deck[ch].dealt = who;
  card = deck[ch];
  return card;
}
```

Keep in mind that the deck array is indexed from 0 to 51. A while statement is another type of looping construction. In most computer programming languages, a while loop is a control flow statement that allows code to be executed repeatedly based on a given Boolean condition; the while loop can be thought of as a repeating if statement. The statements inside the curly brackets will execute as long as the condition inside the parentheses remains true. It is up to the programmer to make sure that this will happen—that the loop won't go on forever. The while loop in our application stops when a card is identified that has not been dealt, that is, its dealt attribute is 0. This function will say there are no more cards when the last card, the fifty-first card, is available and dealt. If the player ignores the message and asks for another card again, the last card will be dealt again.

As an aside, the issue of when the dealer chooses to gather the used cards together or go to a new deck is significant for card counters attempting to figure out what cards remain. At many casinos, dealers use multiple decks of cards to impede card counting. My program does not give the house that capability. You can build on this program to simulate these effects if you want a program to practice card counting. You can put the number of decks under player control, use random processing, or wait until the count of remaining cards is under a fixed amount, or perhaps something else.

The dealer may request another card when the player requests another card or when the player decides to hold. As mentioned earlier, the function to evaluate if the dealer asks for another card is more_to_house. The calculation is to add up the values of the hand. If there are any aces, the function adds an extra 10 points if that will make the total 21 or less—that is, it makes 1 ace count as 11. Then, it evaluates if the sum is less than 17. If it is, it returns `true`, which tells the calling function to request a new card. If the value exceeds 17, it returns `false`.

```
function more_to_house(){
  var ac = 0;
  var i;
  var sumup = 0;
    for (i=0;i<hi;i++) {
    sumup += househand[i].value;
    if (househand[i].value==1) {ac++;}
  }
  if (ac>0) {
    if ((sumup+10)<=21) {
        sumup += 10;
    }
  }
  housetotal = sumup;
    if (sumup<17) {
   return true;
  }
  else {
    return false;
  }
}
```

If you want to experiment with a different strategy for the house, `more_to_house` is the function you change.

Starting a new game can be a challenge for programmers. First of all, it is necessary to understand what starting again means. For this implementation of blackjack, I provide an option to the player for starting a new hand, which means continuing with the same deck. To start with a fresh deck that has no cards dealt out, the player must reload the document. My name for the function that is invoked when the player presses the n key is `newgame`. The required actions are to clear the canvas and reset the pointers for player's and dealer's hands, as well as the variables holding the horizontal position for the next card. This function closes with a call to `dealstart`.

```
function newgame() {
  ctx.clearRect(0,0,cwidth,cheight);
  pi=0;
  hi=0;
  playerxp = 100;
  housexp= 500;
  dealstart();
}
```

Shuffling the deck

The technique for shuffling featured in the concentration game (see Chapter 5) represented an implementation of what my children and I did when playing the game: we spread out the cards and seized pairs and switched their places. For blackjack, a friend pointed me to a website by Eli Bendersky (http://eli.thegreenplace.net/2010/05/28/the-intuition-behind-fisher-yates-shuffling/) explaining the **Fisher-Yates algorithm**. The strategy of this algorithm is to make a random determination for each position in the deck, starting from the end and working toward the start. The calculation determines a random position in the deck from 0 up to and including the current position and does a swap. The main shuffle function follows:

```
function shuffle() {
  var i = deck.length - 1;
  var s;
  while (i>0) {
      s = Math.floor(Math.random()*(i+1));
      swapindeck(s,i);
      i--;
  }
}
```

Recall that `Math.random()` * N returns a number from zero up to but not including N. Taking `Math.floor` of the result returns an integer from zero up to N. So if we want a number from 0 to i, we need to write `Math.floor(Math.random()*(i+1))`. To make the `shuffle` function easier to read, I made a separate function called `swapindeck` that swaps the two cards that are located at the positions indicated by the parameters to the function. To perform a swap, an extra place is needed and this is the variable `hold`. This extra place is needed because the two assignment statements cannot be accomplished at the same time.

```
function swapindeck(j,k) {
    var hold = new MCard(deck[j].num,deck[j].suit,deck[j].picture.src);
    deck[j] = deck[k];
    deck[k] = hold;
}
```

Capturing key presses

The use of the arrow keys was described in the maze game in Chapter 7. This essentially is a repeat of that explanation.

Detecting that a key on the keyboard has been pressed and determining which key is termed **capturing the key strokes**. The code must set up the response to a key event and is analogous to setting up a response to a mouse event. The coding starts with invoking the `addEventListener` method, this time for the `window` for this application.

```
window.addEventListener('keydown',getkey,false);
```

This means the `getkey` function will be invoked if and when a key is pressed.

> Note: There also are keyup and keypress events. The keydown and keyup fire only once. The keypress event will occur again after some amount of time if the player holds down the key.

Now, as you may expect at this point, the coding to get the information for which key involves code for different browsers. The following code, with two ways to get the number corresponding to the key, works for Chrome, Firefox, and Safari:

```
if(event == null)
```

```
{
  keyCode = window.event.keyCode;
  window.event.preventDefault();
}
else
{
  keyCode = event.keyCode;
  event.preventDefault();
}
```

The preventDefault function does what it sounds like: it prevents any default action, such as special shortcut actions associated with particular keys. The only keys of interest in this application are the three keys d, h, and n. The following switch statement determines which key is pressed and invokes the correct function: deal, playerdone, or newgame. A switch statement compares the value in the parentheses with the values after the term case and starts executing the statements with the first one that matches. The break; statement causes execution to jump out of the switch statement. The default clause is what it sounds like. It is not necessary, but if it is present, the statement or statements following default: are executed if nothing matches the case values provided.

```
switch(keyCode)d
{
  case 68:  //d
     deal();
     break;
  case 72:  //h
     playerdone();
     break;
  case 78:  //n
     newgame();
     break;
  default:
     alert("Press d, h, or n.);
}
```

Recall that you can determine the key code of any key by modifying the whole switch statement to have just the following line in the default case:

```
alert(" You just pressed keycode "+keyCode);
```

and doing the experiment of pressing on the key and writing down what number shows up.

Caution: If, like I sometimes do, you move among different windows on your computer, you may find that when you return to the blackjack game and press a key, the program does not respond. You will need to click the mouse on the window holding the blackjack document. This lets the operating system restore the focus on the blackjack document so the listening for the key press can take place.

Using header and footer element types

HTML5 added some new built-in element types including `header` and `footer`. The rationale behind these and other new elements (for example, `article` and `nav`) was to provide elements that serve standard purposes so that search engines and other programs would know how to treat the material, though it still is necessary to specify the formatting. These are the styles we will use in this example:

```
footer {
    display:block;
    font-family:Tahoma, Geneva, sans-serif;
    text-align: center;
    font-style:oblique;
}
header {
    width:100%;
    display:block;
}
```

The `display` setting can be `block` or `inline`. Setting these to `block` forces a line break. Note that forcing the line break may not be necessary for certain browsers, but using it does not hurt. The `font-family` attribute is a way to specify choices of fonts. If `Tahoma` is available on the user's computer, it will be used. The next font to try will be `Geneva`. If neither one is present, the browser will use the `sans-serif` font set up as the default. The `text-align` and `font-style` settings are what they appear to be. The `width` setting sets this element to be the whole width of the containing element, in this case the `body`. Feel free to experiment!

Note that you cannot assume the footer is at the bottom of the screen or surrounding element, nor the header at the top. I made that happen by using positioning in the HTML document.

I used the footer to display the sources for the card images and the shuffle algorithm. Providing credit, showing copyright, and displaying contact information are all typical uses of footer elements, but there are no restrictions on how you use any of these new elements or on where you put them in the HTML document and how you format them.

Building the application and making it your own

The functions used in this game are described in Table 10-1.

Table 10-1. The Blackjack Functions

Function	Invoked / Called by	Calls
`init`	Invoked by the `onLoad` function in the `<body>` tag	`builddeck`, `shuffle`, and `dealstart`
`getkey`	Invoked by the `windowaddEventListener` call in `init`	`deal`, `playerdone`, and `newgame`
`dealstart`	`init`	

Function	Invoked / Called by	Calls
deal	getkey	Two calls to dealfromdeck and one call to more_to_house
more_to_house	deal	
dealfromdeck	deal and dealstart	
builddeck	init	MCard
MCard	builddeck	
add_up_player	playerdone	
playerdone	getkey	more_to_house, showhouse, and add_up_player
newgame	getkey	dealstart
showhouse	playerdone	
shuffle	init	swapindeck
swapindeck	shuffle	

The functions in this example feature a pattern of procedural calls with only init and getkey invoked as a result of events. Please appreciate the fact that there are many ways to program an application, including the definition of functions. Generally, it is a good practice to split code up into small functions, but it is not necessary. There are many places where similar lines of codes are repeated, so there is opportunity to define more functions. The annotated document follows in Table 10-2.

Table 10-2. The Annotated Code for the Blackjack Game

Code	Explanation
`<html>`	Opening tag
`<head>`	Opening tag
`<title>Black Jack</title>`	Complete title element
`<style>`	Opening tag

Code	Explanation
`body {`	Specifies the style for the body element
`background-color:white;`	Sets the background color
`color: black;`	Sets the color of the text
`font-size:18px;`	Sets the font size
`font-family:Verdana, Geneva, sans-serif;`	Sets the font family
`}`	Closes the style
`footer {`	Specifies the style for the footer
`display:block;`	Treats this element as a block
`font-family:Tahoma, Geneva, sans-serif;`	Sets the font family
`text-align: center;`	Aligns the text in the center
`font-style:oblique;`	Makes the text slanted
`}`	Close style
`header {`	Specifies the style for the header
`width:100%;`	Make it take up the whole window
`display:block;`	Treats it as a block
`}`	Close style
`</style>`	Close the style element
`<script>`	Starts the script element
`var cwidth = 800;`	Sets the width of the canvas; used when clearing the canvas
`var cheight = 600;`	Sets the height of the canvas; used when clearing the canvas

Code	Explanation
`var cardw = 75;`	Sets the width of each card
`var cardh = 107;`	Sets the height of each card
`var playerxp = 100;`	Sets the starting horizontal position for the cards in the player's hand
`var playeryp = 300;`	Sets the vertical position for the cards in the player's hand
`var housexp = 500;`	Sets the starting horizontal position for the cards in the dealer's hand
`var houseyp = 100;`	Sets the vertical position for the cards in the dealer's hand
`var housetotal;`	For the total value of the dealer's hand
`var playertotal;`	For the total value of the player's hand
`var pi = 0;`	Index for the next card in player's hand
`var hi = 0;`	Index for the next card in the dealer's hand
`var deck = [];`	Holds all the cards
`var playerhand = [];`	Holds the cards for the player
`var househand = [];`	Holds the cards for the dealer
`var back = new Image();`	Used for the card back
`function init() {`	Function called by `onLoad` in body to performs initialization tasks
`  ctx = document.getElementById('canvas').↪getContext('2d');`	Sets the variable used for all drawing
`  ctx.font="italic 20pt Georgia";`	Sets the font

Code	Explanation
`ctx.fillStyle = "blue";`	Sets the color
`builddeck();`	Invokes the function to build the deck of cards
`back.src ="cardback.png";`	Specifies the image for the back of card (note that only one back appears: the dealer's hidden card)
`canvas1 = document.getElementById('canvas');`	Sets the variable for event handling
`window.addEventListener('keydown',getkey,false);`	Sets up event handling for `keydown`. presses
`shuffle();`	Invokes the function to shuffle
`dealstart();`	Invokes the function to deal out the first four cards
`}`	Closes the function
`function getkey(event) {`	Function to respond to `keydown` events
`var keyCode;`	Holds the code designating the key
`if(event == null)`	Browser-specific code to determine if the event is null
`{`	Open clause
`keyCode = window.event.keyCode;`	Gets the key code from `window.event.keyCode`
`window.event.preventDefault();`	Stops other key responses
`}`	Close clause
`else    {`	`clause`
`keyCode = event.keyCode;`	Picks up the key code from `even.keyCode`

Code	Explanation
`    event.preventDefault();`	Stops other key responses
`}`	Close clause
`switch(keyCode) {`	Header for the `switch` statement based on `keyCode`
`  case 68:`	d key has been pressed down
`    deal();`	Deals out another card to the player and maybe to the dealer
`    break;`	Leaves the `switch`
`  case 72:`	h key has been pressed down
`   playerdone();`	Invokes the `playerdone` function
`   break;`	Leaves the `switch`
`  case 78:`	n key has been pressed down
`   newgame();`	Invokes the `newgame` function
`   break;`	Leaves the `switch`
`  default:`	Default choice, which may be appropriate to remove if you don't feel the need to provide feedback to players if they use an unrecognized key
`    alert("Press d, h, or n.");`	Feedback message
`  }`	Closes the `switch`
`}`	Closes the function
`function dealstart() {`	Header for the function for initially dealing cards
`  playerhand[pi] = dealfromdeck(1);`	Gets the first card for player

Code	Explanation
`    ctx.drawImage(playerhand[pi].picture,↩` `playerxp,playeryp,cardw,cardh);`	Draw on the canvas
`    playerxp = playerxp+30;`	Adjusts the horizontal pointer
`    pi++;`	Increases the count of cards to the player
`    househand[hi] = dealfromdeck(2);`	Gets the first card for the dealer
`    ctx.drawImage(back,housexp,houseyp,cardw,cardh);`	Draws a card's back on the canvas
`    housexp = housexp+20;`	Adjusts the horizontal pointer
`    hi++;`	Increases the count of cards to the dealer
`    playerhand[pi] = dealfromdeck(1);`	Deals a second card to the player
`    ctx.drawImage(playerhand[pi].picture,↩` `playerxp,playeryp,cardw,cardh);`	Draws on canvas
`    playerxp = playerxp+30;`	Adjusts the horizontal pointer
`    pi++;`	Increases the count of cards to the player
`    househand[hi] = dealfromdeck(2);`	Deals a second card to the dealer
`    ctx.drawImage(househand[hi].picture,↩` `housexp,houseyp,cardw,cardh);`	Draws on the canvas
`    housexp = housexp+20;`	Adjusts the horizontal pointer
`    hi++;`	Increases the count of cards to the house
`  }`	Close function
`function deal() {`	Header for the function for dealing through the game
`    playerhand[pi] = dealfromdeck(1);`	Deals a card to the player

Code	Explanation
`ctx.drawImage(playerhand[pi].picture,↪` `playerxp,playeryp,cardw,cardh);`	Draws on the canvas
`playerxp = playerxp+30;`	Adjust the horizontal pointer
`pi++;`	Increases the count of cards to the player
`if (more_to_house()) {`	if function to say there should be more cards for the dealer
`househand[hi] = dealfromdeck(2);`	Deals a card to the house
`ctx.drawImage(househand[hi].picture,↪` `housexp,houseyp,cardw,cardh);`	Draws a card on canvas
`housexp = housexp+20;`	Adjusts the horizontal pointer
`hi++;`	Increases the count of cards to the dealer
`}`	Closes the if-true clause
`}`	Close function
`function more_to_house(){`	Header for the function determining the dealer's moves
`var ac = 0;`	Variable to hold the count of aces
`var i;`	Variable for iteration
`var sumup = 0;`	Initializes the variable for the sum
`for (i=0;i<hi;i++) {`	Iterates over all the cards
`sumup += househand[i].value;`	Adds up value of cards in the dealer's hand
`if (househand[i].value==1) {ac++;}`	Keeps track of the number of aces
`}`	Closes the for loop

Code	Explanation
`if (ac>0) {`	`if` statement to determine if there were any aces
`if ((sumup+10)<=21) {`	If so, asks if making one of the aces take on the value of 11 still yield a total less than 21
`sumup +=10;`	If yes, do it
`}`	Closes inner `if`
`}`	Closes outer `if`
`housetotal = sumup;`	Sets the global variable to be the sum
`if (sumup<17) {`	Asks if the sum is under 17
`return true;`	Returns `true` if so, meaning it's OK to get one more card
`}`	Closes clause
`else {`	Begins `else` clause
`return false;`	Return `false`, meaning the dealer won't get another card
`}`	Closes the `else` clause
`}`	Closes the function
`function dealfromdeck(who) {`	Header for the function to deal from the deck
`var card;`	Holds the card
`var ch = 0;`	Holds the index for the next undealt card
`while ((deck[ch].dealt>0)&&(ch<51)) {`	Asks if this card has been dealt
`ch++;`	Increases `ch` to go on to the next card

Code	Explanation
`}`	Close the `while` loop
`if (ch>=51) {`	Asks if there were no undealt cards
`ctx.fillText("NO MORE CARDS IN↪ DECK. Reload. ",200,250);`	Displays a message
`ch = 51;`	Sets `ch` to 51 to make this function work
`}`	Closes the if-true clause
`deck[ch].dealt = who;`	Stores who, a nonzero value, so this card is marked as having been dealt
`card = deck[ch];`	Sets a card
`return card;`	Returns a card
`}`	Closes the function
`function builddeck() {`	Header for the function that builds the `MCard` objects
`var n;`	Variable used for inner iteration
`var si;`	Variable used for outer iteration, over the suits
`var suitnames= ["clubs","hearts",↪ "spades","diamonds"];`	Names of suits
`var i;`	Keeps track of elements put into the deck array
`i=0;`	Initializes the array to 0
`var picname;`	Simplifies the coding
`var nums=["a","2","3","4","5","6","7",↪ "8","9","10","j","q","k"];`	The names for all the cards
`for (si=0;si<4;si++) {`	Iterates over the suits

Code	Explanation
`    for (n=0;n<13;n++) {`	Iterates over the cards in a suit
`        picname=suitnames[si]+"-"+nums[n]+↪` `"-75.png";`	Constructs the name of the file
`        deck[i]=new MCard(n+1,suitnames[si],↪` `picname);`	Construct an `MCard` with the indicated values
`        i++;`	Increments `i`
`    }`	Closes the inner `for` loop
`  }`	Closes the outer `for` loop
`}`	Closes the function
`function MCard(n, s, picname){`	Header for the constructor function for making objects
`  this.num = n;`	Sets the `num` value
`  if (n>10) n = 10;`	Makes an adjustment in the cases of the face cards
`  this.value = n;`	Set the value
`  this.suit = s;`	Set the suit
`  this.picture = new Image();`	Creates a new Image object and assigns it as an attribute
`  this.picture.src = picname;`	Set the `src` attribute of this `Image` object to the picture file name
`  this.dealt = 0;`	Initializes the `dealt` attribute to 0
`}`	Closes the function
`function add_up_player() {`	Header for the function determining the value of player's hand
`var ac = 0;`	Holds the count of aces

Code	Explanation
`var i;`	For iteration
`var sumup = 0;`	Initializes the sum
`  for (i=0;i<pi;i++) {`	Loops over the cards in the player's hand
`    sumup += playerhand[i].value;`	Increments the value of the player's hand
`    if (playerhand[i].value==1)`	Asks if the card is an ace
`      {ac++;`	Increments the count of aces
`      }`	Closes the if statement
`  }`	Closes the for loop
`  if (ac>0) {`	Asks if there were any aces
`    if ((sumup+10)<=21) {`	If this doesn't make sum go over
`      sumup +=10;`	Makes one ace an 11
`    }`	Closes the inner if
`  }`	Closes the outer if
`  return  sumup;`	Returns the total
`}`	Closes the function
`function playerdone() {`	Header for the function invoked when player says hold
`  while(more_to_house()) {`	While the `more_to_house` function indicates the dealer should get another card
`    househand[hi] = dealfromdeck(2);`	Deals a card to the dealer
`    ctx.drawImage(back,housexp,houseyp,↪` `cardw,cardh);`	Draws the card on the canvas

Code	Explanation
`housexp = housexp+20;`	Adjusts the horizontal pointer
`hi++;`	Increases the index for the dealer's hand
`}`	Closes the `while` loop
`showhouse();`	Reveals the dealer's hand
`playertotal = add_up_player();`	Determines the player's total
`if (playertotal>21){`	Asks if the player was over
`if (housetotal>21) {`	Asks if the house was over
`ctx.fillText("You and house both↪ went over.",30,100);`	Displays a message
`}`	Closes the inner `if` statement
`else {`	Begins `else` clause
`ctx.fillText("You went over and lost."↪ ,30,100);`	Displays a message
`}`	Closes the `else` clause
`}`	Closes the outer clause (player is over)
`else`	else the player is not over
`if (housetotal>21) {`	Asks if the dealer was over
`ctx.fillText("You won. House went↪ over.",30,100);`	Displays a message
`}`	Close the clause
`else`	else
`if (playertotal>=housetotal) {`	Compares the two amounts

Code	Explanation
`if (playertotal>housetotal) {`	Performs a more specific comparison
`ctx.fillText("You won. ",30,100);`	Displays the winner message
`}`	Closes the inner clause
`else {`	Begins `else` clause
`ctx.fillText("TIE!",30,100);`	Displays a message
`}`	Closes the `else` clause
`}`	Closes the outer clause
`else`	else
`if (housetotal<=21) {`	Checks if the dealer is under
`ctx.fillText("You lost. ", 30,100);`	Displays a message
`}`	Closes the clause
`else {`	Begins `else` clause
`ctx.filltext("You won because➡` `house went over.");`	Displays a message (player under, house over)
`}`	Closes the clause
`}`	Closes the function
`function newgame() {`	Header for the function for a new game
`ctx.clearRect(0,0,cwidth,cheight);`	Clears the canvas
`pi=0;`	Resets the index for the player
`hi=0;`	Resets the index for the dealer
`playerxp = 100;`	Resets the horizontal position for the first card of the player's hand

Code	Explanation
`housexp= 500;`	Resets the horizontal position for the dealer's hand
`dealstart();`	Calls the function to initially deal the cards
`}`	Closes the function
`function showhouse() {`	Header for the function to reveal the dealer's hand
`var i;`	For iteration
`housexp= 500;`	Resets the horizontal position
`for (i=0;i<hi;i++) {`	for loop over the hand
`ctx.drawImage(househand[i].picture,↪` `housexp,houseyp,cardw,cardh);`	Draws the card
`housexp = housexp+20;`	Adjusts the pointer
`}`	Closes the for loop
`}`	Closes the function
`function shuffle() {`	Header for the shuffle
`var i = deck.length - 1;`	Sets the initial value for the i variable to point to the last card
`var s;`	Variable used for the random choice
`while (i>0) {`	As long as i is greater than zero
`s = Math.floor(Math.random()*(i+1));`	Makes a random pick
`swapindeck(s,i);`	Swaps with the card in the i position
`i--;`	Decrement
`}`	Closes the while loop

Code	Explanation
`}`	Closes the function
`function swapindeck(j,k) {`	Helper function for the swapping
`var hold = new MCard(deck[j].num,deck[j].↪` `suit,deck[j].picture.src);`	Saves the card in position j
`deck[j] = deck[k];`	Assigns the card in the k position to the j position
`deck[k] = hold;`	Assigns the hold to card in the k position
`}`	Closes the function
`</script>`	Closes the `script` element
`</head>`	Closes the `head` element
`<body onLoad="init();">`	Opening tag to set the call to `init`
`<header>Press d for deal 1 more card,↪` `h for hold, n for new game.</header>`	Header element containing instructions
`<canvas id="canvas" width="800" height="500">`	Canvas opener
`Your browser doesn't support the HTML5↪` `element canvas.`	Warning to noncompliant browsers
`</canvas>`	Closes the element
`<footer>Card images from http://www.eludication↪` `.org/playingcards.html, Creative Common License↪` `(http://creativecommons.org/↪` `licenses/by-sa/2.5/).  `	Opens the footer element, which contains credit for card images and a link to the Creative Common License

`Fisher-Yates shuffle explained at↪`
`http://eli.thegreenplace.net↪`
`/2010/05/28/the-intuition-behind-↪`
`fisher-yates-shuffling`
	Adds the credit for article on the shuffle algorithm

`</footer>`	Closes the `footer`

Code	Explanation
`</body>`	Closes the body
`</html>`	Closes the HTML file

You can change the look and feel of this game in many ways, including offering different ways for the player to request to be dealt a new card, to hold with the current hand, or to request a new hand. You can create or acquire your own set of card images. Keeping score from hand to hand, perhaps including some kind of betting, would be a fine enhancement. Changing the rules for the dealer's play is possible.

Testing and uploading the application

This program requires considerable testing. Remember that the testing is not finished when you, acting as tester, have won. It is finished when you have gone through many different scenarios. I did my first testing of the game with an unshuffled deck. I then put in the shuffling and kept track of the cases that the testing revealed. I pressed the d key for dealing one more card, the h for holding, and the n for a new game in different circumstances. This is definitely a situation when you want to bring in other people to test your application.

Uploading the application requires uploading all the images. You will need to change the `builddeck` function to construct the appropriate names for the files if you use something different than what I demonstrate here.

Summary

In this chapter, you learned how to implement a card game using features of HTML5, JavaScript, and CSS along with general programming techniques. These included

- Generating a set of `Image` objects based on names of external files
- Designing a programmer-defined object for cards, incorporating the `Images`
- Drawing images and text on the screen
- Making use of `for`, `while`, and `if` to implement the logic of blackjack
- Using calculations and logic to generate the computer's moves
- Establishing event handling for the `keydown` event so that the player could indicate a request to deal a new card, hold, or start a new game and using `switch` to distinguish between the keys
- Using the `header` and `footer` elements, new to HTML5, for directions and giving credit to sources

This is the last chapter of this book. I hope you take what you have learned and produce enhanced versions of these games and games of your own invention. Enjoy!

Index

application state
 craps game sample and, 24
 Hangman game sample and, 295, 300
applications
 ballistics simulation. *See* ballistics
  simulation
 building in stages, 38, 66
 examples of. *See* samples
 multilingual, 284
 samples in this book, downloading, 100
 terminology and, 214
arcs, drawing, 70, 32–38
arguments, 11, 26, 76
array of arrays
 audio and, 274
 memory game sample and, 147
 quiz sample and, 184–186, 193
 rock-paper-scissors game rules and, 267
array splice, 110
arrays, 73–75, 101
 everything array and, 101, 103
 gradients and, 74
 Hangman game word list and, 295
 one-dimensional vs. multi-dimensional, 185
arrow keys, responding to, 218, 219, 220
article element, 7, 187
aspect ratio, 72
assignment statements, 26
attributes, 324
audio
 for rock-paper-scissors game sample, 259,
  272–274, 283
 support for, 128
audio element, 272

B

bad/invalid input, 69, 79, 96
ball (sample), illustrating ballistics simulation, 97
Ball function, 102
 for cannonball sample, 103, 111, 118
 for slingshot sample, 129
ballboundx/ballboundy variables, bouncing ball
  sample and, 78
ballistics simulation, 97–140
 ball sample illustrating, 97
 cannonball sample and, 97, 111–128
 slingshot sample and, 98, 107–111, 128–140

ballrad (sample) variable, 78
ballvx/ballvy variables, bouncing ball sample
  and, 78
ballx/bally variables, bouncing ball sample and,
  78
beats array, rock-paper-scissors game sample
  and, 268, 284
best practices
 for comments, 81, 221
 for functions, 80
blackjack card game (sample), 317–346
 building, 330–346
 cards for, 323
 customizing, 346
 d key in to deal new card, 319, 329, 346
 h key in to hold, 319, 329, 346
 n key in to start new game, 318, 320, 327,
  329
 rules of the game, 317
 testing/uploading, 346
body element, 4, 8
 canvas and, 30
 for quiz sample, 189, 193
 rock-paper-scissors game sample score
  and, 268
Boolean values, 27
borders, 8
bouncing ball (sample), 67–96
 in 2-D box, 67, 80–85
 ball replaced with image, 67, 71, 85–91
 ballboundx/ballboundy variables and, 78
 ballvx/ballvy variables and, 78
 ballx/bally variables and, 78
 customizing, 95
 function calls for, 80
 inboxboundx/inboxboundy variables and, 78
 input validation for, 67, 91–95
 moveball function and, 76, 77
 testing/uploading, 96
br singleton tag, 6
break statement, 29
browsers, 1
 audio/video support and, 128, 184, 272
 event handling and, 265
 form input validation and, 79
 keystroke capture and, 220, 328
 local storage and, 224, 226
 mouse event implementation and, 108, 153

CPSIA information can be obtained at www.ICGtesting.com
Printed in the USA
244301LV00009B/4/P